Lazio Rediscovered
Research and Restoration

©
Proprietà letteraria riservata
All right reserved

Gangemi Editore Spa
Piazza San Pantaleo 4, Roma
www.gangemieditore.it

Nessuna parte di questa pubblicazione può essere memorizzata, fotocopiata o comunque riprodotta senza le dovute autorizzazioni; chiunque favorisca questa pratica commette un illecito perseguibile a norma di legge.

No part of this publication may be recorded, photocopied or otherwise reproduced without proper authorisation; doing so constitutes an illegal act that will be prosecuted according to law.

ISBN 88-492-0488-4

Convento di Palazzolo
on the shores of Lake Albano

Edited by Marina Cogotti

Gangemi Editore

Abbreviations

A.C.: Colonna Archives
A.F.R.: S. Francesco a Ripa Archives
A.P.A.: Provincial Archives of Aracoeli
A.S.A.D.P.: Archives of S. Antonio de' Portoghesi
A.S.R.: Rome State Archives
A.V.T.: Tuscolano Episcopal Archives
B.A.V.: Vatican Apostolic Library
Bull.Arch.Sub.: *Bulletin of Underwater Archaeology*
BullCom: *Bulletin of the Municipial Archaeological Commission of Rome*
DdA: *Archaeological Dialogues*
DocAlbana: Documenta Albana
Mél: *Papers of the French School, Rome, Antiquity*
MEFR: *Papers on Archaeology and History*
MemPontAcc: *Notes of the Roman Pontifical Academy of Archaeology*
ParPass: La Parola del Passato
PBSR: Papers of the British School at Rome
QuadAEI: Notebooks of the Study Centre for Etruscan-Italian Architecture
S.B.A.A.L.: Department for the Environmental and Architectural Properties of Lazio
S.B.S.A.R.L.: Department for the Historical and Artistic Properties of Rome and Lazio
V.E.C.: Venerable English College Archives

Contents

Acknowledgements   6

FOREWORD
Pio Baldi   7
Constantino Centroni   9

INTRODUCTION
Marina Cogotti   11

I. THE LANDSCAPE
    Marina Cogotti   13

II. PALAZZOLO IN ANCIENT TIMES
    Giuseppina Ghini   43

III. THE ARTISTIC HISTORY OF CONVENTO DI PALAZZOLO
    Alberto Crielesi   61
    From the beginnings to a Cistercian Abbey   61
    S Maria di Palazzolo: from the Cistercians to the Observantines   73
    Restorations in the 1500s and the enigma of the tomb of Agnesina di Montefeltro   77
    Cardinal Girolamo and Carlo (Dom Egidio) Colonna at Palazzolo   86
    Friar Giorgio Marziale, Minorite architect, and the seventeenth-century work   96
    The 1700s and the Fonseca restorations   108
    Palazzolo in the 19th and 20th centuries   123

IV. THE RESTORATION
    Marina Cogotti   133
    The Project: problems and solutions   133
    The work   141
    The roofing   142
    Restoration of the façades   143
    Restoration of the garden wall
    The garden

V. RESTORATION OF THE SUNDIAL AT PALAZZOLO
    Lucio Baruffi

APPENDICES
Archival and documentary sources   197
General bibliography   199
Index of names   203

In common with the other authors of this volume, I would like to thank the institutions, researchers and individuals who have contributed in various ways to the production of this book, by allowing us to study and publish documents and papers, and by providing suggestions and advice. The long history of the religious house, the owners through time, and the inevitable and valuable references in various archives, have made it possible to pull into one thread the history of this particular place, its buildings and the people who brought the place to life and who, like us, I believe, loved it.

Thanks are due to the Venerable English College, the present owner of Convento di Palazzolo, to both the current Rector, Mgr. Patrick Kilgarriff, and his predecessor, Mgr. Adrian Toffolo; to the Roman Minorite Province of the Holy Apostles Peter and Paul, in particular Fr Aldo La Neve, Brother Nicola Sorbo, Fr Ezio Casella and Fr Antonio Del Vasto, in charge of the Archives of San Francesco a Ripa; to Mgr. Agostinho Da Costa Borges, the Rector of the Portuguese Institute of Santo Antonio in Rome, and Dr. A Cimini; Mgr. Cardoso, the Cultural Affairs Attaché at the Portuguese Embassy to the Holy See; Fr Lino Temperini, Provincial of the Third Order Franciscans; Ambrogio M Piazzoni, Vice-Prefect, and Fr Raffaele Farina, of the Vatican Apostolic Library; Dr Giovanni Castaldo, of the Vatican Secret Archives; Dr Francesco Buranelli and the staff of the Photographic Archive of Pontifical Monuments, Museums and Galleries; the management of the Colonna Gallery in Rome; the architect Francesco Petrucci, custodian of the Chigi Palace in Ariccia; the Aldobrandini family and the archivist, Dr Antonella Fabiani Rojas; the management and staff of the Colonna Archives in Subiaco; Mr. Carlo Silvestri and 'Antichità S. Pancrazio' at Sante Trinca; Enrico and Stefania Albanesi; Dr Piero Scatizzi; Dr Ferruccio Scoccia; Professor Luigi Devoti; members of the Castelli Romani Photo Clubs, Mariano Fanini and Edoardo Silvestroni; Mr Giorgio Guarnieri, from the photographic archives of the Department for the Historical and Artistic Properties of Rome and Lazio; the Rizzi Photography Studio, and the photographers Salvatore Giagnoli (Department for Architectural Properties and the Lazio Countryside) and Gino Viani (Archaeological Department for Lazio).

My personal thanks go to the surveyor Danilo Mattei and the architect Marco Dolce, from the Department for Architectural Properties and the Lazio Countryside, to the professionals and workers who shared the hard work on site, and to Dr Joseph Coughlan of the Venerable English College, for the wise and tactful help he always gave me.

M.C.

At the start of a restoration project there is always the impression of confronting a puzzle. The monument is there with all its inconsistencies, problems, faults, and mysteries: it is always different to what it should be, or, rather, different to how we want it to be.

To begin the restoration of a monument, one needs to find the key or code that will allow us to decipher the secret message.

The path to understanding is always tough. Of course, the thorough intellectual preparation, which, in well-directed restorations precedes and goes apace with the work itself, is a great help, starting with in-depth study of historical changes and then tests and material investigations. Such investigations, however, must be carried out with a precise aim, i.e. that of answering the queries and questions that have been clearly identified. (Restoration reports from recent decades are full of useless, costly analyses aimed simply at substantiating the presumed scientific nature of the work).

But to be in tune with the monument itself, one has to visit it at length, work on site, and work closely with the materials and problems.

C. Brandi's enlightening principle is still very useful. From direct contact with the work he seems able to produce the objective and main result of restoration, that is, an increase in awareness, understanding and appreciation.

From what the authors of this book have written, it seems that becoming attuned to and being able to interpret the monument was attained precisely by a lengthy, patient and well thought out route.

The thorough archaeological appreciation by Giuseppina Ghini and the description of the successive historical-artistic changes by Alberto Crielesi reveal a mass of dates, facts, sources, and information. When checked against the monument itself and critically re-interpreted by Marina Cogotti, they allow us to contextualise and understand not only the modifications which Convento di Palazzolo has undergone in the course of its long history, but also the intentions and the theoretical vision which lay behind each phase of its restructuring.

For example, the meaning of the 18th century work of expansion and decorative re-definition can be understood in the light of the personality and the interests of Josè M. de Fonseca, as can the meaning of the successive 20th century work characterised by the opposing aim of plunder and removal, in the search for an impossible restoration.

This latest series of modifications must be seen within the context of a desire to restore monuments and works of art to an 'original' form which they were presumed to have had at some period of their existence. This desire was one of the most recurring obsessions in the history of restoration in the last century, with the consequence of serious damage inflicted on the entire national cultural heritage.

The choices made for this work are consistent and follow on from this critical plan: the acceptance of the 'shape' of the monument as it is found today with all its changes; the preservation and improvement of the existing parts; the preferential treatment of external surfaces; and the substantial maintenance of the strengthened image.

Finally, rather than just telling us about gaps of three or five centimetres, or the hydraulic mixtures rather than ethyl silicate for reinforcements, an account of any architectural restoration must actually talk about the monument and its significance (*monimentum* means lesson, witness), how history has transformed it and how it has influenced history and the aspect of the place.

This last point (the sense of place) has borne great weight and influence with regard to the choices about aesthetic presentation. In a place as delicate and fragile as the eastern side of the Lake Albano basin which the site occupies, it was clearly proper to safeguard the rediscovered nature of the place in its balanced link with the surrounding countryside.

Restoration – of which this is an elegant example – is not simply a matter of solving technical problems, but of providing a credible historical and theoretical interpretation of the phenomena and facts, translating them into a coherent, formal aesthetic vision and, finally, in preparing its technical realisation.

Pio Baldi

The publication of this book is the natural conclusion to the patient and rigorous restoration work carried out at Convento di Palazzolo, Rocca di Papa, by the Department for Architectural Properties and the Lazio Countryside, as one of its restoration projects for the Great Jubilee of the year 2000.

Credit is due to those who carried out the work and further completed it with this offering, the fruit of further intellectual effort, an invaluable account of the planning choices and problems involved in the restoration. It would be wonderful if this were done for every operation carried out on buildings of historical and artistic interest. The chosen site, part of a series of twenty restored thanks to Jubilee funds, is one of the most enchanting places near Rome, and the destination of countless scholars interested in the antiquities and history of the Castelli Romani.

In the imagination of scholars, the place has been a focus of special sacredness, where, according to one legend, there are the remains of an ancient city, where the first founders of Rome came from. Even if this has not been scientifically proven (in fact, the tendency is to discount the theory), the site nevertheless remains a place of archaeological and historical interest, full of character and enigma and one of the most studied in Lazio.

Situated on the crater of an extinct volcano, it is today one of the most evocative places in the countryside. It offers both traces and considerable remains of structures from all historical periods, which make it even more interesting. After the year 1000 Benedictine monks arrived, followed by Cistercians and finally Franciscans. At the beginning of the twentieth century, the place underwent such serious changes that, to a certain extent, its whole physical nature was changed. The co-existence of evidence from various historical periods posed serious problems with regard to preservation and evaluation. The evidence was thoroughly examined and is described by the authors, who explain their work with a profound awareness of the condition of the place and its historical evolution, emphasising above all the relationship between nature and history, landscape and culture, which represents the most authentic and well-known characteristics of Lazio and other Italian regions.

A heartfelt thanks are extended to the authors, whose work has come to fruition with the publication of this book, a sound and important cultural success, which, we hope, will be a good omen for other restoration projects.

Costantino Centroni

Introduction
Marina Cogotti

> Alice added: "Would you tell me, please, which way I ought to go from here?" "Well, that depends a good deal on where you want to get to", replied the Cat.
> (Lewis Carroll, *Alice in Wonderland*)

Anyone working regularly in the field of restoration, and especially in that of architectural restoration, knows that one cannot count on the final results not changing. The inevitable processes of the ageing of materials; natural factors such as the work of atmospheric or human agents such as atmospheric pollution; alterations to the very form of the monument, in order to satisfy ever changing functional needs; or even just negligence and lack of maintenance, eventually limit the benefits gained from restoration itself. Although this can be a source of concern, it is also necessary to assume a 'decay' factor as one of the givens of the problem, while adopting all possible protection to reduce or delay the process of decline over time.

But there it is. No restoration, however important, is definitive; and all of them, even the most thorough or prestigious, represent a chapter, sometimes even just a paragraph, to be added to the long history of an architectural monument. There is no work, not even that which appears most marginal to the formal and material integrity of a monument, which does not open a channel of communication between the object of the restoration itself and whoever is working on it. In a different way, any intervention on an historical building takes something original from it while introducing something new; if this is not at a purely formal level, it certainly happens at the level of the very material texture, which is not separable from the first aspect. Until the habit of constant maintenance becomes common practice, it will be necessary to proceed with work that will be known for its radical nature which, no matter how thorough and respectful it is, entails levels of greater tampering.

This relationship of give and take in terms of a monument undergoing restoration calls for intelligent and well-informed management, in order to be able to unravel the many threads competing for decisions, where there is always more than one path which could be taken and the choice of a particular path presupposes clarity about the final objective. The "puzzle" to be put together again is then enriched by elements deriving from a range of recognised tools: the search for historic fact, investigations about the structure and materials, specialist analyses, critical comparisons. It is a collection of knowledge that forms and grows as the work progresses and which, if it is not shared, risks disappearing once the work is over. Every architectural restorer is familiar with the importance of finding an historical document concerning the object of the work, perhaps a money order containing the description of mortar or colouring; or is lucky enough to be able to arrange information gathered in the course of preceding restorations, thus avoiding the often useless (and at times offensive) inquiries into current material. The precise communication of this collection of knowledge enables the experience of restoration to live on, extending its benefits beyond the limits of time as a perfect witness left to the people who, after us, in a few or many years, may find themselves restoring the architectural monument again.

It is for this reason that the Department for Architectural Properties and the Lazio Countryside has agreed, with the publication of this first volume connected with restoration work carried out on the Convento di Palazzolo on the occasion of the Jubilee, to publish a series entitled *"Lazio Rediscovered – research and restoration"*. The primary aim is to not squander the heritage of knowledge acquired during the restoration work and, in parallel, to collate the choices made, explaining the motivation and the thought processes behind them.

It is not just restoration, however; nor is it just building site reports, even if these are extremely useful. The series, of which this book is the first volume, follows the criterion of providing an exhaustive picture of knowledge about the monuments treated, as well as touching on more specialist aspects, in the wider framework of a "handy" graphic format which uses a rich display of images.

In this way we believe we are providing a service for the community of scholars, for those who work in the area of restoration and for whoever develops an interest in culture, thereby hoping to contribute to the knowledge and preservation of the architectural heritage of Lazio.

I. The landscape
Marina Cogotti

The irreversible building process throughout the country over the last fifty years has changed profoundly the physical aspect of some of the most enchanting Italian landscapes. Nor has it spared the hilly district south-east of Rome known as the 'Castelli Romani'. Nevertheless, those who pass through the area along the trunk road, the Via dei Laghi, or stop at one of the viewpoints on the ridge of the crater which acts as a basin for Lake Albano, cannot but notice the foreshortened panorama glimpsed from the steep slopes of the south-eastern side of the lake. Here, the secluded architectural outline of the Palazzolo complex[1] stands out (figs. 1-3). It is an image which still allows one to experience fully those feelings of "spatial harmony", of which travellers and tourists less distracted by current events have felt the need to leave evidence down the centuries (figs. 4-5).

Undoubtedly, if one simply glances up to follow the rising skyline towards Monte Cavo, the ancient *Mons Albanus*, the forest of antennae which today dominates the top and the explosion of the built-up area of the town of Rocca di Papa below lead again to thoughts of other delicate issues, to the several ways in which the land has been used (figs. 6-7). Fortunately, the most recent building developments have largely spared the slopes of the lake where Palazzolo stands, thus safeguarding that intimate relationship which binds every monument to the environmental context in which it finds itself. This is a particularly determinant relationship in the case of Palazzolo, which arose from, and was modified down the centuries, precisely in relation to the landscape. Indeed, Palazzolo itself has contributed to reshaping that landscape, from its establishment in ancient times with the tremendous carving through the rock (fig. 8), to the panoramic comparison with the other emerging monuments, the first of which was the villa wanted by Urban VIII looking out from the opposite side of the lake and universally known, since then, as the summer residence of the Popes (fig. 9).

This relationship with the landscape could not be otherwise. It can be seen even today by anyone who, leaving the main road on the ridge, goes back down the steep slope along the ancient path which leads to the Capuchin Priory at Albano and passes Palazzolo: while the view of the lake gradually opens out to the right, the peperino hillside out of which the path is hewn reveals various aspects, depending on the indications left by human work on it: breathtaking hacks into the rock, caves, wild vegetation, even a rocky tomb (figs. 10-11). Palazzolo, too, extending along the terracing standing out from the hilly nature of the site, continues to follow its ancient layout with the long terrace garden, until it rejoins the tufa hillside close to the mysterious caves (figs. 12-14).

There are many elements that contribute to this extraordinary setting. Firstly, the pleasant nature of the site, those unique mountainous and physical conditions which, in themselves, offer a history more ancient than that of humanity itself, for the whole district of the Castelli Romani is well-known for its physical characteristics which derive from the geographical system of the Latian Volcano, the most complete of the volcanic features in the Lazio region.

Dating back some 700,000 years or so, when the first products of

---

[1] The present place-name is "Palazzola", a relatively recent deformation of the more ancient name "Palazzolo". This is a direct derivation of "Palatium" relating to the Roman settlement. Medieval variations are listed by L. JANAUSCHEK in his *Originum Cistercensium*, Vindobonae, 1877, p. 244, n. 637. The authors have chosen to use the more ancient name.

1. Panoramic view of the south eastern slope of Lake Albano with Convento di Palazzolo and the Villa Colonna, today called "Villa del Cardinale", which overlooks it

volcanic activity were deposited on the broad plain extending from the coast to the Apennines, the hilly system that arose through geographic events today covers an area of about 60 km. It is made up of an external craterous surround, still preserved in a south-south-east arc and in the south-west. Here it is fringed by the formation of outlying secondary craters, in which lie the origins of Lakes Albano and Nemi. The principal crater at the centre of the volcanic system consists of a rim about 2 km in diameter. It came about through the elevation of a final cone formed on a new volcano within the preceding one in a period between 500,000 and 300,000 years ago. Monte Cavo and Mascho delle Faete, with a height of about 950 metres, emerged as part of this process. After a long, dormant period, which allowed this central funnel-shaped gap to cool, and the subsequent blockage by deposits of magma (resulting in the formation of the plateau of the present Campi di Annibale), the pressure released by the products of the volcano's internal activity coming into contact with underground waters resulted in a series of explosions, which caused the surface crust to break and secondary craters to form, between 70,000 and 30,000 years ago (figs. 15-16). Within and around these craters, the eruptive material gradually built up due to repeated wa-

2. View of the Convento from the gardens of the Villa del Cardinale.

ter-bearing explosions, resulting in the formation of huge deposits of peperino. This can still be seen today at Palazzolo, high up on the vertical wall where the layer of peperino has been excavated to make way, first for the Roman settlement, and then for the successive religious houses[2] (figs. 8, 17).

For centuries, the products of the Latian Volcano were the mainstay of the Roman construction industry: tufa, ash and lava, later hardened into stone-like tufa (peperino), leucocyte lava (flint) and, to a lesser extent, spurs and basalt. They have contributed decisively to both the structural and formal aspects of architectural achievements, as well as to the colourful composition of the local landscape.

The image of Palazzolo is inseparable from the rocky material which characterises not only the site itself but also the material

[2] Cf. M. FORNASERI – A. SCHERILLO – U VENTRIGLIA, *La regione vulcanica dei Colli Albani*, Rome 1963; also *Geomorphological features of the Latian Volcano* (Alban Hills, Italy) in "Geologica Romana", Vol. XIII, Rome 1974; C. CIVITELLI – R FUNICIELLO – M PAROTTO, *Caratteri deposizionali dei prodotti del vulcanismo freatico nei Colli Albani*, in "Geologica Romana", Vol. XIV, Rome 1975.

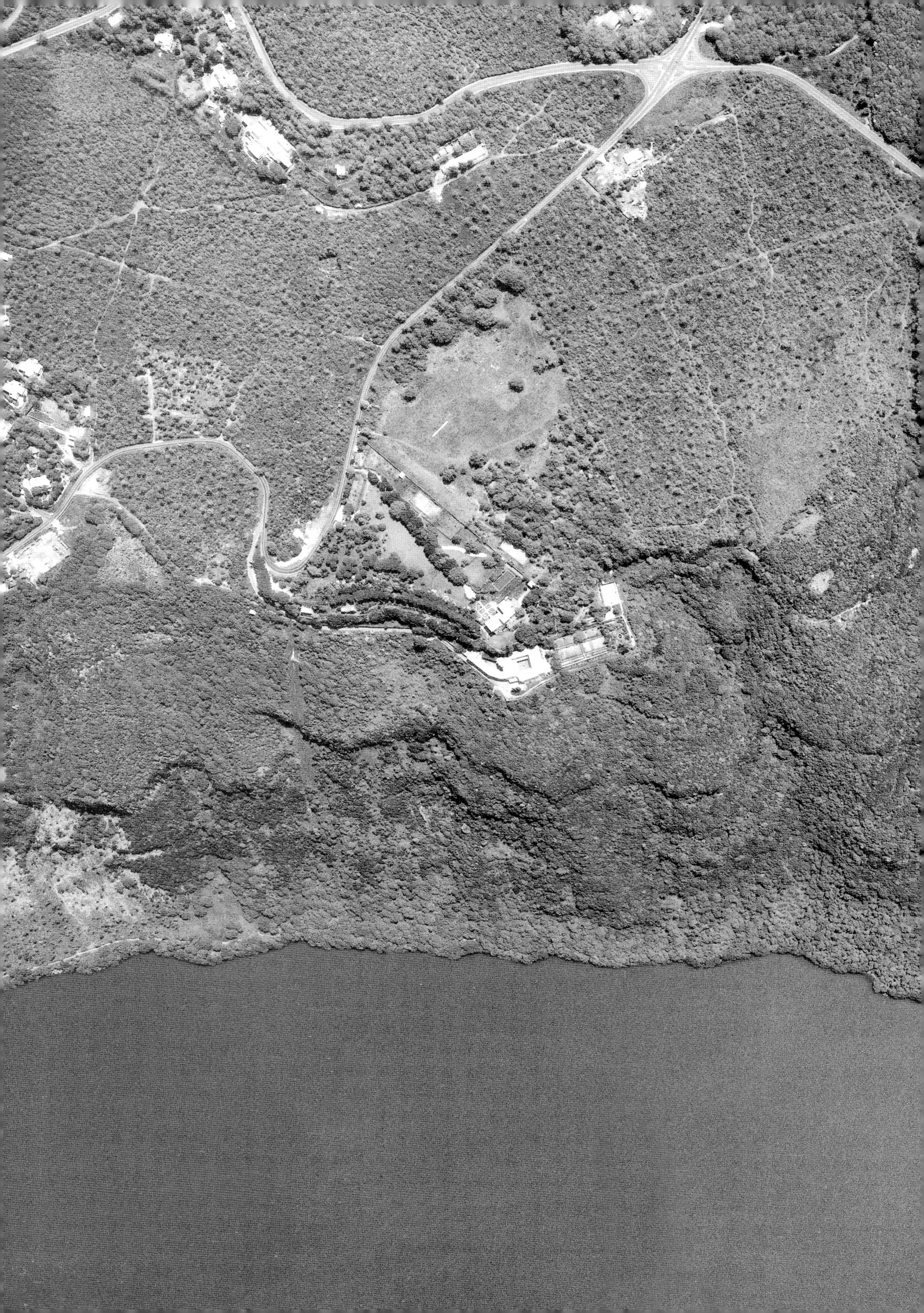

3. Aerial photo of the area around Palazzolo (S.A.R.A. – Nistri: 1982).

THE LANDSCAPE 17

4. J. C. Reinhart, "Pallazzola", 1792 (private collection).

[3] Cf. D. Esposito, *Tecniche costruttive murarie medievali*, Rome 1997, p. 79.

used for it, such as the buttress stone with which all the Tuscolan villas were built, or the little flint bricks which are characteristic of a medieval building technique in tufa blocks known as 'opera veliterna'. The peperino stone at Palazzolo (the vitruvian *Lapis albanus*), characterised by its excellent workability, is a clear, grey, stone-like tufa, made up of ash with limestone of varying properties and particle size depending on the distance from the centre of eruption. It is present in the whole area from Marino to Grottaferrata[3]; it was the principal building material in the area, used in ancient projects and right up to the last ten years or so, when the quarries were exhausted (fig. 18).

Over time, the hollows of the secondary craters of the volcano filled with water to form lakes, of which those of Albano and Nemi remain, while those of the Valley of Ariccia and the Marciana Valley were reclaimed. Together, the lakes form an '8' due to the basin originally being formed by two or perhaps more adjoining cones, united by the destruction of the intermediate septa due to successive explosions. For a long time the mountainous formation of their origin has protected the banks of the two lakes, with the steep slopes above the level of the lake, the wild woods covering the slopes and the au-

5. N. BOUGET-DIDIER, View of Lake Albano with the Priory, end of 18th – early 19th century (Istituto Nazionale per la Grafica).

ra of mystery. They were places known for their magical and religious significance, especially in the case of Lake Nemi, which even today remains one of the most complete corners of the Castelli Romani, despite the untidy presence of predominantly agricultural construction on the north-east side and the hydro-biological problems which affect it.

Lake Albano, on whose slopes sits Convento di Palazzolo, overlooked by the "Villa del Cardinale", is the largest of the two surviving lakes (fig. 19); the expanse of water, conveniently absorbed into an ellipse, has a maximum length of 3.5 km and an average width of 2.5 km. The surrounding crater is over a kilometre wider than the size of the lake itself; close to the centre the maximum depth today reaches 170 metres[4]. There is a vast bibliography about this lake, whose history down the centuries is deeply connected with that of Rome. Its volcanic origins; the legends linked to the city of Alba Longa and the building of an outlet - a true masterpiece of hydraulic engineering still working today; the building on ancient sites of both medieval settlements and later the great baroque villas which make up part of the panorama; all have made it a place of continuing interest for artists, poets and scholars. Down the centuries they have repeatedly de-

[4] In the past, the depth was much greater; Tomassetti talks of 217 metres: cf. G. TOMASSETTI, *La Campagna Romana Antica, Medioevale e Moderna* (1910-1926), new edition edited by L. Chiumenti and F. Bilancia, Florence 1979-80, Vol. II, p. 206.

6. Palazzolo today; in the background are the slopes of Monte Cavo and the forest of antennae dominating the peak.

8. The vertical cut through the rock-face; in the foreground is the old barn.

scribed and represented this scene, in some cases quite openly re-interpreting it (figs. 20-21).

The "architecture" of this volcanic landscape, with its pleasant unevenness and variety of views and heights, and with the presence of the lakes and forests, the variety of the panoramic viewpoints, the mildness of the climate and the healthy air, has always favoured settlements conditioned by the physical structure of the great volcanic edifice. This began with the pre-Roman settlements, and the choice of the highest point of the central crater (*Mons Albanus* or Monte Cavo) as a religious focal point, and includes the constellation of little centres, including the powerful and extended Alba Longa, later destroyed by the Romans.

The physical geography of the area was a primary factor in the form that the settlements took, with the transformation of the hard conditions imposed by the mountainous landscape extolling the choice of location. The nucleus of Palazzolo, extended on a base carved from natural material, just like the palace at Castel Gandolfo, represents various ways of responding to the suggestions that the site itself provides. It is interesting to see how even the most recent studies on Alba Longa – whose very name is significant when consider-

7. Panoramic view of the lake from Castel Gandolfo; to the left of Monte Cavo is the town of Rocca di Papa, and to the right is Palazzolo.

ing its form – suggest research starts from the design of the city as a response to a geographical condition, in this specific case as a "ridge illuminated by the sun"[5].

The suggestive but weak hypothesis that the location of the lost city was to be found precisely at Palazzolo, encouraged by observations shared and proposed by various scholars, disappeared some time ago. However, there remain reasonable theses to support the identification of the site on the opposite side of the lake, corresponding to Castel Gandolfo, a site certainly inhabited by an advanced civilisation some centuries before the foundation of Rome, as proved by the burial-grounds discovered there. However, the presence of caves, the tomb and the ancient outline of a path at Palazzolo, does not exclude the fact that this side of the lake, too, belonged to the territory of Alba Longa; it is certain that from the start of the 9th century B.C. the site was inhabited, shown by the necropolis of Vigna Trovalusci[6].

Even when the supremacy of Rome was well-established and the centre of settlements had shifted from the craterous rim towards the plain, the great infrastructures, such as the roads, the aqueducts and the suburban villas, ensured the permanence of the old centres of the Latin tribes; the lake, with its inhabited sites, along with Albano, Ar-

[5] Cf. A. ARNOLDUS-HUYZENDVELD, *Nota preliminare sull'interpretazione di Alba Longa come "dorsale illuminata dal sole"*, in "Documenta Albana", IIs., n. 21, 1999, pp. 25-42.

[6] For the archaeological aspects see chapter II: G. GHINI, *Palazzolo in ancient times*, and the General Bibliography.

THE LANDSCAPE 21

9. Panoramic view of the lake and the town of Castel Gandolfo, dominated by the architecture of the Papal residence.

iccia and Nemi, gravitated around a sphere of influence connected to the Via Appia which had a strategic role due to its position as a point of transit for traffic heading towards the south and the east. Furthermore, communications between the Alban Hills and Rome benefited from a good local and territorial road network dating back to the time of ancient *Latium*. In 312 B.C., the Via Appia, following the path of the ancient Via Albana linking Rome to the community of Alba Longa, was added to the Via Castrimeniense and the Via Latina, which, in linking Rome with Capua, climbed back up the north-west side of the crater heading towards the Valle del Sacco, passing through Grottaferrata; the Via Tuscolana guaranteed links with the town of Tuscolo and the gentle north-western slopes, which became the panoramic viewpoint from the hills towards Rome.

Many of the achievements of this period, which would be decisive centuries later in choosing where to make settlements, left a clear mark on the Alban landscape. Such is the striking case, for example, of the phenomenon of the prestigious out-of-town residences in the Tusculum area, chosen in Imperial times and later on, during the baroque period. The correspondence between the new settlements and the old ones is of interest not only for the choice of the site, but because it also affects the relationship with the surrounding territory. This means constructions which, starting from the significance of the landscape in which they find themselves, tend to exploit all the intrinsic possibilities that this relationship provides, boldly and skilfully reshaping the features in order to draw comfort and pleasure from it. At the same time they increase its value: imaginative planning links, enormous excavations, terracing and gaps fit in harmoniously with the variety of nature, and still offer today a lesson in landscape architecture which it is sometimes difficult to find in contemporary achievements.

To a lesser extent, due to the more difficult landscape conditions and accessibility, the same phenomenon affects the villas built on the slopes of Lake Albano, including the site of Palazzolo, which owes its place name to the first Roman construction. Even if it is not certain

10. The path, today suitable for vehicles, leading from the Via dei Laghi to the Priory, showing the now semi-destroyed fountain in the wall. In the background, in a gap in the vegetation, the rock tomb can just be seen.

11. The same view at the time of this drawing by Labruzzi at the end of the 18th century; C. LABRUZZI, *"Le Antichità di Albano delineate da suoi avanzi"*, 1854.

Monumento Sepolcrale à Palazzuolo | *Monument Sépulcral à Palazzuolo*

THE LANDSCAPE 23

12. The final part of the path to Palazzolo, running past the most recent buildings.

13. The path alongside the great supporting wall of the Priory's terrace garden.

[7] For a general analysis of the genesis and transformations of the settlement and land system in the Castelli Romani, cf. T. PARIS (editor), *L'Area dei Castelli Romani*, Rome 1981, pp. 33-47.

[8] For the historical events and relative sources see the detailed and well-documented chapter: A. CRIELESI, *The Artistic History of Convento di Palazzolo* and the General Bibliography

[9] The document, dated 8 February 1269, names the two buildings in a description of the boundaries of Palazzolo's property. Cf. CASIMIRO DA ROMA, 1744, p. 326.

that the Roman construction (whose original dedication is lost) had fallen into ruin when a group of hermits found refuge there, it is certain that great excavations had already taken place and that for a long time the old structures were adapted. With the dissolution of the Roman political and economic structure and the barbarian invasions which followed the fall of the Empire, the Alban Hills, like the whole of the *Ager*, saw the abandonment and destruction of the great patrician villas, deforestation and damage, and the consequent depopulation of the settlements.

With the spread of Christianity in the centuries immediately following the fall of the Empire, numerous centres of worship arose in suburban territory, just as at Palazzolo, often in buildings dating from the Roman era; it is noteworthy how from this first, embryonic ecclesiastical structure, with the support of a solid land base, via the phenomenon of *domuscultae*, the 8th century saw a restructuring of the agricultural and social organisation of the territory by Pope Zacharias, with definite physical changes to the landscape. The successive Muslim invasions led to the introduction of a defence system of towers and the first fortified fortresses of the widespread *domuscultae* type, an easy prey for plundering.

It is the start of that process which, for defensive motives, caused the population to move from the countryside to fortified centres built on the highest ground and with eye contact between each other, thus bringing about that settlement system which is still seen today in this territory, although many of the defensive structures have now disappeared or are in ruins. This system was strengthened in the last decades of the first millennium when, through the processes triggered by the institution of long-term leases and renting, there came the first perpetual leases, which slowly ensured that political control passed from the bishops to the baronial families[7].

The events that followed the abandonment of Palazzolo's imperial villa and the other Roman settlements are recorded; the first documents referring to the locality date back to the first decades of the 11th century[8] and speak of the existing church of *Sancta Maria de Palatiolis*. As has already been said, it can be presumed that this little settlement had not been in continuous use, but was soon turned into a place of worship; remains of the Roman construction can still be seen, despite the plundering of successive eras, in the materials reused in the construction of the church or incorporated in various parts of the building or the garden (fig. 22). Remains of the *opus reticulatum* (lattice-pattern brickwork) are still visible in the lower part of the walls of the oldest part of the building, adjoining the tower. But the church, with its little religious house attached, was not the only building to occupy this steep part of the lakeside. It was declared an Abbey by Pope Innocent IV in 1244, but a document dating from just after its actual habitation by hermits mentions, in the vicinity, the little *ecclesia sancti Angeli post lacum* and the *castrum Maleaffictum*[9].

The ruins of these buildings, found on the slope south-east of Palazzolo, are still visible today, even though they are almost completely covered by thick vegetation. However, the destruction of the castle, at least, dates back a long way, as is also shown by ancient car-

14. W. F. GMELIN, "View of the volcanic cave at Palazzuola", 1812.

Veduta della Grotta vulcanica di Palazzuola

tography (figs. 23-24). Taken over via a transfer in 1277 by Riccardo from the late Mattia Annibaldi, all trace of it is lost for the next two hundred years. Then, in a 1428 document, ratifying the sale by Nicolò Savelli, whose family took over the Annibaldi estate, to Antonio Colonna, Prince of Salerno, the castle is described as *dirutum et inhabitatum*[10]. It is probable that the defensive structure functioned as a lookout post for the Rocca della Molara, guarded by the Annibaldi, but its importance should not be underestimated as possibly controlling the water springs there, which were well known and had already been used for centuries. Today, little remains of the castle. It returned to the Savelli, who disposed of it, along with Ariccia, in 1661, on behalf of the Chigi. The castle was rectangular with square towers at the corners, the western side vertically above the lake, which is perhaps the origin of the term 'Malafitto' ('badly placed'?). It was built with peperino bricks, using a technique which can be still found

[10] Cf. V. TOMASSETTI, op. cit., p. 199.

15. Evolutionary phases of the Latian Volcano.
A) First period: 700,000 years ago.
B) Second period: 500,000 years ago.
C) Third period: 500,000 – 300,000 years ago.
D) Fourth period: 70,000 – 30,000 years ago (from *Un parco naturale regionale nei Castelli Romani*, Velletri 1980).

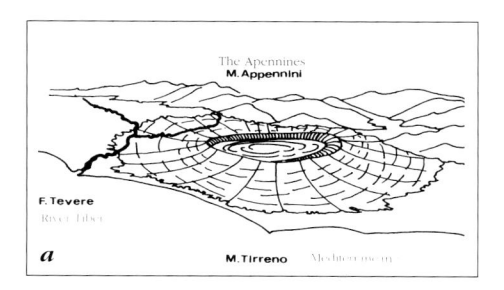

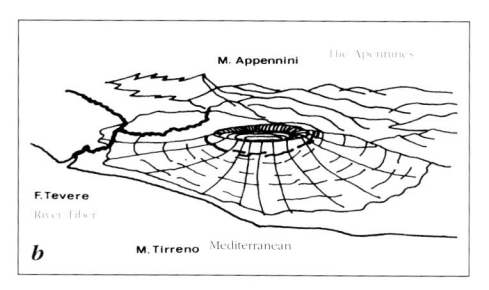

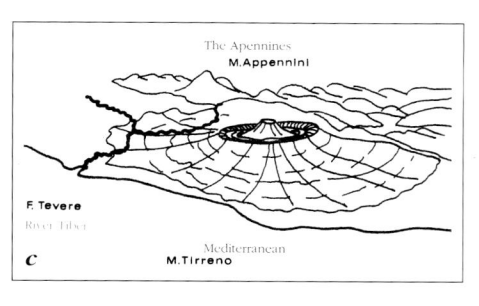

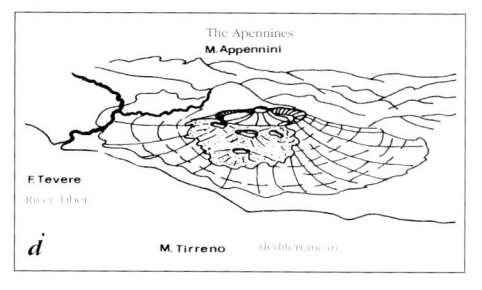

in contemporary buildings of a similar type, such as Castel Savello at Albano Laziale or the medieval tower at Convento di Palazzolo itself. The corner towers had a high base in squared-off peperino (fig. 25).

The fate of the S. Angelo hermitage, situated on the steep slope beneath Palazzolo, was no better than that of the *castrum*. It was mentioned in a Papal Bull of Paschal II in 1116 and was demolished by Cardinal Colonna in 1773 as part of a number of measures taken against brigands. The original building must have been on different levels, given the nature of the slope on which it was built, and included a little church with a bell tower and a monastery attached, with arched rooms supporting the upper floors and perhaps basement rooms carved into the rock itself. The state of the stones, which collapsed, and the presence of vegetation do not make for an easy reconstruction of the plan of the complex. It was built of blocks of peperino and flint, with variations of flint and peperino chips; until recently, traces of plasterwork and fresco could be seen inside (fig. 26).

After the fall of the Counts of Tusculum, the powerful and warlike family which for two centuries had stood up to Rome, commanding a well-defended territory extending from the Tusculan Hills to the Pontine Marshes, a number of the Roman hill towns returned to the jurisdiction of the churches and monasteries, which, in some cases, such as the Abbey of Grottaferrata, were large property owners. The Roman families, such as the Savelli, the Colonna, and the Annibaldi, already beneficiaries of the new temporary leases which were then transformed into definite acquisitions, assumed greater prestige when, following the Avignon period of the papacy, which loosened ecclesiastical control over the kingdom, poverty and famine forced many Romans to move into the countryside to follow their lords and masters. Another migration followed in the middle of the 16th century, from which comes the name Castelli Romani, given to the Tusculan and Alban Hills.

After the devastation following the defeats inflicted upon the Colonna and Savelli families, the 16th century saw the re-discovery of the Roman buildings, particularly the great villas. Admittedly, it was a little later with respect to the proper 'Roman' society, but there was a rediscovery of the past and the birth of a taste for antiques and collections. The new Roman aristocracy, linked to the Pontiff of the time, once more adopted the settlements already seen in Roman times, particularly on Tusculum, but also on the slopes of Lake Albano. The landscape of the Castelli Romani was revitalised by a series of projects and link roads, which remodelled entire areas of the countryside, according to the contemporary concept of the villa. This was an estate, which provided for a prestigious residence, the house and estate served by agricultural land – orchards, olive groves, and vineyards. The whole was almost always enclosed in a large park, itself consisting of well-designed gardens, embellished with avenues, panoramic viewpoints and fountains.

The most significant modifications to the Alban landscape and, thus, to the site of Palazzolo, came in the time of Pope Urban VIII (1623-1644), who in 1624 decided to start work on the construction

16. Volcanic material and sediments (from *Un parco naturale regionale nei Castelli Romani*, Velletri 1980).

17. Full view of the garden; in the background can be seen the rock-face which was cut away to make the terrace.

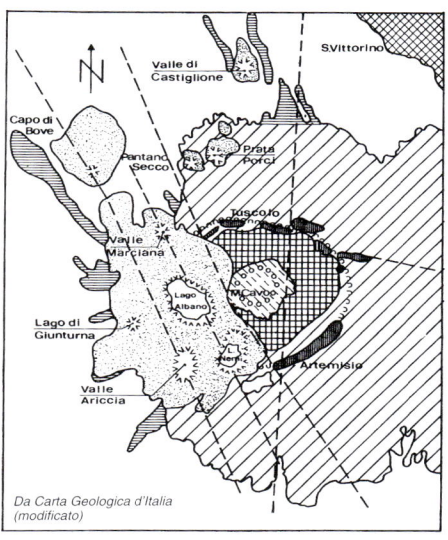

18. Peperino brickwork characteristic of the Priory's medieval buildings.

19. Panoramic view of the whole of Lake Albano.

THE LANDSCAPE 27

20. C. ZIMMERMANN, "Kloster Palazzola", from *Rom und seine Imgebung*, 19th century (private collection).

21. N. BOUGET-DIDIER, Panoramic perspective of the lake with the Palazzolo buildings, end of 18th-start of 19th century (Istituto Nazionale per la Grafica).

28   CHAPTER I

of his own summer palace at Castel Gandolfo, where he already owned a modest residence. As the plan for another villa to be built close to Palazzolo shows (fig. 24), the Barberini Pope carefully assessed the possibility of having the palace in an area of the lake less bound by concerns of height. Arrigucci prepared a project whose apparent rigidity in terms of the ground plan (fig. 27) was due precisely to its location on a narrow plateau wedged between two narrow valleys[11]. Its actual construction, described in the documents of *"Castello Sud"*, was amazing for its magnificence and the stress on its relationship with the lake below, towards which it was pointed like a missile; the villa itself faced directly the panorama with its façade pierced by a portico. It boasted a vast terrace whose supporting portico was built against a double flight of steps that overcomes the jump in height between the wood beneath and the monumental *belvedere*[12].

The presence of the Papal court in the territory of Albano led to building activity of the highest order in the area, and was also the reason for the construction of a Villa on the plateau immediately above Convento di Palazzolo. In much of the Palazzolo iconography, the view of this Villa is inseparable from that of the Convento itself (figs. 28-30). It was built by Cardinal Girolamo Colonna, after Pope

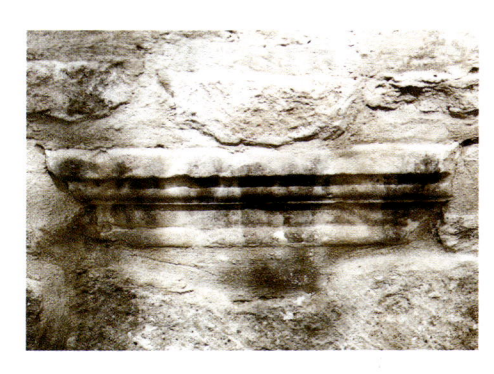

22. Marble fragment built into the wall in the Priory garden.

23. ANONYMOUS, Planta, et descriptio Status, ac Territori, 1588. Frascati, Aldobrandini Archives.

[11] VATICAN CITY, Vatican Apostolic Library, henceforth B.A.V. *Disegni e Piante diverse*, Chigiani Manuscript, P. VII, 12. *Territorio di Castel Gandolfo, con sue strade, Palazzuolo, Casini e strade diverse con il Lago dove Papa Urbano hebbe disegno di fare un Castello, et il disegno lo fece Arrigucci*, fol. 2.

[12] B.A.V., *Disegni e Piante diverse*, Chigiani Manuscript, P. VII, 12. *Pianta del Castello sud fatto da Luigi Arrigucci*, fol. 3.

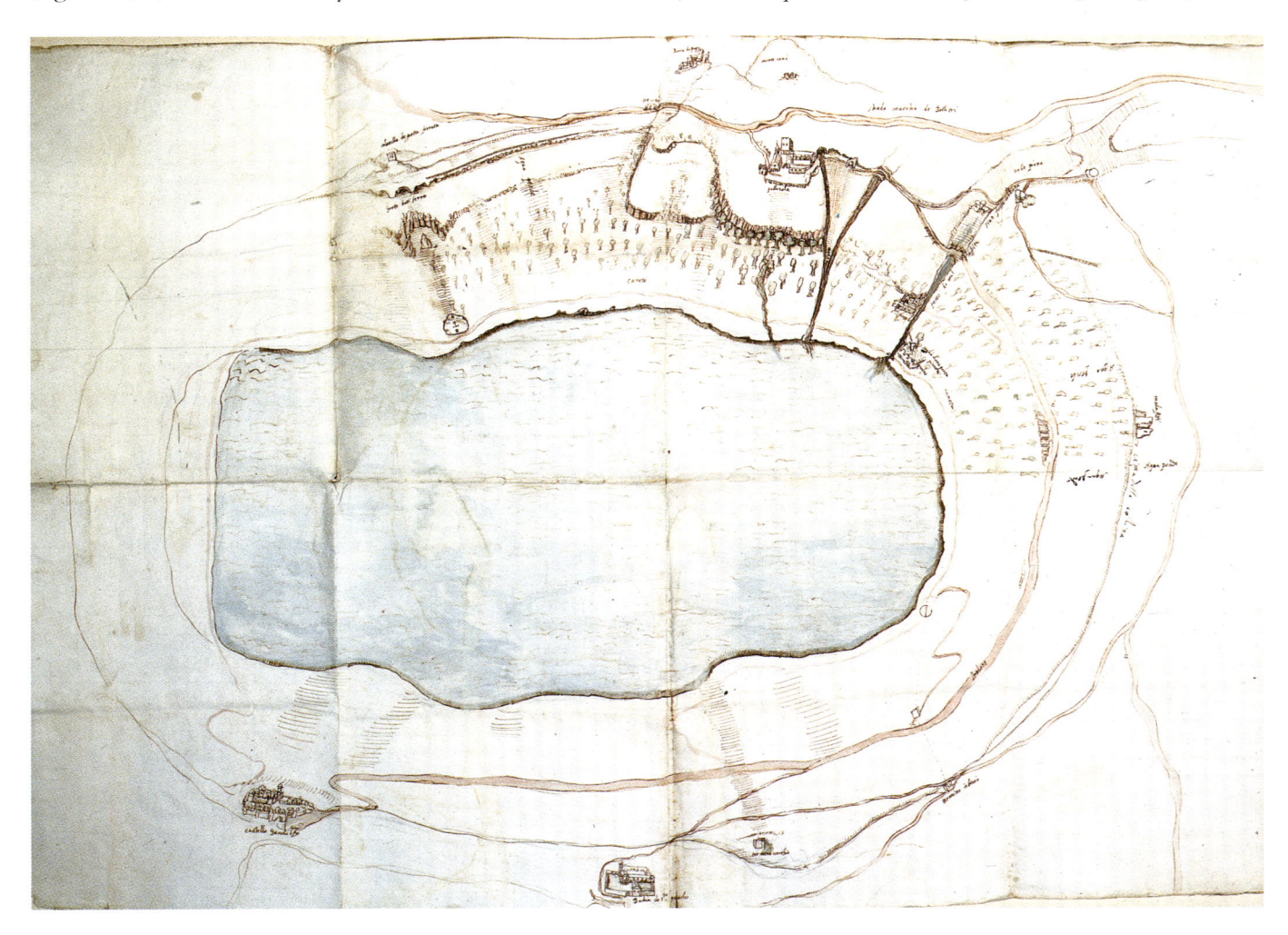

THE LANDSCAPE

24. The Palazzolo area in a map by Arrigucci showing the planned location of Urban VIII's un-built castle (17th century). B.A.V., Disegni e Piante diverse, Chigiani Manuscript, P. VII, 12, fol. 2.

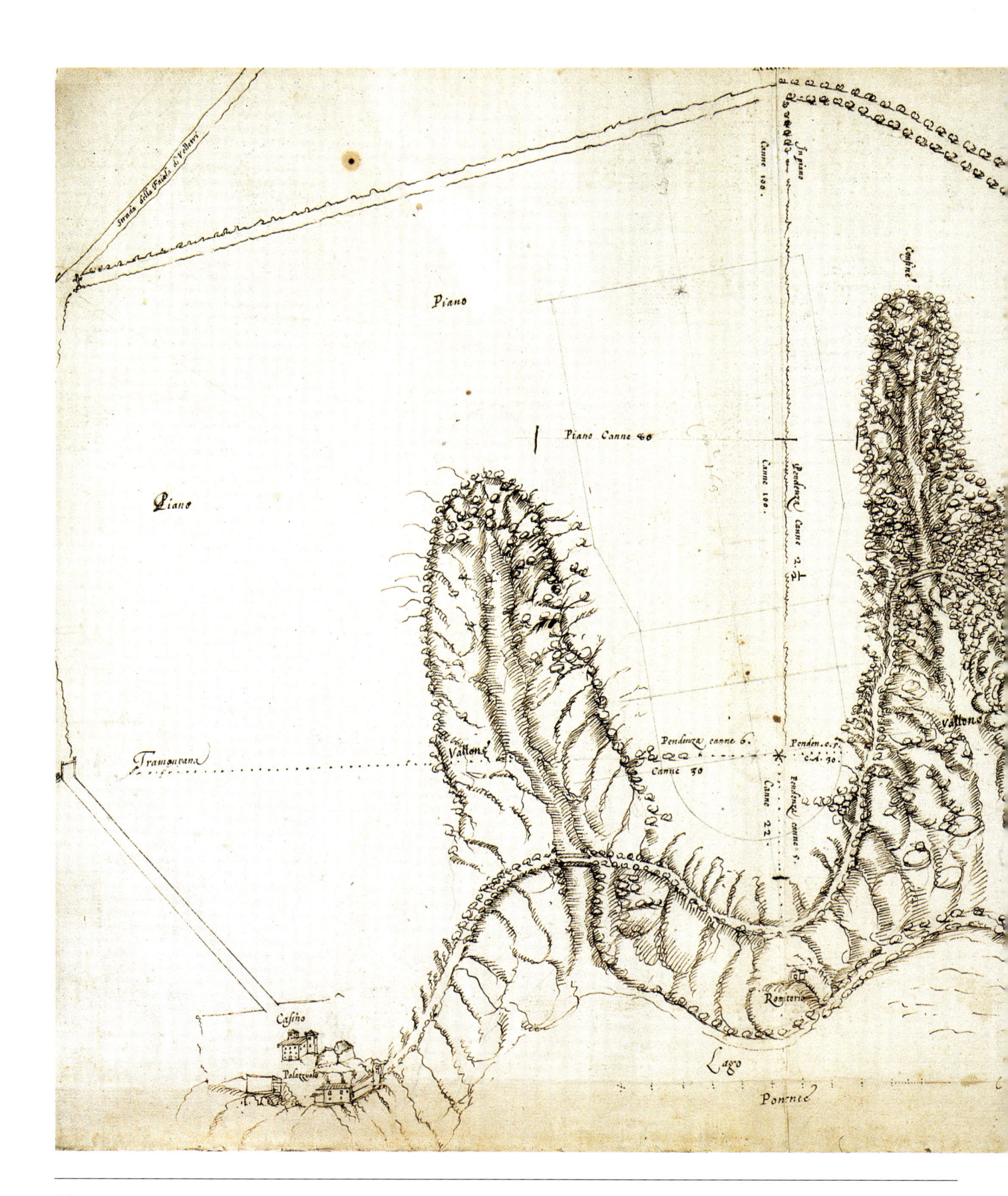

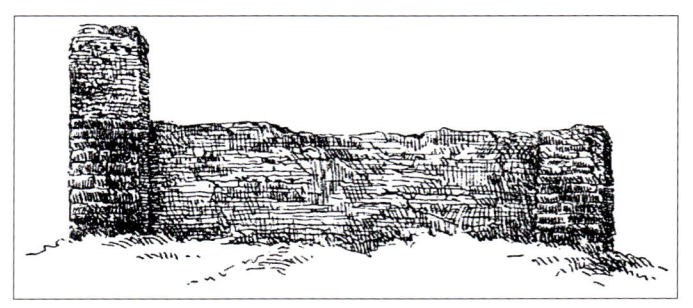

25. The Malaffitto Castle (from G. TOMASSETTI, *La Campagna romana antica, medioevale e moderna*, Rome 1910).

26. The Hermitage of S. Angelo in a period photograph (from G. TOMASSETTI, *La Campagna romana antica, medioevale e moderna*, Rome 1910).

THE LANDSCAPE

27. LUIGI ARRIGUCCI, Plan for a castle for Urban VIII, B.A.V., Disegni e Piante diverse, Chigiani Manuscript, P. VII, 12, fol. 3.

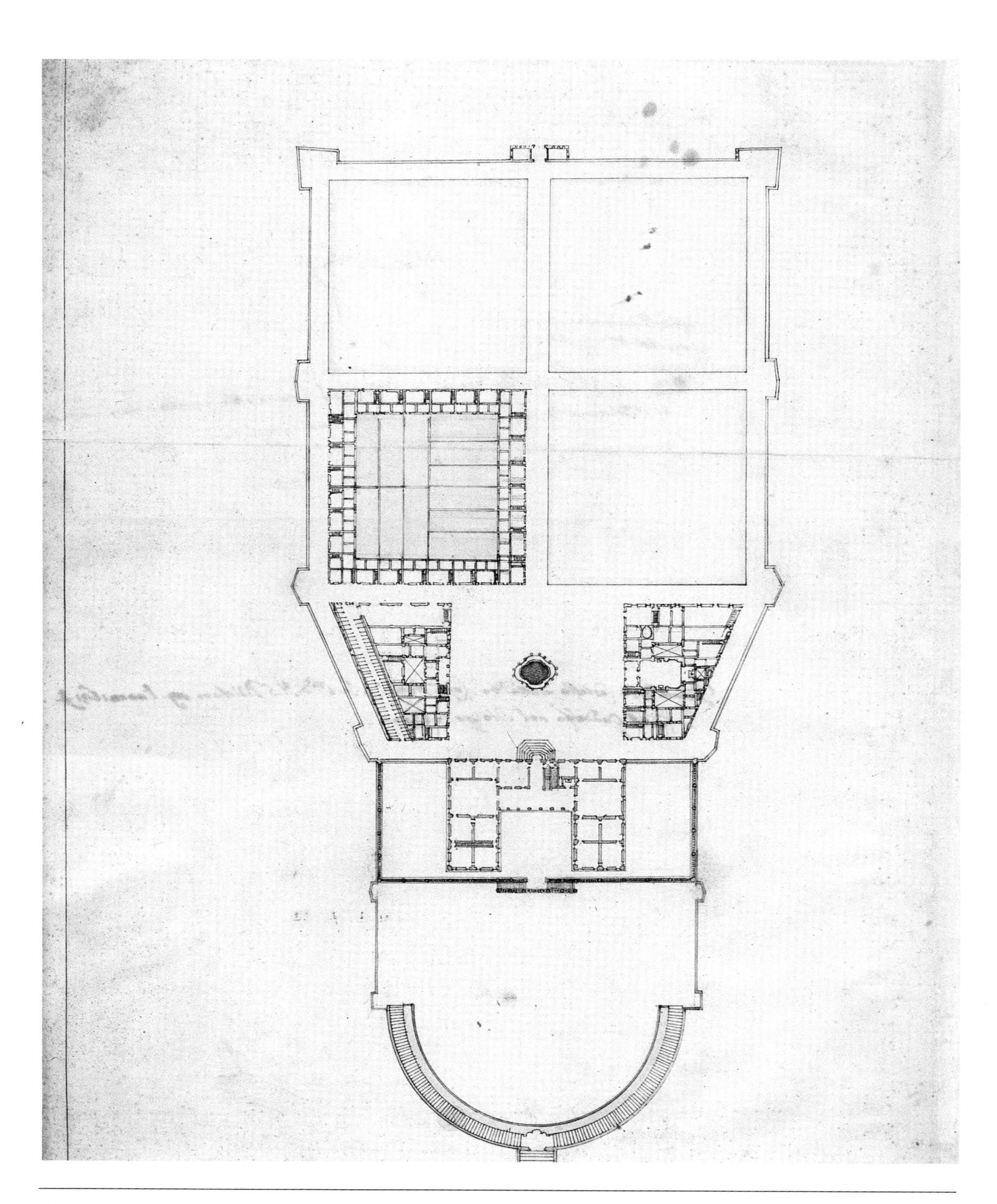

28. L. CAVALIERI, "Palazzuolo", from Italia illustrata, mid-19th century (private collection).

Urban VIII, in 1629, gave him some property belonging to the Friars, "six *rubbie* [a medieval measurement] of land attached to the Priory"[13]. Previously, there had been a lodge and a medieval tower on this land. The building of the Villa was part of a vast property operation conducted by the Colonna family throughout the Marino territory they had controlled from the first decades of the 15th century. The "Colonna" achievements can be seen substantially in two building phases: the first, which chiefly concerned the town of Marino and its immediate neighbourhood, began in the years immediately following the Sack of Rome. It was largely the work of Marcantonio II and his son Cardinal Ascanio, who were responsible for a complex which included not just the palace itself, but also the arrangement of a vast park area, with a layout of land, the creation of a network of paths and gardens, embellished by sculptural and architectural creations which, in its final phase, also had the collaboration of Girolamo Rainaldi.

The second phase can be dated to the first decades of the seventeenth century, when the Lord of Marino, Duke since 1606, was Philip I. The achievements of this High Constable, who with his consort, Lucrezia Tomacelli, enjoyed lengthy stays at Marino, are buildings jutting out onto the landscape; the drawings of Van Wittel are

[13] A.C., III BB XV n. 637.

THE LANDSCAPE

29. CHAMPIN, Les bord du Lac d'Albane, from *Album Portatif de l'Italie*, c. 1850 (private collection).

well-known, portraying the Marinese panorama respectively from the terrace of the Bel Poggio hunting lodge – at the time the Villa Desideri – or from the Costagnana terrace, then a villa named 'La Baldacchina'. Better than any discussion these show the value of the 'privileged view points' which these buildings possessed. Another achievement of this period was the completion, under Cardinal Girolamo, fourth Duke of Marino, of the villa situated in the Colonna estate at Frattocchie, known as the "Villa della Sirena" after the feminine figure that decorated the outside; and it is this same Cardinal to whom we owe the building of the Villa above Palazzolo.

The Villa was built on the terracing immediately above that occupied by the Priory, on the area which had probably formerly been occupied by the Roman villa already mentioned. It made use of a clear plan and varying heights of façade, due to the slope which became more pronounced close to the edge of the cut through the peperino. With a little Italian garden in front, the present building (figs. 83-84) is the fruit of a substantial reconstruction which took place in the 1930s, under Guido De Cupis who had bought it in a state of advanced disrepair in 1924. Clearly, the Colonna family interest in owning Palazzolo had disappeared some time before, perhaps with the death of Girolamo and Egidio Colonna.

30. E. Cicéri, Lac d'Albano (from a drawing by F. Bourgeois de Mercey), lithograph from *c.* 1850 (private collection).

Certainly, there was no further repetition of the favourable conditions that led to the building of the Villa at the time of a general appreciation of the area which took place, above all, under Urban VIII and then Alexander VII. To the Chigi Pope, in particular, is due the re-organisation of roads in the whole area. There remains the interesting testimony of someone with the job of *magister viarum*, Domenico Jacovacci, from Albano, and author, among other things, of a manuscript about the area complete with illustrations. It was perhaps commissioned by the Pontiff with a view to property developments to be carried out in the area[14] (figs. 31-32).

From our point of view Plate III is very interesting. It contains a bird's-eye view of the whole volcanic landscape of the Alban area, showing a complete picture of the area's road network at that time. The work from the time of Alexander VII, aimed at improving the links between Castel Gandolfo and the nearby towns, incorporated into the new system the network of paths undertaken some years before by Urban VIII, the 'Upper Path' and the 'Lower Path' which linked Castel Gandolfo to the Capuchins and to Albano. With the extension of the Upper Path through the Capuchin priory, Alexander's road now reached Ariccia; from here a link was established towards Genzano,

[14] Cf. F. Petrucci, *Architettura* in "L'Ariccia del Bernini", pp. 44-49.

THE LANDSCAPE 35

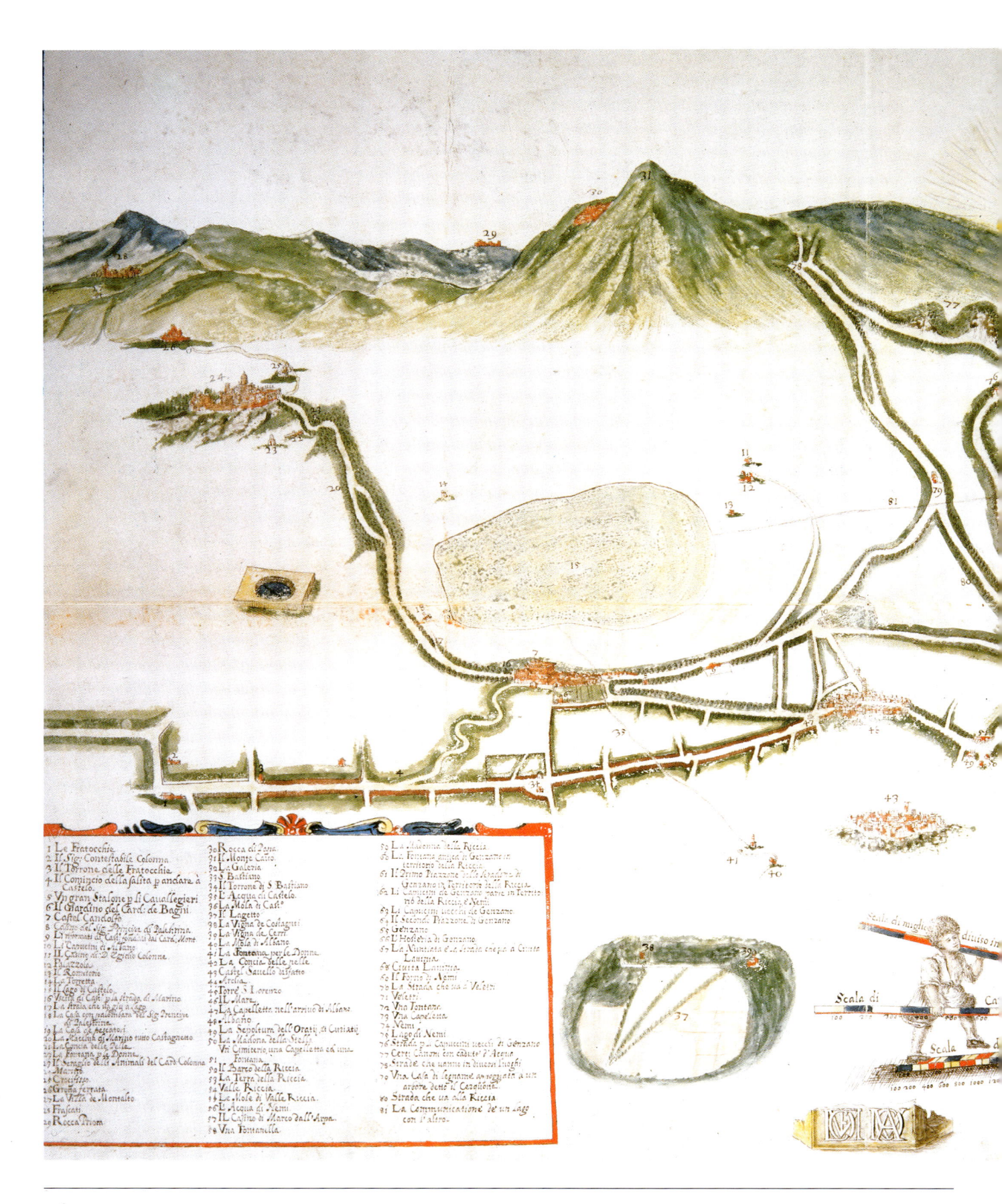

1 Le Fratocchie
2 Il Sigr Contestabile Colonna
3 Il Torrone delle Fratocchie
4 Il Cominecio della salita p andare à Castelo
5 Vn gran Stalone p li Cauallegieri
6 Il Giardino del Card: de Bagni
7 Castel Gandolfo
8 Casino del Sigr Prencipe di Palestrina
9 Li nominati Casi fondati dal Card: Mont
10 Li Capucini di Albano
11 Il Casino di D Egidio Colonna
12 Piazzola
13 Il Romitorio
14 La Torretta
15 Lago di Castelo
16 Vscita di Cast. p la strada di Marino
17 La strada alla legnia de'88
18 La Casa con vn semina del Sigr Prencipe di Palestrina
19 La Casa de' pescatori
20 La Macchia di Marino tutto Castagneto
21 La Concia delle Pelle
22 La Fontana delle Donne
23 Il Serraglio de l' Animali del Card: Colonna
24 Marino
25 Crocifisso
26 Grotta ferrata
27 La Villa de Montalto
28 Frascati
29 Rocca Priora
30 Rocca di Papa
31 Il Monte Cairo
32 La Galeria
33 S. Bastiano
34 Il Torrone di S. Bastiano
35 L' Acqua di Castelo
36 La Mola di Castº
37 Il Lagetto
38 La Vigna de' Castagni
39 La Vigna de' Cerri
40 La Mola di Albano
41 La Fontana per le Donne
42 La Concia delle pelle
43 Castel Gandello disfatto
44 Arcia
45 Torre S. Lorenzo
46 Il Mare
47 La Capelletta nell'arriuo di Albano
48 Albano
49 La Sepoltura dell' Oratij et Curiatij
50 La Madona della Stella Vn Cimiterio una Capelletta ed una Fontana
51 Il Barco della Riccia
52 La Terra della Riccia
53 Valle Riccia
54 Le Mole di Valle Riccia
55 L' Acqua di Nemi
56 Il Casino di Marco dall' Arpa
57 Vna Fontanella
58 La Madonna della Riccia
59 La Fontana antica di Gensano in territorio della Riccia
60 Il Primo Piazzone della Strada de Gensano di territorio della Riccia
61 Li Capucini de Gensano nuovi in territorio della Riccia, e Nemi
62 Li Capucini vecchi de Gensano
63 Il Secondo Piazzone di Gensano
64 Gensano
65 L' Hosteria di Gensano
66 La Nunziata e la strada che va a Ciuita Lauinia
67 Ciuita Lauinia
68 Il Fonte d' Agnis
69 La Strada che va a' Veletri
70 Veletri
71 Vna Fontana
72 Vna Capelletta
73 Nemi
74 Lago di Nemi
75 Strade p. Capucini vecchi di Gensano
76 Certi Chioni ton caduti l' Acqua
77 Strade che vanno in diuersi luoghi
78 Vna Casa di legname appoggiata a un arbore detto il Cauatiore
79 Strada che va alla Riccia
80 La Communicatione de' un lago con l' altro

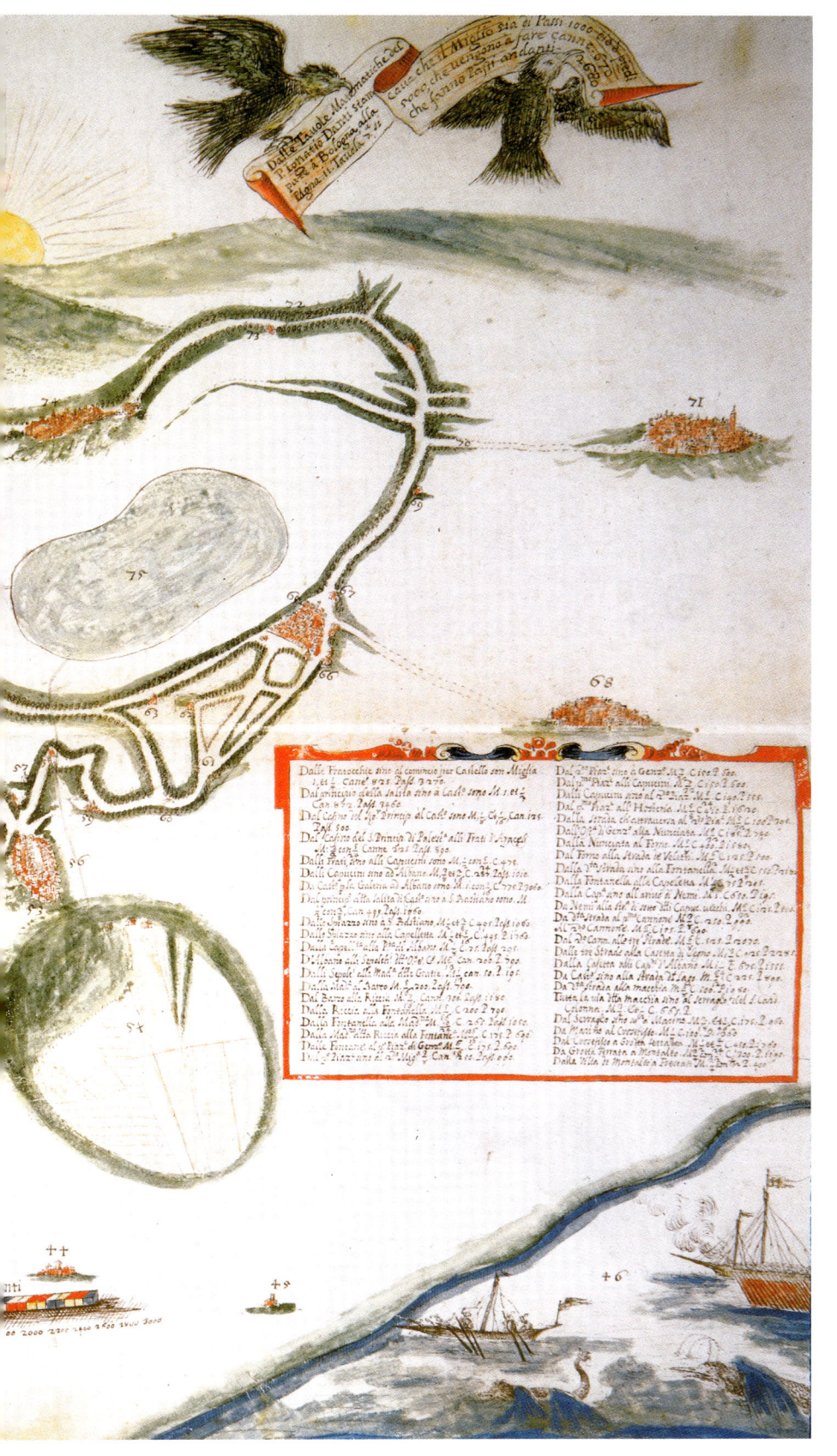

31. D. Jacovacci, "The road from Frattocchie to Castello, from Castello to Albano, to Riccia, to Genzano and to Nemi", c. 1658, folio III, Ariccia, Chigi Palace Library.

1 Roma
2 Torre di mezza uia d'Albano
3 Torre di mezza uia di Marino
4 Diuerse Torri antiche per la Campagna
5 Le Fratocchie
6 Il Casino del Contestabile Colonna
7 Il Torrone delle Fratochie
8 La Vigna di Domenico Fonthta
9 Vigna del Capitano Buticelli
10 Il Casale Palauerta
11.12 Strada che ua a Castello
13 Castel Gandolfo
14 Vigna del Principe de Palestrina
15 Il Torrone di S. Bastiano, e S. Bastiano
16 Torre Chiesa di Bartolomeo Batij
17 Vigna de Bartolomeo Batij
18 Strada che ua alla mola, et al lagetto
19 20 21 Strada da Roma ad Albano
22 Torre falcone del Contestabile
23 Vigna de Domenico Berti
24 Mola di Castello
25 Vigna d'Alberto Pauolone
26 Vigna di D Olimpia Sotto falcognano
27 Falcognano
28 Vigna della Serra
29 Vigna del Costaguti
30 Vigna e Torretta del Cerri
31 Il Lagetto
32 Vigna del Card: Frenzola
33 Vigna de D. Olimpia
34 Vigna de Gio' Luca de Franchi
35 Vigna dell'Abbate Zarotti
36 Vigna del Bresciani incontro l'host. del lag...
37 Vigna delli Gesuiti
38 Vigna dell' Card: Sauelli
39 Vigna delle Monache di Torre de Specchi
40 La Torre di Pagliara
41 Pratica de Borghesi
42 Torre Maggiore
43 La Torretta del Card: de Bagni
44 Strada che ua alla mola d'Albano
45 Le Case delli Gesuiti
46 Vigna dell'Arcolani
47 Vigna de Gioseppe Benedetti
48 49 50 Anticaglie nella uigna de Gesuiti
52 Vigna de Gesuiti di Castello
53 La mola d'Albano
54 Vigna di Gierolamo
55 Monte Sauello Castel diruto
56 Torre Cancelliera
57 Casaletto de Val de Pozzi
58 Ardia del Duca Cesarini
59 Torre S. Lorenzo
60 Il Mare

61 Campo Morto
62 Vigna del Valletti
63 Vigna del Brandani
64 Vigna del Caualier Marando
65 Vigna della Prinesa Sauelli
66 Vigna del Caualier d'Asti
67 Vigna de Marconi
68 Vigna de Domenico Adamo
69 Giardino del P[ri]pe de Palestrina
70 Vigna delli Gelsi
71 Albano
72 Strada arborata da Castel alli Capuccini
73 Le due Torre del Duca Cesarini
74 Li frati riformati di S. francesco
75 Strada arborata alli Capuccini
76 Li Capuccini d'Albano
77 Il Casino de Monsig[.] Colonna
78 Palazzola
79 Vigna de francesco Barsega
80 Romitorio di Palazzola de Zoccolanti
81 Monte Cauo, anticamente Alcido
82 Rocca di Papa
83 Rocca Priora
84 Il Tuscolano sono tutte uigne de frascati
85 Vigna della Vigenana
86 Villa de Montalto
87 Grotta ferrata
88 Crosesto de Marino
89 Marino
90 La Mad[onn]a delle Gratie di Marino
91 Strada che ua a Marino
92 Dierse Vigne e' Poderi
93 La Casa de Pescatori
94 La strada che ua giù al lago
95 Il lago de Castello
96 Casino con palombara del P[ri]pe de Palest[rina]
97 Le Maccie delle Coste del lago
98 Torre di Carlo Antonio Magnini
99 Il Castellaccio
100 Vigna del Caualier Muti
101 Vigna de S. Spirito
102 Torre Pauola
103 Vigna de Mons[.]
104 Vigna del francese
105 Vigna di Marco Antonio
106 Il Casaletto
107 Montagna di Sant'Oresto
108 Monticelli
109 Sant'Angelo
110 Cretone
111 Palombara
112 Montagna de Tiuoli
113 Strada dietro al Castello

32. D. JACOVACCI, "View of the living quarters from above the Castello Palace", c. 1658, folio V, Ariccia, Chigi Palace Library.

THE LANDSCAPE 39

33. P. A. GIORNI, "Plan concerning the aqueducts and underground springs of the Albano community", designed as part of the restoration work of the springs and aqueducts begun in 1789, Albano 1791.

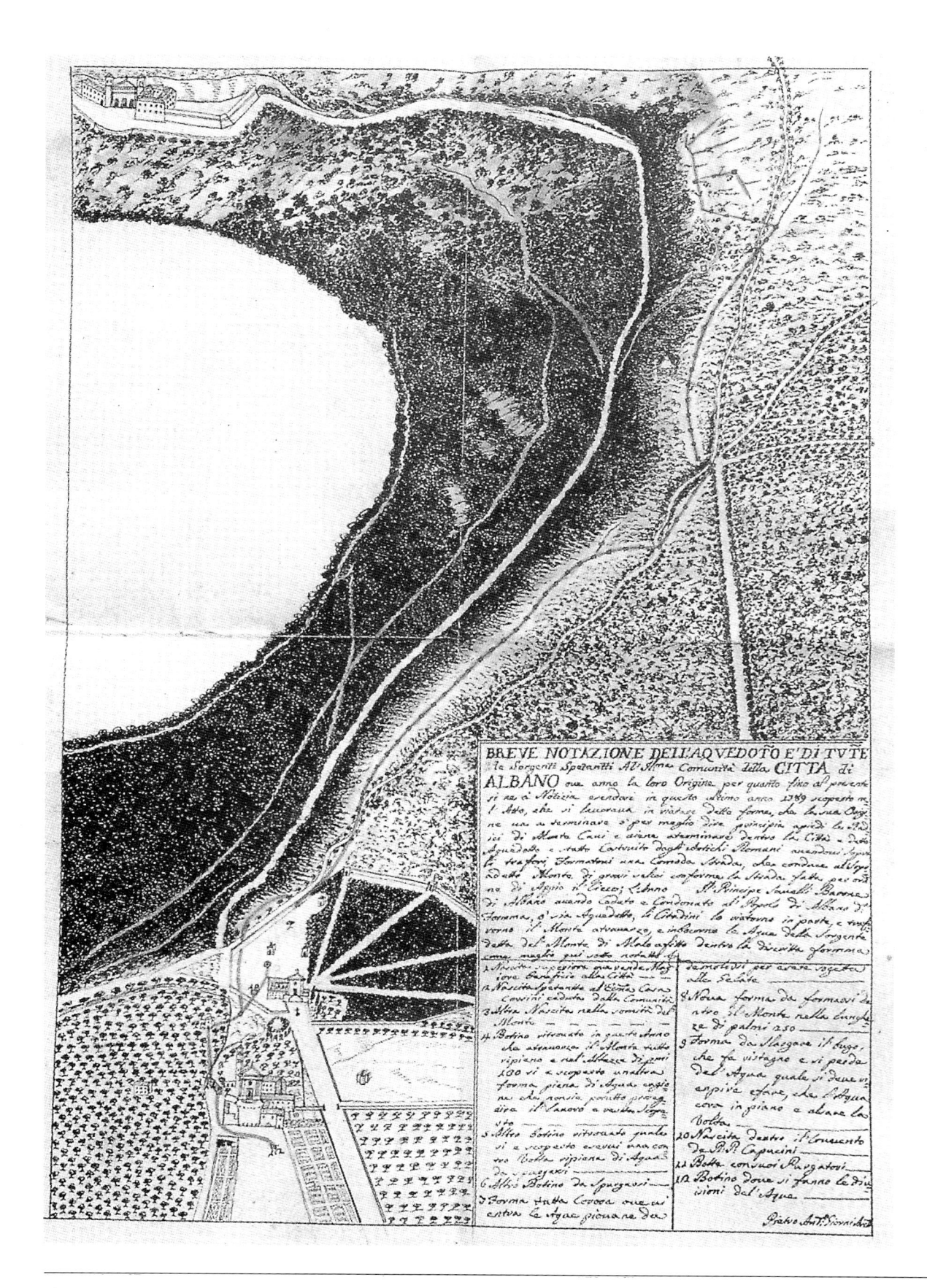

Lanuvio and Velletri, and another between Ariccia and Albano, passing through the Convento della Stella.

Among the new paths aimed at linking the other diocesan centres of worship, one was destined for Convento di Palazzolo itself. The opening of the road for Palazzolo coincided with the presence in the Priory of Friar Giorgio Marziale, an interesting figure in Franciscan architecture. He played an active role in much of the building work in the area on behalf of the Chigi family, who maintained a friendly relationship with him, and Egidio Colonna, as revealed in the documents concerning the visits he made to the Colonna Villa and the Priory[15]. Without entering into the merits of the historical events linked to the construction of the road, covered elsewhere in this publication, it is interesting to note here the landscape significance of the path, a real panoramic trail linking the two monuments at either end (fig. 33). It was furnished with peperino seats placed half a mile apart and fountains to refresh travellers; of both, sadly, virtually nothing remains. The economic effort spent on the programme of re-forestation connected to the opening of the new road, which saw the planting of 60 elms and "1098 trees along the above-mentioned new road"[16], is further confirmation of the attention and care given even to a decidedly functional task as a road network.

Successive eighteenth century works on the land immediately surrounding Palazzolo simply reinforced the Alexandrian system. This included the work carried out by Friar Josè de Fonseca on the Priory itself which, apart from extensions, followed exactly the work done by Brother Marziale. With the declining presence of the Colonna family in the Villa Palazzolo and papal interest in the site dwindling, the nineteenth century saw little work of any great note. Interest in the Palazzolo property, both the Villa and the Priory, was rekindled in the first years of the twentieth century; precisely in that period and for different reasons, they became separated. Enlargements, restoration and restructuring changed the aspect of the buildings; the thickets, hedges, scrubs and the land were rented out and then sold in part to private individuals; access was improved with the enlargement and tidying up of the old mule track which led to the Priory and, later, the construction of the Via dei Laghi, partly following the path already there.

The building boom did not arrive until after the Second World War, from the 1960s onwards, first of all as a phenomenon linked to second homes, but in the last two decades essentially due to illegal building, a problem in the whole Castelli region. The landscape, which for centuries had maintained an essential balance in the relationship between the country and the lake, has seen an ever-more rapid increase in land occupation in recent decades, going way beyond the physical population increase. This has particularly affected the north-west bank of the lake, characterised by more accessible landscape conditions.

Even if the picture of the Priory with the Villa above, with the exception of the significant modifications which these buildings have undergone in the course of time, still represents a substantially complete panoramic piece, the outline of some of the most recent constructions

[15] For further information about Friar Giorgio Marziale, cf. A. CRIELESI, *Fra Giorgio Marziale di Ponzano*, in "Atti del Convegno Ponzano di Fermo tra Medioevo e Rinascimento", Ponzano 19 July 1998, pp. 20-33; cf. also chapter III of this book where the theme is studied in depth.

[16] A.S.R., Giustificazioni di Tesoreria e dei Mandati Camerali.

just on the ridge of the crater, to the right of the Palazzolo complex, makes us acutely aware of the vulnerability of this surviving heritage. We hope in these pages to contribute to proving how one can view the countryside, a common good entrusted to each one of us. We are no longer simply the legitimate heirs of those who owned it before, but users of an inheritance given to us on trust for our children, to whom we have the duty of passing it without loss of value.

II. Palazzolo in ancient times
Giuseppina Ghini

Lake Albano fills one of the secondary craters of the Latian Volcano, which only finished erupting in the Upper Paleolithic era (about 30,000 years ago), although secondary activity, as attested by ancient sources, continued up to the historic era.

Titus Livius[1] wrote that under King Tullus Hostilius, towards the middle of the 7th century BC, "stones rained down on Monte Albano" and "one heard a powerful voice from the sacred forest at the top of the peak". Following such extraordinary events the *Feriae Latinae* were instituted in honour of *Iuppiter Latiaris*[2], during which the Alban people sacrificed an ox or white bull, sharing the meat as a sign of their equality and their common descent from Aeneas[3]. During these feasts, offerings of various kinds, especially the produce of the earth, were brought to the Sanctuary of *Iuppiter Latiaris* on the summit of *Mons Albanus* (Monte Cavo), while the inhabitants of the villages around the lake brought the *piscatorium aes*, an offering aimed at gaining a good catch[4]. Some experts have identified this with the numerous pieces of *aes rude* present in the votive firewood found at the top of the mountain[5]. Here, along the northern slope, in the final phase of the Bronze Age (13th-12th century BC) a settlement began which was to last until the first era of the Iron Age (11th-8th century BC)[6] (fig. 34).

The oldest settlements identified around Lake Albano are to be found along the southern and north-western banks, where the nature of the land, sloping gently towards the water, made occupation easier than on the north and north-eastern slopes[7].

In 1984, at the Casa del Pescatore, a pile-dwelling habitation was discovered which dated from the transition period between the Ancient and Middle Bronze Ages (18th-17th century BC). It was called the "village of the millstones" because of the vast quantity of lava millstones found there. It was a settlement whose economy, like that of the rest of the villages in the area, was based on sheep-farming, hunting, agriculture and fishing, as shown by the number of fishing weights found there[8]. It was, therefore, an economy that already showed a certain permanence[9].

In the passage from the Bronze Age to the Iron Age (10th century BC), the Alban area maintained a certain continuity with the preceding phases: the small inhabited settlements on the high ground and around the lake remained, gravitating, economically and "politically", around a greater centre, identified as Alba Longa[10].

Experts have still not reached an unambiguous answer about the site of Alba Longa. The most likely suggestions are those that place the ancestral city of Rome in relation to Castel Gandolfo or Albano, on the Hill of the Capuchins[11]. Pottery dating from the first Iron Age (10th century BC), attributable to small habitations, has been found at both sites.

It is now generally accepted that in the first stages of Latian civilisation, the population was made up of separate settlements, headed by single family groups, in some cases bound by a hierarchical relationship within a fixed territory, but without a real principal centre[12]. A determining factor in the choice of sites was the exploitation of the natural resources, especially water, and control of the routes for moving livestock, which went from the Alban Hills towards the coast and inland.

Between the final Bronze and first Iron Ages (12th-10th century BC)

---

[1] Tit. Liv., I, 31.
[2] Dio. Hal., IV, 49, 2; Cic., *Ad Att.*, I, 3, 1; about the Sanctuary of *Iuppiter Latiaris* see: C. Cecamore, *Il santuario di Iuppiter Latiaris sul Monte Cavo: spunti e materiali dai vecchi scavi* in "Bull. Comm." XCV, 1993, pp. 19-44; EAD., *Nuovi spunti sul Santuario di Iuppiter Latiaris attraverso la documentazione d'archivio*, in *Alba Longa 1996*, pp. 49-66; A. Pasqualini, *I miti albani e l'origine delle Feriae Latinae*, in *Alba Longa 1996*, pp. 217-253.
[3] Arnob., II, 68;
[4] Fest., p. 230 L
[5] Cecamore 1993, pp. 34-35; Cecamore 1996, p. 60.
[6] P. G. Gierow, *The Iron Age Culture of Latium: II Excavations and Finds*; 1, *The Alban Hills*, Lund 1964, pp. 274, 281ff; P. Chiarucci, *Colli Albani. Preistoria e protostoria*, in "Doc. Albana", I s., 5, 1978, pp. 167-168; A. Guidi, F. Di Gennaro, M. Pacciarelli, *Rinvenimenti di età pre e protostorica a Grottaferrata e a Monte Cavo*, in "QuadAEI", 1, 1978, pp. 84-86.
[7] P. Chiarucci, *Materiali dell'età del bronzo nelle Acque del Lago Albano*, in "QuadAEI", VII, 1985, pp. 36, 38-39.
[8] P. Chiarucci, *Il villaggio delle macine sommerso nelle acque del Lago Albano*, in "Bull. Arch. Sub.", n. 1-2, Anno II-III, Rome, 1995-96, pp. 175-183.
[9] A. Guidi, in *Enea nel Lazio, Archeologia e mito*, Rome 1981, pp. 88-94; G. Chiarucci, *Guida al Museo Civico Albano*, Albano Laziale 1996, pp. 63-66.
[10] On this complex question, refer to the summary articles: G. Lugli, *Dove sorgeva Alba Longa?*, in *Studi minori di topografia antica*, Rome 1965, pp. 353-358; L. Crescenzi, E. Tortorici, *Alba Longa*, in *Enea nel Lazio, Archeologia e mito*, Rome 1981, pp. 18-19; S. Quilici Gigli, *A proposito delle ricerche nell'ubicazione di Alba Longa*, in "ParPass", 38, 1983, pp. 140ff.; A. Arnoldus-Huyzendveld, *Nota preliminare sull'interpretazione di Alba Longa come "dorsale illuminata dal sole"*, in "Doc. Albana", II s., 21, 1999, pp. 25-42.
[11] Gierow 1964, pp. 285, 287-288. 290ff., 309; Chiarucci 1978, pp. 60-72, 171-174; P. Chiarucci, *La documentazione archeologica pre-protostorica nell'area albana e le più recenti scoperte*, in *Alba Longa 1996*, pp. 1-27.
[12] A. Guidi, *Alcune osservazioni sul popolamento dei Colli Albani in età protostorica*, in "DdA", IV, 1982, pp. 31-34; A. P. Anzidei, A. M. De Santis, A. M. Bietti Sestieri, *Roma e il Lazio dell'età della pietra alla formazione della città*, Rome 1985, pp. 156-157.

34. The Alban area in the pre-historic era: 1) Monte Cavo, settlement; 2) Lake-dwelling habitation (village of the millstones); 3) Habitation at Castel Gandolfo; 4) Habitation of the Capuchins; 5) Habitation at Pentima Battiferro; 6) Habitation at Palazzolo; 7) Habitation at Pescaccio; 8) Necropolis of Vignatrovalusci; 9) Necropolis of Divin Maestro; 10) Habitation at Prato della Corte; 11) Habitation at Monte Crescenzio; 12) Habitation at central Marino.

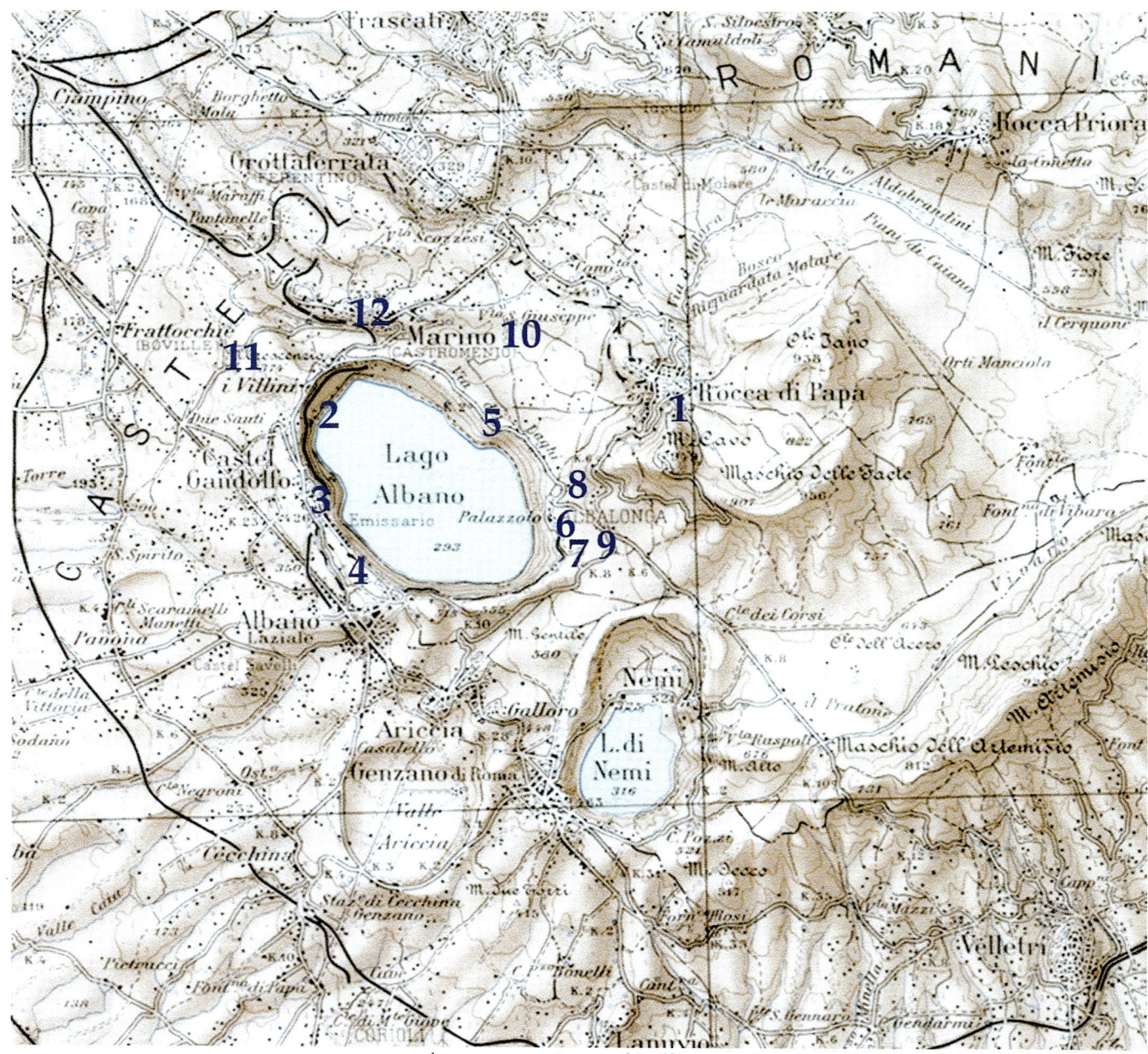

there was a "cave-dwelling" at Pentima Battiferro, on the north-eastern ridge of Lake Albano [13].

In the second Iron Age in Lazio (9th-start of 8th century BC), Palazzolo[14] and Pescaccio were also inhabited, adding to the already existing villages around the lake. The necropolis of Vigna Trovalusci, on the plateau above Palazzolo, and that of Divin Maestro near Pescaccio are probably linked to this[15].

By the time of the Fourth Iron Age in Lazio (730-580 BC), the archaeological evidence is concentrated on the areas of Marino and Castel Gandolfo, the sites of the settlements of Prato della Corte, Monte Crescenzio and central Marino[16]. It is in this period, or, more precisely, towards the middle of the 7th century BC, that sources place the destruction of Alba Longa by Tullus Hostilius[17].

[13] CHIARUCCI 1978, pp. 155-156; CHIARUCCI 1985, p. 35.
[14] GIEROW 1964, pp. 282ff.; CHIARUCCI 1978, pp. 101. 154; CHIARUCCI 1987, pp. 205-207.
[15] GIEROW 1964, pp. 245ff., 260.
[16] GIEROW 1964, pp. 282ff.; CHIARUCCI 1978, pp. 101, 154; P CHIARUCCI, *Nuovi materiali e recenti scoperte della civiltà laziale nell'area albana*, in "QuadAEI", VIII, 1987, pp. 205ff.
[17] Tit. Liv. I, 29.

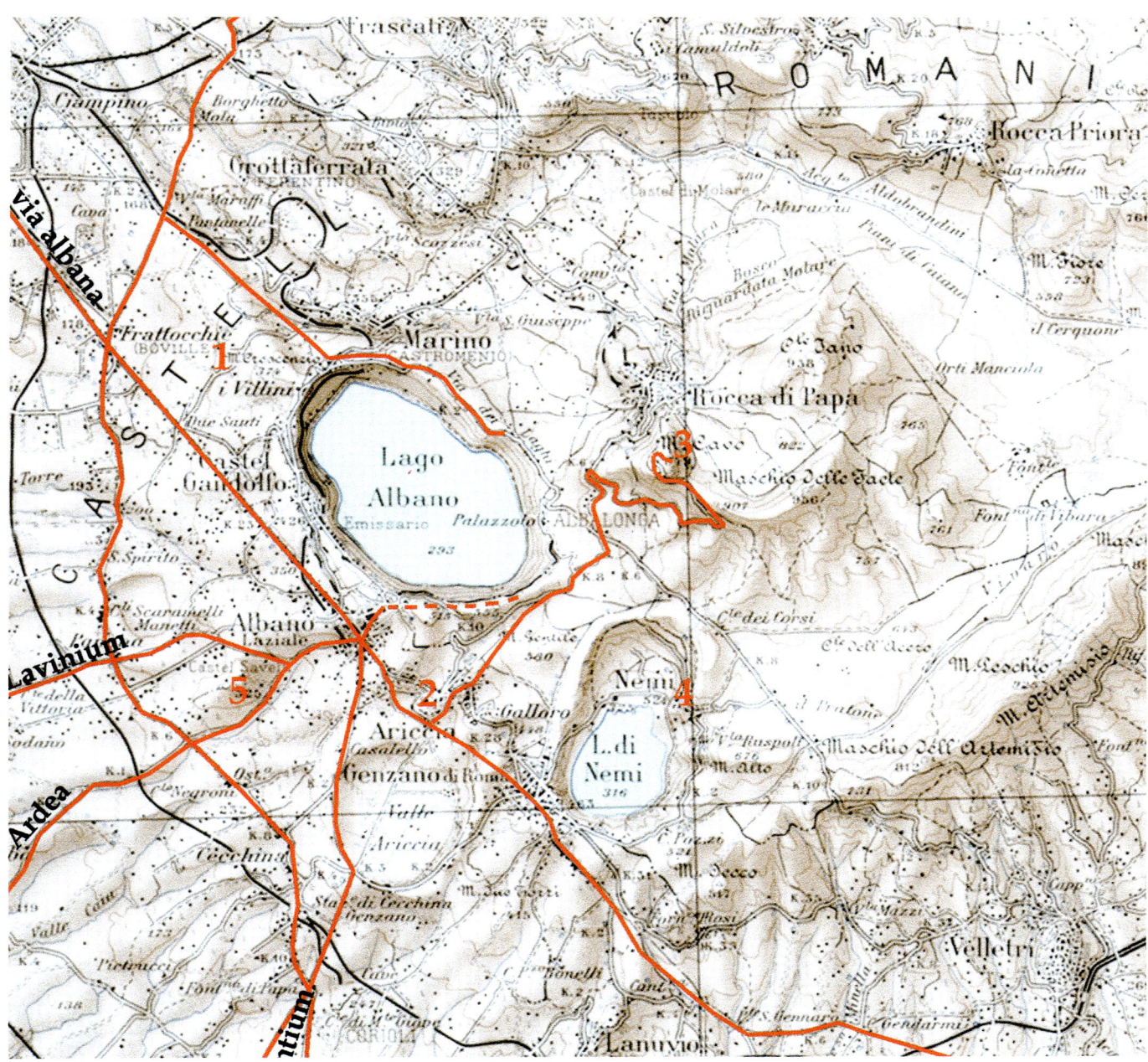

35. The Alban area in the Archaean era: 1) Bovillae (archaean dwelling); 2) Aricia; 3) Sanctuary of Iuppiter Latiaris; 4) Lucus Dianae; 5) Lucus Ferentinae.

From the start of the Archaean Age, the Alban area saw the birth of new centres, real cities, such as *Aricia* and *Bovillae*, and the start of a transport network laid out over earlier prehistoric tracks[18] (fig. 35). These routes followed a northwest-southeast orientation (the future Via Appia, Via Anziate, Via Satricana), crossed by roads that went from the Alban Hills to the coast; Lake Albano thus found itself at the centre of this network.

Along the north and north-western side of Lake Albano runs a path, partly traced by the Via dei Laghi. At Monte Crescenzio this path meets a road leading to Anzio towards the south-west (the Via Cavona and Anziate). Almost parallel to the first path runs the ancient Via Albana (later Via Appia), which at Castel Savelli (the ancient *Lucus Ferentinae*) meets a path for *Lavinium* (Pratica di Mare) and one for

[18] On the road system in this period see: P. CHIARUCCI, *Viabilità arcaica e luoghi di culto nell'area albana*, in *Alba Longa* 1996, pp. 317-333.

PALAZZOLO IN ANCIENT TIMES   45

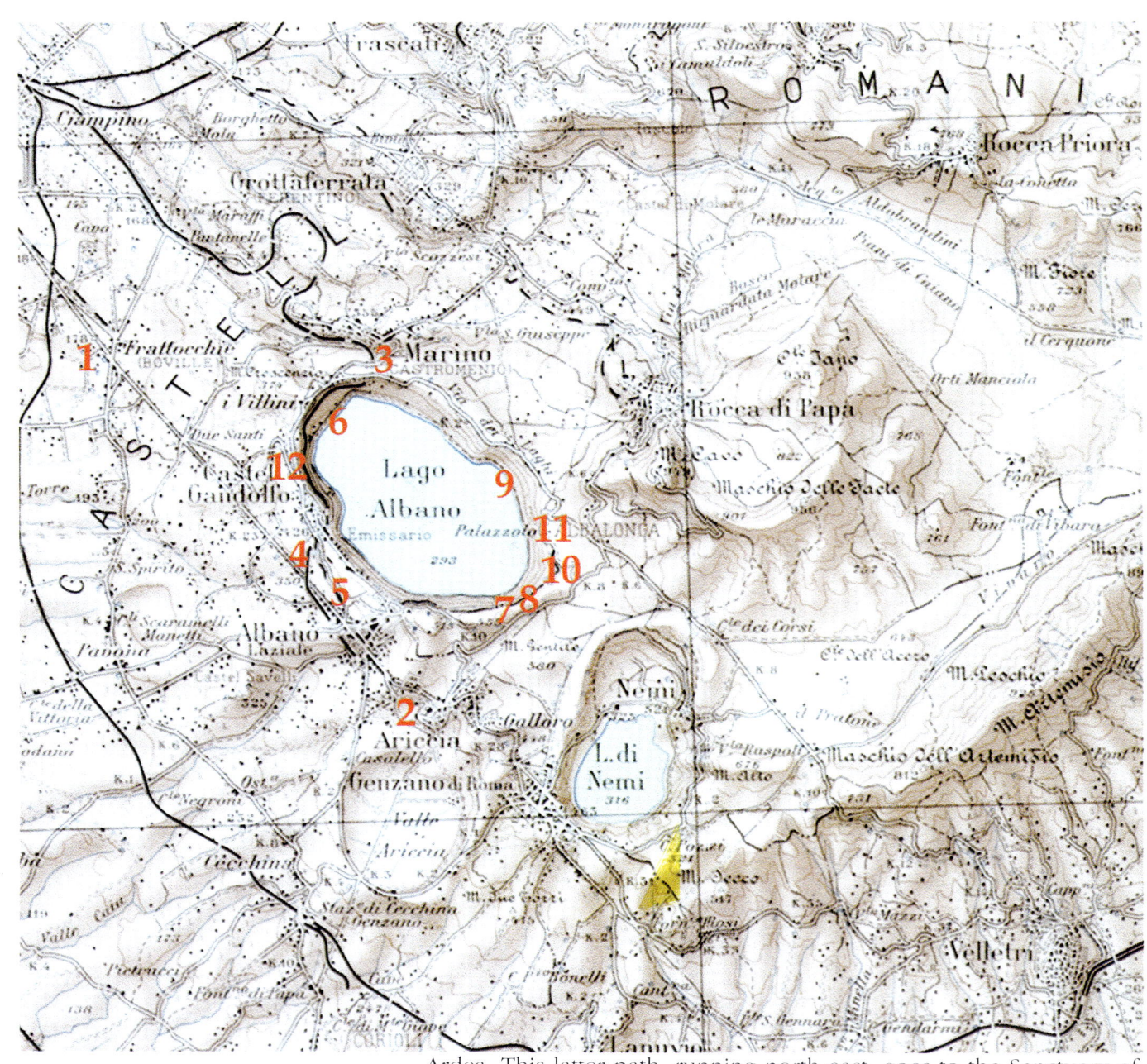

36. The Alban area in the Roman era: 1) Bovillae; 2) Aricia; 3) Castrimoenium; 4) Clodio's Villa; 5) Villa of Pompey the Great; 6) Quays alongside Lake Albano; 7) Polygonal wall; 8) Villa or sanctuary; 9) Augustus' Villa; 10) Malaffitto Villa; 11) Villa Palazzolo; 12) Domitian's Villa.

[19] Tit. Liv., V, 17, 1; F. COARELLI, *Gli emissari dei laghi laziali*, in "Gli Etruschi maestri d'idraulica", Perugia 1991 (edited by M. BERGAMINI), pp. 35-41; V. CASTELLANI-W. DRAGONI, *Opere arcaiche per il controllo del territorio: gli emissari sotterranei artificiali dei laghi albani*, ibid., pp. 43-65.

[20] G. UCELLI, *Le navi di Nemi*, Rome 1950, pp. 39-56; COARELLI 1991; CASTELLANI-DRAGONI 1991.

Ardea. This latter path, running north-east, goes to the Sanctuary of *Iuppiter Latiaris* on *Mons Albanus*, hugging the southern ridge of the lake and rising through hairpin bends up to the summit (Via Sacra or *Via Triumphalis*). In turn, this path meets a trail that in part follows faithfully another bit of the Via dei Laghi (the ancient *Via Castrimoeniensis*) to head off towards the coast in the direction of *Satricum*. Another road from *Mons Albanus* reached Ardea via *Aricia*.

During the Republic there was substantial change in the area, due to considerable engineering works: during the Veii War (406-396 BC) an outlet was constructed to control the waters of Lake Albano and carry them to the Tiber[19]. This was a century after the opening of the outlet from Lake Nemi to the Fosso dell'Incastro, at Ardea[20].

37. Lattice-pattern brickwork in the wall of S. Maria di Palazzolo.

38. The cut through the rock-face.

Earlier paths which in the pre- and post-historic periods linked Etruria with central-southern Italy, crossing or skimming the Alban Hills, were straightened and paved on the stretches near Rome, making up the Via Appia, Via Latina, Via Labicana and Via Prenestina.

The construction of the first large arterial road, the Via Appia, in 312 BC, caused the inhabitants of *Bovillae* to move towards the road, from Casale Licia towards the area of Frattocchie and *Aricia*, and from the rock at the actual town centre down to Vallericcia[21].

From the start of the second century BC this area saw the transformation of many agricultural settlements into residences. While activity based on land exploitation continued, these were places of rest for rich entrepreneurs, politicians and Roman and, in some cases, Alban scholars. Both here and in the Tusculan, Tiburtina and Prenestina areas, the fertility of the land, its beauty, and the proximity to Rome encouraged the proliferation of residential settlements linked to the city and each other by a detailed network of roads and byways.

Events at the start of the 1st century BC had a notable influence on the area. Social wars caused the partial destruction by Mariane troops, and the successive reconstruction by Sulla, of urban centres loyal to him (*Aricia* and *Lanuvium*), and the distribution of the territories of *Bovillae* and *Castrimoenium* (Marino) to veterans (fig. 36).

In the second half of the 1st century BC, the Alban territory was gradually occupied by residential complexes of often remarkable dimensions, such as the villa of Clodius, which reached the southern bank of Lake Albano from the XIII mile on the Via Appia, or that of Pompey the Great, which occupied part of the future *Castra Albana*.

39. The rock tomb.

[21] GIEROW 1964, pp. 114-119; G. M. DE ROSSI, *Bovillae*, in "Forma Italiae", R. I. vol. XV, 1979, p. 290.

40. The rock tomb in a drawing by Abbot Riccy, detail of the decoration (from GUERRINI 1969).

41. The access corridor to the burial chamber.

[22] G. LUGLI, *La Villa di Domiziano sui Colli Albani. Topografia generale*, in "Bull.Comm.", 1917, pp.29ff..; ibid., *La Villa di Domiziano sui Colli Albani. Le costruzioni sparse*, in "Bull.Comm.", 47, 1919, pp. 153ff.; P. CHIARUCCI, *Indagini sul Lago Albano*, in "DocAlb", II s., 9, 1987, pp. 19-28; G. GHINI, *Prospezioni subacquee nei laghi albano e nemorense*, in "Bull. Arch. Sub.", n. 1-2, Anno II-III, Rome 1995-96, pp. 185-191.

[23] G. LUGLI, *La Villa di Domiziano sui Colli Albani. Le costruzioni sparse*, in "Bull.Comm.", 47, 1919, p. 182.

[24] P. CHIARUCCI, *Rinvenimenti presso il Lago Albano*, in "QuadAEI", 1981, 5, pp. 191-197; ibid., *Nuove considerazioni su alcune sostruzioni in opera poligonale sui Colli Albani*, in "1° Seminario nazionale di studi sulle mura poligonali", Alatri 1988, pp. 65-69; P. CHIARUCCI, in Alba Longa 1996.

During this period the lake was equipped with quays for private landing places, built in squares of peperino, and a harbour, situated along the north-eastern side, in the Cantone area[22].

A long piece of later-style polygonal masonry, preserved for about 1 kilometre on the north-east and south-east sides of the lake can be dated to a period preceding the Republic. Some scholars[23] claim it is foundations of a villa or a road around the lake, others[24] attribute it to a Sanctuary, consisting of vast platforms surrounded by a winged portico.

At the start of the 1st century AD, under Augustus, many properties of the late Republic were already becoming part of the imperial patrimony (the *Albanum Caesarum*); this is what happened to the villas of Pompey the Great, Clodius, Malaffitto and Palazzolo, which were incorporated by Domitian into his imperial residence. This extended from the southern slopes of Monte Cavo in a southerly direction to the Via Appia, eastwards to Monte Gentile,

42. The right-hand wall of the burial chamber.

43. The left-hand wall of the burial chamber.

and westerly as far as the Via Due Santi[25]. To have some idea of the dimensions involved, it contained Lake Albano and the present towns of Castel Gandolfo and Albano, just brushing past Marino.

The main part of the complex, laid out along four terraces and going as far as the Via Appia, was developed within the present-day Pontifical Villa at Castel Gandolfo, where the first two terraces are preserved along with the monumental remains of a cryptoporticus, a theatre, a façade with nymphs and the remains of the palace itself. Along the third terrace was the circus, while the entrance on the Via Appia, corresponding to the fourth terrace, had a series of buildings, including a nymphaeum[26]. Two other nymphaea adorned the residence on the opposite side, facing the lake: the Doric nymphaeum, from the Republic, and the Bergantine nymphaeum, inspired by the Tiberian one at Sperlonga[27].

The complex was supplied by numerous reservoirs, in turn supplied by three aqueducts that picked up the waters from the springs at Malaffitto and Palazzolo.

[25] G. LUGLI, *Le antiche ville dei Colli Albani prima dell'occupazione domizianea*, in "Bull.Comm.", 42, 1915, pp. 251-316; F. COARELLI, *Dintorni di Roma*, Bari-Rome 1981, pp. 67-80.

[26] G. LUGLI, *La villa di Domiziano sui Colli Albani. Le costruzioni centrali*, in "Bull.Comm.", 46, 1918, pp. 3-68; L. CRESCENZI, *La Villa di Domiziano a Castel Gandolfo: nuove prospettive*, in "QuadAEI", IV, 1981, pp. 181ff.

[27] N. NEUERBURG, *L'architettura delle fontane e dei ninfei nell'Italia antica*, Naples 1965, pp. 158-159; A. BALLAND, *Une transposition de la grotte de Tibère à Sperlonga: le ninfeo Bergantino de Castelgandolfo*, in "Mel", LXXIX, 1967, pp. 421-502; B. AMENDOLEA, *I due ninfei del Lago Albano in alcune disegni ed incisioni del XVII, XVIII e XIX secolo*, in "DocAlb", II s, 9, 1987, pp. 29-49.

The monumental complex which developed on the south-east side of the lake between the late Republic and the early Empire was probably also incorporated in the imperial property. This site, which from the Middle Ages became part of the Priory and Church of S. Maria di Palazzolo, was a 1st century AD villa, of which a wall in *opus reticulatum* (lattice-pattern brickwork), now part of the present structure (fig. 37), is still visible. So too is a cut through the rock (fig. 38), carried out to provide access to the residence, and a rock tomb (fig. 39).

There is vast amount of literature about the tomb suggesting different dates and attributions and its architectural characteristics have aroused considerable interest since the time of the Renaissance. It is worth mentioning the most salient facts, starting with a description of the monument, and referring to the bibliography for the more detailed explanations of the most recent studies[28].

The tomb is carved out of a peperino wall. It consists of a square base surmounted by a truncated pyramid with seven steps, carved on only three sides; the base, which is about 6.50 metres in length and 2.65 metres high, bears a bas-relief decoration which is barely legible but which Dionisi accurately described at the end of the 1960s[29]. The central part is decorated with a *sella curulis* (the seat reserved for consuls), surmounted by a cushion on which are laid headgear or a crown and a sceptre with an eagle (the *scipio eburneus*); under the seat is a little footstool (*suppedaneum*), at the sides of which are two male busts (believed by Dionisi to be prisoners or Telamones), on whose shoulders rest two erotes holding a cloth. In turn, the frame of the seat is decorated with a bas-relief with a lighted candelabra in the centre and, at the sides, two cupids, spiral plants and two medusa heads[30] (fig. 40).

To the right and left of the *sella curulis* are two groups of six fasces, another symbol of consular power. It would have been precisely these that inspired the archaeologist Giacomo Boni in the choice of this motif as the sign of the Fascist Party[31].

Under the relief the rock has a smooth section, on which, according to Lucia Guerrini, an inscription with the name of the owner could have been placed[32].

At the moment very little can be seen of this complex decoration: the *sella curulis*, the sceptre, the twelve fasces and the much-worn male busts. Such a relief functioned as a base for a seven-step pyramid which probably supported a sculptural group of the deceased and his wife or simply the figure of the deceased; Lucia Guerrini has hypothetically attributed to this a headless feminine torso in limestone preserved in the garden of the Villa Colonna or Villa del Cardinale[33].

The tomb is found on the left of the base and is reached via seven steps perpendicular to the pyramid, leading to a corridor covered by a barrel vault that opens into a burial chamber (fig. 41). Carved out of the rock, it is rectangular (2.60 m x *c*. 2.30 m x 2.10 m high) and covered by a cross vault; inside are two niches, with a depth of 97 cm: one is on the back wall, one on the right, and each must have contained a sarcophagus, while on the left-hand wall there is a supporting shelf surmounted by an arcosolium, probably to hold the plate and funeral offerings (fig. 42-44).

On the basis of the description provided by Father Casimiro ("an

---

[28] There is ample literature about the monuments at Palazzolo. Here the most recent works, themselves inclusive of the preceeding bibliography, are cited: Th Ashby, *Classical Topography of the Roman Campagna*, in "PBSR", 1910, V, p. 27; ibid., *The History of Palazzola. Palazzola in Ancient Time*, in "The Venerabile", n. 4, April 1924; F. Dionisi, *L'artistico sepolcro rupestre di Palazzola non è del console Cornelio Scipione Ispalo*, in "Studi Romani", XVII, 1969, pp. 405-424; L. Guerrini, *Il monumento rupestre di Palazzolo*, in "Archeologia Classica", XXI, 1969, pp. 227-245; G. Tomassetti, *La Campagna Romana Antica, Medievale e Moderna*, ed. Rome 1976, pp. 194ff.

[29] Dionisi 1969, pp. 405-409; Coarelli 1981, p. 112.

[30] Such a motif is also confirmed by the design of Abbot Riccy (G. A. Riccy, *Osservazioni archeologiche sopra un antico mausoleo consolare incavato nel Monte Albano presso il convento di Palazzolo*, Rome 1828) mentioned also in Guerrini 1969, plate LXXVII (fig. 19).

[31] Dionisi 1969, p. 408, note 6; Coarelli 1981, p. 112.

[32] Guerrini 1969, p. 243.

[33] Guerrini 1969, plate LXXXIV, 1.

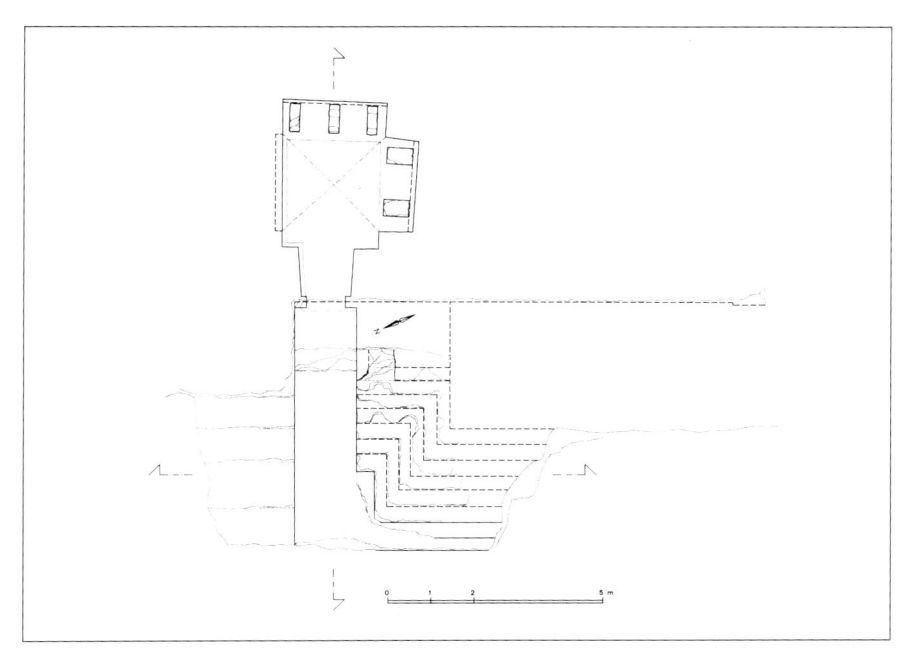

44. Plan and sections of the tomb (Soprintendenza Archeologica del Lazio, rilievo e restituzione grafica by M. Marchetti).

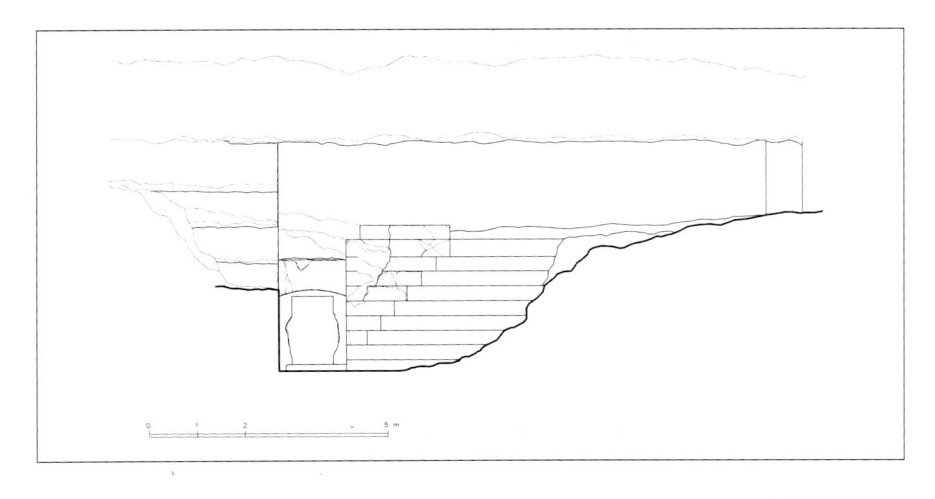

PALAZZOLO IN ANCIENT TIMES 51

45. Villa del Cardinale: striated marble sarcophagus.//
46. Villa del Cardinale: striated travertine limestone sarcophagus.

47. Villa del Cardinale: tombstone altar of an Isiac priestess.

48. Villa del Cardinale: marble sarcophagus with ancient basket design.

PALAZZOLO IN ANCIENT TIMES 53

49. Villa del Cardinale: marble frieze with cupids racing on chariots.

50. Villa del Cardinale: male marble bust.

urn of streaked marble which the friars used for gathering water in the garden")[34] and above all by Riccy[35], Guerrini has suggested the identification of one of the two sarcophagi as being the marble one kept in the garden of the Villa Colonna (or del Cardinale), decorated with a rectangular *tabula* without a title in the centre and strigil marks at the side[36] (fig. 45). There remains some doubt as to whether this is the same one bought in 1792 by the Count of Sousa, Portuguese Ambassador to the Holy See[37] or another one, a twin, which has remained in the property. What is certain is that from the moment the tomb was discovered in 1576 there has only ever been talk of one sarcophagus.

In the garden of the Villa there is a second limestone sarcophagus of uncertain authenticity. It is striated travertine with little columns and corinthian lateral capitals and a central rectangular *tabula* bearing an inscription to *A. Sergio patrono*; the short sides are each decorated with two crossed oval shields[38] (fig. 46).

In addition, both inside the building and in the garden, other finds are preserved. Their origins, however, are unknown and were neither seen nor mentioned by Lucia Guerrini nor by Francesco Dionisi. They include a funeral altar in travertine limestone dedicated to a certain Amanda, priestess of Isis by her husband C. Vibio; on the sides, sculptured in relief, there is a sistrum and a pod-shaped *umbilicata* broad, flat dish[39] (fig. 47).

There is also a third sarcophagus, of marble, almost completely blank on the simple, roughly-hewn long sides, while on the short sides there is a beautiful decoration with an intertwined *kalathos* and fruit[40] (fig. 48). There is also a millstone in earthenware stone with *catillus* and *meta*, a marble frame decorated with indentations, and a marble column base, probably all coming from excavations carried out in the area[41].

---

[34] Casimiro Da Roma, *Memorie Istoriche delle Chiese e dei Conventi dei Frati Minori della Provincia di Roma*, Rome 1764; Guerrini 1969, p. 242.

[35] Riccy 1828, p. 48.

[36] Guerrini 1969, plate LXXXVI, 2; for the type of sarcophagus compare R. Calza, *Antichità di Villa Doria Pamphilj*, Rome 1977, pp. 237-238; plate CLVIII, 283 (the example is dated 230-240 B.C.).

[37] Dionisi 1969, pp. 417-418.

[38] Length 210 cm; width 70 cm; height 45 cm; to compare type see Calza 1977, p. 239; table CLVIII, 285 (first half of the 3rd century A.D.).

[39] Height 103 cm; width 58x56 cm; on the upper part there is a circular groove with a diameter of 26 cm to hold the funeral urn.

[40] Length 210 cm; width 67 cm; height 65 cm.

[41] A plinth measuring 85x85 cm; superior diameter of the base 70 cm.

In one of the separate buildings of the Villa is embedded a fragment of a marble frieze with cupids racing on two-horsed chariots[42] (fig. 49).

Inside the Villa there is a marble bust, which could possibly have belonged to the sculptured group which decorated the top of the tomb, according to Canina's reconstruction[43] (fig. 50); in one of the corridors there is a marble sarcophagus belonging to a baby, with a cushion and a hollow for the head. It has been re-used as a basin and bears the date 1776[44].

Of all the material described above, only the striated marble sarcophagus and the marble bust can be linked in any definite way to the tomb, while one can only guess that the others come from the area.

The tomb was unknown to ancient sources and was first described in 1463 by Enea Silvio Piccolomini, Pope Pius II, in his *Commentarii*[45]; more than a century later, in 1576, the Friars at the Priory opened the tomb and, according to the testimony of Francesco Gonzaga, found "by a stroke of luck a treasure of not negligible value"[46], obviously the funeral trappings, of which nothing else was heard.

In 1629 Lucas Holstein was the first to attempt some identification of the tomb and the nearby villa, based on a passage of Dion Cassius[47] which he believed concerned the place where the consuls stayed when they went to *Mons Albanus* for the *Feriae Latinae*[48]. The same year, Cassiano Dal Pozzo discovered an inscription concerning a Lucilla Pira and her husband Aesop Apsyrtiano, *dispensator* (bursar) of the Emperor Augustus[49]. Further identifications of the tomb followed, however highly improbable, such as that of Kircher, who attributed the tomb to a monument of Alba Longa then used for King Tullus Hostilius[50].

At the end of the 17th century, excavations carried out by the Friars led to the discovery of inscriptions bearing the name of the Tarquinii[51] and at the start of the following century "were unearthed heads, arms, torsos and a little horse in marble, in whose saddlecloth was written a memorial in Greek lettering"[52].

The first person to suggest that the Palazzolo tomb might be that of a consul was Father Casimiro da Roma[53], in 1755, on the strength of the testimony of Francesco Gonzaga. At the same time, Abbot Jean-Jacques Barthèlemy began a philological study of the monument, noting similarities to the Halicarnassus mausoleum, dedicated by Artemisia to her brother and husband, Mausolus, Satrap of Caria[54].

At that time, then, controversies about the tomb began. Abbot Bertrand Capmartin de Chaupy dated it to the start of the 1st century AD[55], Piranesi – who provided a suggestive but fanciful engraving (fig. 51) – to the royal era[56], Carlo Fea to the late Republic or early Empire[57]. Both for the date and to whom the tomb belonged, the opinion of Giovanni Antonio Riccy is fundamental. In an accurate study of Alba Longa and the Alban area[58] he thought that the tomb could be attributed to the consul Cn. Cornelius Scipio Hispalus, who died in 176 BC after falling from his horse returning from *Mons Albanus*[59].

Other suggestions, in part fanciful views or descriptions of the rock tomb, are those dating from the early to mid-19th century by Gmelin[60], Labruzzi[61] (fig. 52), Rossini[62], Canina[63] (fig. 53) and Vecchi[64].

Riccy's attribution to the consul C. Cornelius Hispalus, accepted

[42] Length 60 cm.
[43] cf. fig. 53.
[44] Length 120 cm; width 45 cm; height 30 cm.
[45] E. S. Piccolomini, *Commentarii rerum memorabilium*, Rome 1584, p. 568.
[46] F. Gonzaga, *De origine Seraphicae Religionis Franciscanae*, Rome 1587, p. 183.
[47] Cass. Dio., *Hist. Rom.*, LIV, 29.
[48] L. Holstenii, *In Italiam Antiquam Philippi Cluverii Annotationes*, Rome 1666, p. 180.
[49] *CIL XIV*, 2259; Dionisi 1969, p. 422.
[50] A. Kircher, *Latium*, Amsterdam 1671, p. 34.
[51] The inscription would have been found in underground vaults in the priory in the 17th century; it was reported by Friar Casimiro da Roma in the priory archive but was not subsequently confirmed (Dionisi 1969, p. 422).
[52] Casimiro Da Roma 1764, p. 244; Dionisi 1969, p. 422; Guerrini 1969, p. 234; the whereabouts of these finds is unknown.
[53] Casimiro Da Roma 1764, p. 244.
[54] *Mémoires sur les anciens monuments de Rome* by M. l'Abbè Barthèlemy, in *Mémoires de Littérature...de l'Académie Royale des Inscriptions et Belles Lettres*, Paris 1761, p. 588; Riccy 1828, p. 18.
[55] B. Capmartin De Chaupy, *Découvert de la Maison de Campagne d'Horace*, Rome 1767, vol. II, pp. 109-113.
[56] G. B. Piranesi, *Antichità d'Albano e di Castel Gandolfo*, 1762-1764, plate III, chapter II, p. 7.
[57] C. Fea, *Varietà di notizie...*, Rome 1820, p. 10.
[58] Riccy 1828, p. 74.
[59] Tit. Liv., XLI, 16; XLII, 21; XLV, 15.
[60] P. Arrigoni, A. Bertarelli, *Piante e vedute di Roma e del Lazio conservate nella raccolta delle stampe e dei disegni. Castello Sforzesco*, Rome 1939, n. 4387; Guerrini 1969, plate LXXV, 2.
[61] Th Ashby, *Dessins inédits de Carlo Labruzzi*, in "MEFR", XXIII, 1903, p. 398, nos. 18-19; Dionisi 1969, Plate LXXII, 2.
[62] Guerrini 1969, plate LXXVI, 2.
[63] L. Canina, *Gli edifizi antichi dei contorni di Roma*, Rome 1856, vol. V, pp. 58ff.; vol. VI, plate LXXI.
[64] Vecchi's drawings are kept in the library of the Palazzo Venezia in Rome (see n. 14; G. Lugli, *La Via Trionfale a Monte Cavo e il gruppo stradale dei Colli Albani*, in "MemPontAcc", I, 1923, p. 258).

51. G. B. Piranesi, *Le Antichità d'Albano e di Castel Gandolfo*, 1762-64.

[65] A. Nibby, *Analisi storico-topografico-antiquaria della Carta de' dintorni di Roma*, Rome 1848, vol. I, p. 75.

[66] Lugli 1915, pp. 295ff.; Lugli 1923, p. 258.

[67] A. M. Colini, *Il fascino littorio di Roma*, Rome 1932, pp. 75ff.

[68] J. W. Salomonson, *A Roman Relief in Copenhagen with Chair, Sceptre and Wreath and his historical Associations*, in "BullAntB", XXX, 1955, pp. 1ff.; ibid., *Chair, Sceptre and Wreath*, Groningen 1956.

[69] F. Coarelli, *Su un monumento funerario romano nell'abbazia di San Guglielmo a Goleto*, in "DdA", I, 1967, pp. 58, 69; Coarelli 1981, pp. 111-112.

[70] Lugli 1915, p. 298; Lugli 1923, p. 257; Guerrini 1969, pp. 237-240.

[71] Casimiro Da Roma 1764, p. 228; Lugli 1915, p. 298; Ashby 1924.

by various experts and scholars, including Nibby[65] and Lugli[66], was, for a long time, held to be precise, up to the time when Colini lowered the date to the era of Caesar[67], and Salomonson[68], followed by Coarelli[69], to the 2nd century AD.

The conclusion is that at Palazzolo there is a unique monumental complex, which includes not just the tomb but also the remains of a late Republican villa in *opus reticulatum* and other varied brickwork, linked to the road which went up to *Mons Albanus* (the Via Sacra or *Via Triumphalis*) by a path which was made possible by a deep cut in the rock which is still visible, even if partially hidden by vegetation[70] (figs. 38, 54). Apart from the meagre structures still visible, rooms of once considerable dimensions also belonged to the villa. The Priory garden rested on these, perhaps corresponding to one of the terraces of the Roman villa[71].

Lugli maintains that, at the time of Augustus, the residential com-

52. Inside the tomb, from an engraving by Labruzzi (from Dionisi 1969).

53. The rock tomb in a drawing by Luigi Canina (from Guerrini 1969)

Palazzolo in ancient times 57

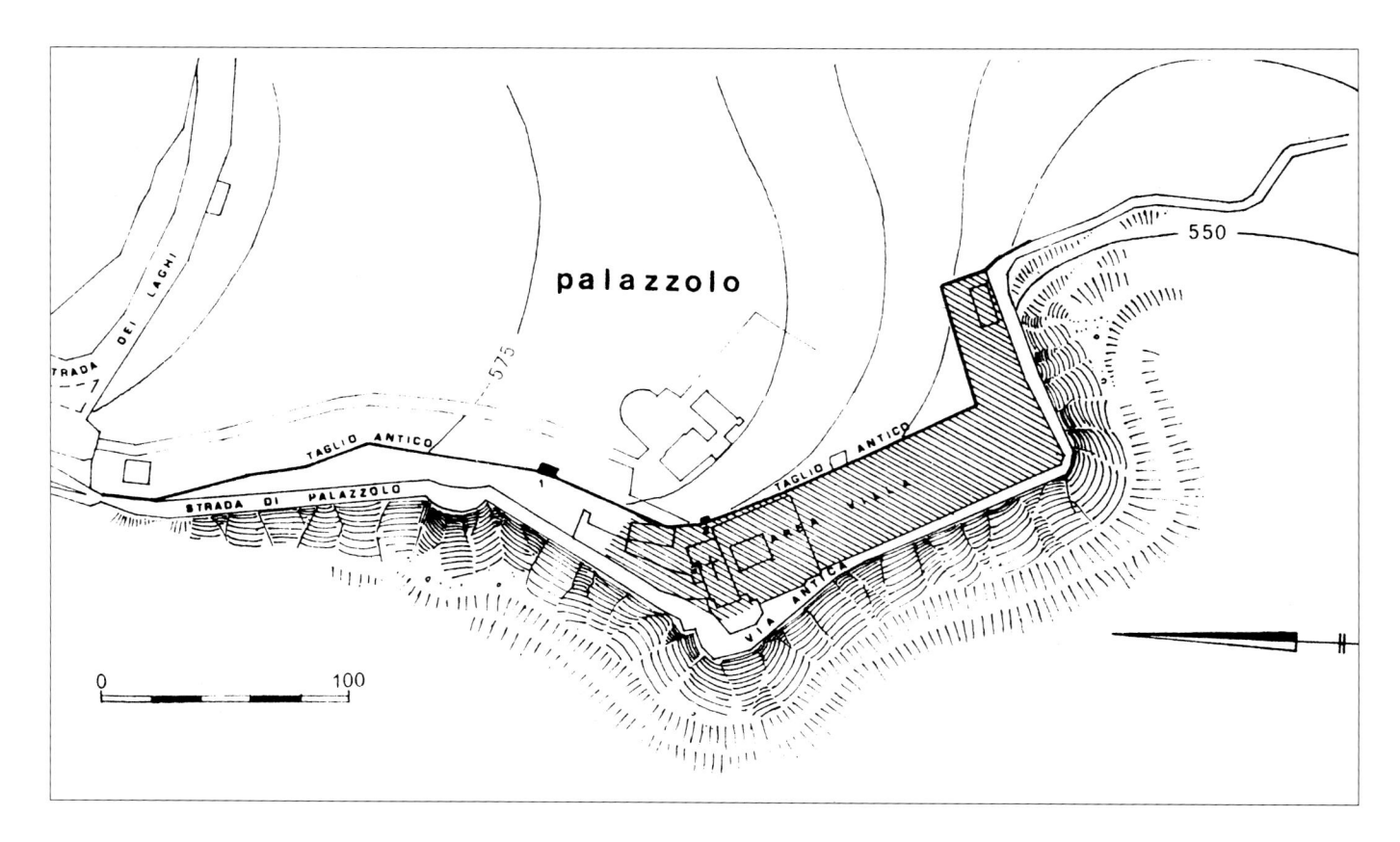

54. Plan of Palazzolo (by C. F. Giuliani in GUERRINI 1969).

[72] LUGLI 1923, p. 258.
[73] *CIL* XIV 4091; XV 2336, 2.
[74] LUGLI 1923, p. 258.
[75] The dating of the medieval period is confirmed by the fact that a Roman tunnel was cut to make the cave (DIONISI 1969, p. 424, note 51).

plex was already part of the *Albanum Caesarum*[72] and such a suggestion is supported by the 17th century discovery of the funeral inscription of Lucilla and her husband mentioned above. The discovery, among the ancient structures, of seals on bricks from the Successiane workshops[73], dated to the turn of the 1st and 2nd centuries, confirms that the residence, dating back to the late Republican era, underwent restorations and restructuring in this period under the new owner, realistically the one to whom the tomb belonged.

The question about his name still remains: if, in fact, the whole property was already part of the *Albanum Caesarum* in the early Empire, as Lugli pre-supposes[74], such an hypothesis can hardly be reconciled with the idea that the villa was the residence of consuls who were going to sacrifices on *Mons Albanus* and that one of these consuls was buried there in the 2nd century AD, an idea formerly proposed by Holstenius and accepted by Lugli.

The villa wanted to extend its property to the present Villa del Cardinale, and it is only from that property that the funeral monument can be reached. An important characteristic of the residence, besides the beauty of the panorama over Lake Albano, was the presence of springs of hot and cold water, used in ancient times to supply the villas in the area and in particular that of Domitian. It was still active in modern times, so much so that it was used by Ruthenian Cardinal Isidore of Thessalonica, who liked to rest in a cave – probably dating back to the Middle Ages – called the 'Grotta di Gasperone', named after the 19th century brigand who sheltered there[75]; in his *Com-*

55. Villa del Cardinale: "Gasperone's cave" in one of the painted rooms.

mentarii[76] Piccolomini also talks about *vivaria* full of fish, while Holstenius refers to "crypts, nymphaea, fountains and aqueducts hollowed out of the rock in a wonderful manner"[77] (fig. 55).

At the start of the 17th century Clement VIII built the aqueduct that supplied the Pontifical Villa at Castel Gandolfo and notably impoverished the springs[78]; in fact, in 1740 Father Casimiro da Roma noted that the hot and cold water supplies had almost dried up[79].

Today, the rock tomb at Palazzolo is semi-hidden by the vegetation and this, combined with the relative height of the monument from the road, is probably why it has not been subjected to desecration or vandalism.

Its decorated face continues to look out over the lake below, still keeping the secret of the name of its owner.

[76] PICCOLOMINI 1584, p. 568; LUGLI 1915, p. 299.
[77] GUERRINI 1969, p. 238, note 42.
[78] FEA 1820, p. 11.
[79] CASIMIRO DA ROMA 1764, p. 244.

III. The artistic history of Convento di Palazzolo
Alberto Crielesi

From the beginnings to a Cistercian Abbey

The architectural complex of the former Minorite Priory of S. Maria di Palazzolo[1] has, for centuries, been favoured as one of the most suggestive and enchanting corners of the Alban Hills: perched above Lake Albano, the clear brilliance of its profile stands out against the dark green of the plants which wildly invade the greyish peperino cliffs providing us with one of those scenes so dear to landscape painters of the past.

Besides the Priory, there are other elements that are inseparable from the context, all united by a virtual optical axis: the Lake, the Villa Colonna and the ubiquitous Monte Cavo, focal point of the Alban Hills (figs. 1, 6, 7).

Without doubt the most beautiful view is precisely the one from Palazzolo itself: from here, like a fantastic observatory, one gazes down below to the mirror of the lake, across to Castel Gandolfo sheltered on the top of the bank, and, beyond the Campagna, the Mediterranean as a final boundary.

Here, to use De Cupis' words, "An indefinable sense of calm, and of mysticism is all around in the air, eloquently revealing the supreme wisdom of the Creator of such a splendid and varied horizon!"

But the image and sensation are not just simple stylistic concessions. Note the air of history and legend, which, despite the various and debatable modernisations, is still in the air, and envelopes in particular the adjacent enigmatic garden tomb (fig. 56). Hewn from the Alban stone, this remains an ever-fascinating archaeological mystery in whose burial chamber, according to Gonzaga in 1756, a reasonable treasure was found[2].

According to one of the more insistent opinions of times past, Palazzolo was the site of the citadel of the mythical Alba Longa, jealous custodian of another much more fabulous treasure, in search of which past scouts worked so hard, to no avail, not least a certain Antonio Calcini "a Bolognese gentleman, furnished with the necessary licence" [...] who in July 1701 – as Casimiro recalls[3] – "excavated in the sacristy"; and finding there only pure, hard stones, resigned himself and abandoned the arduous task, on the grounds "that with the passage of time the gold and silver will have turned into these".

Without going back to the mythical Alba Longa, the origins of S. Maria di Palazzolo date back to ancient times: the name itself seems to derive either from the Latin *Palatium*[4], along with its medieval diminutive form *Palatiolum*, or perhaps from an ancient Roman construction in which historians of past centuries recognised a mythical Consuls' palace, obligatory resting-place for the high-ranking State officials about to face the steep slope of the *Via Sacra* which led to the summit of Monte Albano to celebrate victories or the *Feriae Latinae*.

Gonzaga referred to the ruins on which the complex is built, and Father Casimiro echoed this when he noted: "...And furthermore it is certain that the garden attached to our Priory is built on the great vaults of an ancient edifice, divided into several rooms..."[5].

As confirmation of this, some studies[6] have shown that the mea-

---

[1] The subjects treated in this chapter were in part anticipated by a series of articles published from 1995 onwards. The unpublished information and the knowledge acquired during research carried out by the Department for the Environmental and Architectural Properties of Lazio allows the presentation here of an organic and exhaustive body of knowledge about Palazzolo. Cf.: A. CRIELESI, *Santa Maria ad Nives di Palazzolo*, Rome 1997; ibid., *L'eredità del Fonseca a S. Maria ad Nives di Palazzolo*, in "Castelli Romani" A. XXXV Monograph 1995, pp. 5-26; ibid., *Santa Maria ad Nives in Palazzolo*, in "Frate Francesco" n. 3, July-September 1997, pp. 5-24; ibid., *Palazzolo, Splendori e miserie dell'atica abbazia nullius di S. Maria della Neve durante i secoli*, in "Lazio Insolito", Montecompatri 1998, pp. 22-30.

[2] F. GONZAGA, *De Origine Seraphicae Religionis Francescanae*, Rome 1587, p. 183.

[3] CASIMIRO DA ROMA, *Memorie istoriche delle Chiese e dei Conventi dei Frati minori della Provincia Romana*, Rome 1744 (1845), pp. 321-346.

[4] G. MAROCCO, "*Monumenti dello Stato Pontificio e relazione topografica di ogni paese*", *Lazio e le sue memorie*, Rome 1853, vol. VIII, pp. 164-5: "*Various experts agree that the name derives from Palatium, maintaining that the Roman consuls went there when sacrifices were offered to Latian Jupiter, because it was just situated on the path to Monte Cavo which one ascended along a magnificent path of enormous flint paving stones, traces of which can be seen at various points up there*".

[5] CASIMIRO 1744, p. 228.

[6] F. CHIARELLI – G. MORELLI, *Palazzola*, Restoration thesis II, Faculty of Architecture, "La Sapienza" University of Rome, Professor G. Miarelli Mariani, Rome 1988/89.

56. J. J. Middleton, The rock mausoleum of a Roman Consul, from *Grecian remains in Italy, a description of Cycloplian walls and roman antiquities, with topographical and picturesque views of ancient Latium*, London 1812.

57. V. VECCHJ, "Attempt made at the Convento di Palazzola on Lake Albano 28 March 1833 to discover the remains of the consular house and the entrance to the underground galleries of the terrace garden above the ancient vaults belonging to the same consular house...". Taken from: *Collezione di 24 vedute quasi tutte inedite rappresentanti monumenti e luoghi celebri esistenti nelle vicinanze di Rome disegnate dal vero dal Dottor Vincenzo Vecchj*, Rome 1866. Plate 14.

surements of the space of the present church and the area of the cloister can be expressed exactly in Roman feet.

These ancient burial remains under today's buildings – belonging to the hypothetical consular *domus* or, more probably, to a Roman villa – were inspected by the doctor and painter Vincenzo Vecchi on 28 March 1833. In captions to his drawings (fig. 57) he wrote:

"...*one entered via a covered drain, serving the cloister, situated on the external façade of the Priory, and seen from inside there is a very high modern vault, and to the right a hole which one can easily pass through, [...] and once inside [...] one went along an ancient vault 40 handbreadths long with another modern one above 3 handbreadths higher. At the end of the walk one could see that the ancient vault had a hole [...] once down [...] one could see two rooms or rather two spaces which were joined one to the other by an arched little portico which, together with the external walls, seemed to be 1,000 year-old constructions, since they were all rectangular bricks made of local stone, and the internal wall was largely covered by an ancient lattice-pattern common in the first of the two little rooms or spaces, the one in which one was let down, and you could see that on the part adjoining the large garden there was an opening higher than a man but later walled up...*"[7].

Unfortunately, Vecchi's attempt to go into the rooms underneath the terrace garden failed because of the smoke produced by the torches.

Thomas Ashby, as reported by Garvin, also repeated the experiment at the start of the century. Like Vecchi, the results were poor[8].

As to when a church was built over the Roman ruins and when a monastic community moved in – whether that might have been a number of detached cells for monks with no rule or superior, or a Benedictine monastery – these are both questions which are wrapped

[7] V. VECCHJ, *Collezione di 24 vedute quasi tutte inedite rappresentanti monumenti e luoghi celebri esistenti nelle vicinanze di Rome disegnate dal vero dal Dottor Vincenzo Vecchi,*, Rome 1866. Plate 14. "*An attempt made at the Convento di Palazzolo on Lake Albano 28 March 1833, to discover the remains of the consular house and the entrance to the underground galleries of the terrace garden above the ancient vaults belonging to the same consular house...*"

[8] Cf. also T. ASHBY – J. GARVIN, "The history of Palazzola", *The Venerabile*, I, 4, 1924, pp. 289-297. ibid., "The history of Palazzola", *The Venerabile*, II, 1, 1924, pp. 3-13. ibid., "The history of Palazzola", *The Venerabile*, II, 2, 1925, pp. 132-146. ibid., "The history of Palazzola", *The Venerabile*, II, 3, 1925, pp. 222-230. Cf. also C. DE CUPIS, *La villa e l'eremo del Cardinal Girolamo Colonna (senior) sul lago Albano*, undated, (copy with the author) p. 23.

58. S. Maria di Palazzolo, marble lunette with Agnus Dei (?13th century), whose original purpose is completely unknown (formerly in the garden and re-used as a water butt, now in the church). Archivio Fotografico della Soprintendenza Beni Storici e Artistici di Roma e del Lazio.

[9] A. FORBIGER, *Handbuch der Alten Geographie*, Leipzig 1822-1848, II, pp. 322-456, notes that the numerous Palazzolo throughout Italy (Palazzolo sul Serio, sull'Oglio, della Stella, etc.) betray an early-medieval rather than Roman origin. J. MABILLON, *Annales O.S.B.*, vol. 6, Lutetiae Parisorum 1739-1745, I; pp. 337-338-448; II, pp. 131-195; III, pp. 3-90-160-195; IV, pp. 12-136-388; refers to some religious houses with the name Palazzola in France, Belgium, and two in Italy: the first, in Tuscany, dates back to the second half of the 8th century and the other is in the Ravenna area. C. HUELSEN, *Le chiese di Roma nel Medio Evo. Cataloghi ed appunti*, Florence 1927, p. 352, para. 70, cites the name Palazzolo as an example of early-medieval constructions. CASIMIRO 1744, p. 326, recalls in the city of Rome "...*a little mountain also bearing the name of Palazzolo*" (the last spur of the Gianiculum) mentioned in the biography of Gregory VII, when, in 1083, the Emperor Henry came to Rome with his army and installed himself "*juxta S. Petrum, quemdam Monticulum nomine Palatiolum*".

in the many silences of history: the very name *Palatiolo* – common to many churches of medieval origin[9] – has certainly not helped to unravel this mystery. If certain dubious references to the locality are excluded – such as that which mentions Saint Romuald, founder of the Camaldolese Order, who in 986 had ear-marked certain sums of money for the restoration of "Palatioli" monastery[10]; or the mention by Padre Uberto, who, in his "*Memorie di Montecassino*"[11], recalls how in 1023 three Benedictines lived in the then grange; and that of 1050, reported by Tomassetti[12], and consequently by Galieti[13] and by Carafa in *Monasticon Italiae*[14] – the only certain mention of S. Maria di Palazzolo is that of 1109.

September 6 that year saw the completion of the sale of a piece of land named "*Grotule*" after the many caves of the ancient peperino quarries spread throughout the area, belonging to the Roman monastery of S. Maria in Campo Marzio[15] and bordering on "*Sancta Maria de Palazzo*". It is clearly Palazzolo and not to be confused with a church of the same name near the ruined Roman amphitheatre in Albano called, in the Middle Ages, *Palatio*[16].

Two similar land documents, dated respectively to 1086 and 1151[17], seem to refer to the Castelli religious house.

To these documents must be added a 1227 legacy from Cardinal

Guala Bicchieri to the "*Ecclesia et fratribus de Palazzolo*"[18] which testifies, as later documents will confirm, to the presence of a stable monastic community at Palazzolo.

But it is the Bull of Pope Innocent IV, published on 19 January 1244[19], just on the eve of his decision to abandon Rome and take refuge in France, which, besides conferring the title of 'Abbey' on S. Maria di Palazzolo, offers us a real historical *excursus* on the thirteenth century church and community.

It must be borne in mind that this document is full of supplements. In fact, it bears a letter (1237) from the Abbot General of the Cistercian Order addressed to his religious brother, Abbot of the Roman monastery of S. Anastasio, which in turn transcribes a Bull of Gregory IX addressed to the same Abbot General, dated Viterbo, 13 August of the same year, which in turn refers to preceding letters, among which are two of great importance from Innocent III and Honorius III.

Going back chronologically over the essential dates of these documents, it is possible to provide an adequate reconstruction of the events surrounding the church and monastery at Palazzolo in the medieval period (fig. 58).

From the Bull of Gregory IX[20] – merged into the one of Innocent IV – it is clear that at the time of Innocent IV the "*Ecclesia S. Mariae de Palatiolis*" already belonged, with all its property and possessions, to the Cistercian Abbey of SS. Andrea e Saba on the Aventine Hill. Furthermore, at the suggestion of the same Pope, who was from the Conti di Segni family, for the annual sum of two pounds of wax it had all been given to a certain Sixtus, Prior of the community of hermits installed at Palazzolo (1204); this was to be as long as they kept the Rule they observed, with the proviso that should the Rule be broken in any way through their own fault, the church would return to the possession of S. Saba.

For his part, in 1204 the Abbot of S. Saba did not hesitate in complying with what the Pope had decided[21].

On the death of Innocent III, his successor Honorius III (Savelli) attempted to bring some rule to the myriad communities of hermits and penitents proliferating in the bosom of the Church. At times, through their observances they were straying into being more or less heretical movements. So, in 1220, when he discovered that at Palazzolo none of the approved Orders of the Church were being followed, he made the brothers there embrace the Rule of St Augustine[22].

Then Cardinal Stefano de' Normanni – joined by the better-known Jacoba de' Settesoli, 'Brother' Jacoba, friend and follower of St Francis of Assisi, wife of Graziano Frangipane, Lord of Marino – persuaded the "penitents" of Palazzolo to embrace a real monastic Order. Through Cardinal de' Normanni, the Prior of Palazzolo, a Brother Romano, agreed with the Abbot of Tre Fontane at the *Aquae Salviae* (SS. Vincenzo e Anastasio) to the incorporation of the church at Palazzolo into the Roman abbey, and the acceptance of the Rule of St Bernard on behalf of his brothers.

For its part, the Roman Cistercian Abbey arranged to send there a "crowd" of 12 lay brothers, with the relevant "family" who would

[10] G. B. Mittarelli – A. Costadoni, *Annales Camaldulenses*, Venice 1755, I, p. 119. See also footnote 7, which makes reference to the Roman church of the same name, within the Leonine city (see also the preceeding footnote).

[11] Uberto, *Memorie di Montecassino*, p. 123, in "G. Torquati, *Studio Storico, Archeologici.*," MS., I, church of S. Barnaba, Marino, undated. cf. Ashby 1924 II, 1, p. 3.

[12] G. Tomassetti, *La Campagna Romana Antica, Medioevale e Moderna (1910-1926)*, new edition edited by L. Chiumenti and F. Bilancia, Florence 1979-80, vol. II, p. 198, with reference to Vat. Lat. 7931, f. 100, containing eighteenth-century copies of Galieti taken from the same Archive of S. Maria in Campo Marzio. Cf. successive footnotes.

[13] A. Galieti, *Contributi alla storia della diocesi suburbicaria di Albano Laziale* (Vatican City, 1949) p. 50.

[14] F. Caraffa, *Il monachesimo a Roma (e nel Lazio) dalle origini al secolo XX*, in "Monasticon Italiane", Cesena 1981, vol. I, Rome and Lazio, p. 148 n. 128. Cf. also L. Janauschek, *Originum Cistercensium*, Vindobonae, 1877, p. 244, n. 637.

[15] F. Caruso, *Cartario di S. Maria in Campo Marzio (986-1199)*, Rome 1948, p. 55. The same or a similar document is the one indicated by Tomassetti with the date 1050.

[16] Galieti 1948, p. 117.

[17] Ashby 1924, II, p. 3, which also refers to the quote from Galieti mentioned and to Vat. Lat. 7929, f. 11 (21) and f. 28 (54). Other documents dated 1185, 1205 and 1228 show an "*Ecclesia S. Mariae de Palazolo*" with its property subject to the Chapter of St Peter's (*Bullarium Basilicae Vaticanae*, Rome 1747, I, pp. 69, 83,113). Furthermore, in an inventory of St Peter's Chapter Archive, between the end of the 14th century and the start of the 15th, there is recorded an "*instrumentum S. M. de Palazolo subiecta nostrae Basilicae*" in the "Archivio Soc. Romana Storia Patria", XXIV, 1901, p. 424 (it certainly refers to the Roman church mentioned in footnotes 12 and 13).

[18] A. Paravicini Bagliani, *I testamenti dei cardinali del Duecento*, Rome 1980, p. 115. Cf. R. Lefevre, *L'Abbazia medievale di Palazzolo sul lago Albano*, in "Lunario Romano 1988", Rome 1987, XVII, pp. 173-191.

[19] F. Ughelli, *Italia Sacra sive di Episcopis Italiane*, Venice, 1717-1722, 1, col. 259ff.

[20] Cf. L. Auvray, *Les resgistres de Grégoire IX*, Paris, 1896-1955, vol. II, p. 869 n. 4043. In some texts, the Bull of 13 August 1237 is dated 27 August 1237.

[21] Ibid.

[22] Ibid.

59. S. Maria di Palazzolo, present-day church façade.

take up residence at Palazzolo to reform it, working to preserve its benefits[23].

The agreement also contained a clause common to the Cistercian Order: if, at some future stage, the Palazzolo community should become economically autonomous to such an extent that it could decently maintain the monastery, it could attain the title of Abbey *sui juris* becoming a "daughter house" of Tre Fontane[24].

In the meantime, the Abbot of S. Anastasio had Palazzolo freely at his disposal *"tam in spiritualibus quam in temporalibus et tam in personia quam rebus"*, with the authority also to have the entire Abbey, or part of it, to stay there in the summer, depending on their needs, since in the great summer heat malaria raged at the Abbey of Tre Fontane[25], just as it did over a good part of Rome.

In Gregory IX's arrangements for the community at Palazzolo (1237), the payment of two pounds of wax to the Abbey of SS. Andrea and Saba remained in force, as did the condition that the Cistercian Rule should always be kept there[26].

On receiving the Papal Bull, the Abbot and General Chapter at Cîteaux, at the behest of Cardinal Stefano de Normanni and other Cardinals, complied with the order received, giving *"tempore Capituli Generalis a. D. 1237"* the necessary arrangements to the Abbot of S. Anastasio[27]. For his part, in a Brief from the Lateran dated 16 January 1238, the Pope hastened to inform the *"priori et fratribus Ecclesie S. Mariae de Palatioli Cisterciensis ordinis, albanensis diocesis"* of the confirmation of their incorporation into the Cistercian Order and union with the Abbey of S. Anastasio[28].

It is not out of place to record here that, besides Palazzolo, Nemi and Genzano[29] also belonged to Tre Fontane, which makes one think of a precise plan of patrimonial expansion on the part of the Roman Abbey towards the Alban Hills and, what is more – in conformity with one of the Church's plans – the idea of recovering impoverished monastic communities in order to place them back under a stronger Rule.

But, continuing to look at the essential points of the 1244 document, it is clear that after a few years the community, having grown economically[30] and being fit to assume, according to the agreement, the title of an independent Abbey, was raised by the Abbot of Tre Fontane *"ad titulum Abbatiae"*, through the intervention of the then Bishop of Albano, Cardinal Pietro di Collemezzo, in place of the consensus of the General Chapter.

This is what can be learned from the group of documents inserted into the Bull of Innocent IV dated 19 January 1244.

Thus, S. Maria di Palazzolo had its own Abbot, patrimonial and administrative autonomy, its own novitiate, with monks bound by the vow of stability, independent from other authorities, with the exception of the *vinculum* or *jus paternitatis* of subordination to the Abbot of Cîteaux and to the *linea* from which the Abbey came; in the case of Palazzolo it was that of Clairvaux, one of the four "daughter houses" of the mother Abbey of Cîteaux (*Cistercium*), which in turn was once (1140) the "mother house" of the Roman Abbey of Tre Fontane when Abbot Paganelli, the future Eugenius III, took possession in the

[23] ibid.
[24] ibid.
[25] ibid.
[26] ibid.
[27] For *L'Epistola del Capitolo Generale cistercense all'Abate di S. Anastasio* cf. I. M. CANIVEZ, *Statuta Capitolorum Generalium Ordinis Cistercensium*, Louvain 1933-1941, vol. II, p. 171, n. 14.
[28] AUVRAY, II, col. 868 n. 4041, which quotes Reg. 18, f. 351 v. (a. XI c. 363): *"Cum igitur nuper vobis assumentibus Cisterciensis Ordinis instituta dilecti filii abbas et generale capitulum cistercienses ecclesiam vestram, iuxta mandatum nostrum super hoc eis directum, monasterio S. Anastasii de Urbe ipsius Ordinis duxerint uniendam et incorporaverint Ordini memorato, prout in eorum litteris inde confectis plenius continetur; Nos, vestris precibus inclinati, quod super hoc ab eis provide factum est, auctoritate apostolica confirmamus et presentis scripti patrocinio communimus; ad maiorem rei evidentiam tenorem litterarum ipsarum de verbo ad verbum presentibus inseri facientes, qui talis est* (om.)".
[29] N. RATTI, *Storia di Genzano*, Rome 1797, Doc. nn. I, II, III, IV, pp. 93-104.
[30] Among other things, the monks at S. Maria di Palazzolo paid a sum of two "cents" to the Lateran Basilica for certain of their properties in the "Sulforata" area. Cf. GALIETI 1948, p. 50, footnote 196: *"Ecclesia seu monasterium S. Mariae de Palazzolo, Albanensis diocesis, Ordinis Cistercensis, pro uno castellare et certis terris positis in loco ubi dicitur Sulforata, sub annuo censu duorum solidorum"* (Arch. Basil. Later., cod. 71, f. 9).

60. S. Maria di Palazzolo, present-day interior of the church.

name of St Bernard of Clairvaux. Thus the Abbey of Palazzolo was added to the other branches of the Roman Abbey, which at its height had reached five: Casanove in Abruzzo (1165); Arabona, in the diocese of Chieti (1209); S. Agostino di Montalto (1234); Palazzolo; and finally S. Maria di Ponza (1245).

The arrival of the Cistercians at Palazzolo saw the start of the rebuilding of the old abbey, adapting it, where possible, to the building regulations then in force in the Order, as the restrictions of the place did not allow the construction of Cistercian prototype buildings[31] which had been happily tried out and applied in other places. The very location of S. Maria di Palazzolo, even if not through choice, was in stark contrast to the Bernardine theories which were preferred for the Order's establishments, open and well-served spaces in order to best manage the agricultural economy of which the monks had made themselves pioneers and innovators.

[31] F. Federico – I. Fontana, *L'organizzazione dei Cistercensi nell'epoca feudale*, Calamari 1988, pp. 257-265.

61. S. Maria di Palazzolo, present-day side-view of the narthex.

    The famous saying "Benedict prefers the mountains, Bernard the valleys" remains an indication of the fundamental difference between the two models of Western monastic establishments of the time.

    For the Abbey of S. Maria di Palazzolo, it was, therefore, a matter of adjustment rather than building from scratch, as shown by the existence of large pieces of *opus reticulatum* – masonry work which in all probability preceded the arrival of the Cistercian monks – visible outside on the apsidal part of the building and the left side of the church (fig. 37).

    Following the adaptations, the complex formed a *unicum* with the buildings for the monks, the cloister, the church; the latter fitted into the particular typology of minor Cistercian churches with a single nave, constituted by the fusion of typical elements: gothic vault in two spans; a choir lower than the nave and a flat apse; a façade made more beautiful by a multi-foil rose window in white marble; lateral sides marked by buttresses into which single-lancet windows opened (figs. 59-60). To these were added elements of a more Roman tradition, such as the portico – like that of the church of the mother Abbey at Tre Fontane – supported by pillars and columns with re-used capitals and obvious Cistercian origins (figs. 61-63).

Even after many twists and restorations, the architectural mark of the monks of St Bernard is still visible in some parts of the former Abbey, as, for example, in the room now used as a Library, which, according to the canonical disposition of rooms, corresponds to the old Cistercian refectory; or in the rooms to the left of the church (today the sacristy and preparatory area), in which, beneath the eighteenth century stucco, the medieval cross vaults resting on corbels can be made out (fig. 64).

The initial estate of S. Maria di Palazzolo, which enabled it to be raised to an Abbey, is worth a brief mention: its contents can be understood from a deed of 8 February 1269 which fixed the extent of the Cistercian property, situated "*una cum hortis, vineis, silvis, fontibus, viis et inviis, cryptis et rupibus, arboribus fructiferis e infructiferis*" on a hill overlooking Lake Albano, at the foot of Monte Cavo, adjoining the properties of S. Maria di Grottaferrata (...*S. Mariae de Crypta Ferrata...*), of the Church – now ruined – of S. Angelo sul Lago (...*S. Angeli post lacum sunt pentoria rubea...*), of the castle of Rocca di Papa (...*Castrum Rocchae de Papa...*); and that of Malaffitto (...*Castrum quod dicitur Maleaffictum...*), whose ruins still dominate the steep slope of the Lake[32].

In the second half of the 13th century, contrary to what Casimiro states, believing that the place was more or less uninhabited from 1249, the Abbey played an active part in the life of the Order; the same Abbot of Palazzolo who was denounced for not attending and participating, for unknown reasons, in the General Chapters of the Order at Cîteaux, was, in 1263 and 1267[33], given inquisitorial roles with regard to other abbeys by the General Chapter, in 1263, 1264, 1270, and 1282[34].

We should also note that in 1285, at the request of the Abbots of S. Paolo de Urbe and "*Palassolis, Albanensis Diocesis*", Honorius IV (Savelli) intervened for a transfer of their funds to the farmhouses of S. Proculo and Cerqueti[35]; in 1286 the same Honorius IV sanctioned the transfer of a ruined castle from the already-mentioned estate of Solforata or Solforatella on behalf of the Lateran Basilica to the Abbot of Palazzolo[36]; in 1288 a letter from the Franciscan Nicholas IV concerning the payment "*pro Abbate et conventu monasterii S. Mariae dei Palactiolis, cisterciensis ordinis, Albanensis diocesis*" of a tithe owing from the Bishop of Ferentino[37]; and again in 1289 the General Chapter at Cîteaux commissioned the Abbots of S. Anastasio and Palazzolo to "*capere*", or capture, the fugitives from the Order taking shelter in Rome, with the help, if possible, of the secular powers, "*invocato ad hoc, si necesse fuerit, auxilio brachii saecularis*"[38].

Still in the middle of the 13th century there is another document which merits particular attention: it bears the date 1253 and concerns what Cardinal Stefano de' Normanni, principal promoter of the Palazzolo monks' incorporation into the Cistercian Order and the affiliation of their church to the Abbey of S. Anastasio at Tre Fontane, asked and

---

[32] "...*Anno MCCXLIX Apostolica sede vacante, indicatione XII, mense Februarii, die VIII, facta est praescriptio bonorum omnium immobilium Coenobii S. Maria de Palatiolis cistercensis ordinis, quod Coenobium situm est una cum hortis, vineis, silvis, rivis, fontibus, viis et inviis, cryptis, e rupibus, arboris fructiferis, e infructiferis per gyrum in quodam colle, super lacum Albanensem, suae in pede Montis Cavae inter hos fines...*". Cf. CASIMIRO 1744 p. 326. The document quoted is shown with the date 1248, corrected to 1268 by Tomassetti, IV, p. 187. Cf. LEFEVRE 1987, p. 182.

[33] CANIVEZ 1933-41, III p. 14 n. 36 ; p. 56 n. 59.

[34] *ibid.*, p. 17 n. 59; p. 20 n. 20; p. 86 n. 30; p. 257 n. 53.

[35] M. PROU, *Les registres d'Onorius IV*, Paris, 1888, n. 49.

[36] P. PRESSUTTI, *Regesta Honoris papae III*, Rome 1886, I, pp. CX-CXI.

[37] E. LANGLOIS, *Les registres de Nicolas IV*, Paris 1886, p. 10.

[38] CANIVEZ 1933-41, III, p. 244 n. 10. In the registers of the three-year Tithe of 1298-1301, the figure of 20 pounds is mentioned given to the monastery of S. Maria di Palazzolo by a certain lay brother Friar Martino. Cf. G. BATTELLI, *Ratones decimarum nei secoli XIII e XIV, Latium*, Vatican City 1946, p. 15 n. 3.

62. S. Maria di Palazzolo, present-day detail of the columns of the narthex with shaft and re-used ionic capital, Archivio fotografico S.B.S.A.R.L.

63. S. Maria di Palazzolo, detail of the columns of the narthex with capital with a typical Cistercian moulding, Archivio fotografico S.B.S.A.R.L.

obtained from the General Chapter at Cîteaux: that after his death, during the Mass for the dead, there would be recited every day a special prayer for his own soul and only in the "*Abbatia de Palatiolis quam ipse fundavit*", that is, in the Abbey which he had founded[39].

Perhaps it was to him, as founder of the Abbey, that a worn, rough and difficult to read epigraph was dedicated, visible before Fonseca's restorations, engraved on the threshold of the church of Palazzolo and beseeching eternal peace for a Stefano linked to the Abbey itself?[40]

But to return to the Abbey's property. Besides the neighbourhood of the Alban Hills, its property was also to be found outside the Castelli area: the destroyed church of S. Lorenzo at Tivoli and the impoverished Abbey of S. Angelo in Valle Arcese, still in the Tivoli estate, as can be seen from some documents of 1301 and 1302.

Confirmation of the first, S. Lorenzo, comes from a Bull of Boniface VIII, who, from Velletri on 18 April 1301, sanctioned possession of the church in Tivoli with the relative governance and care of souls[41] on behalf of the monks of Palazzolo: the "*ecclesia S. Lauren-*

[39] CANIVEZ 1933-41, II, p. 391 n. 7 : "*Petitio rev. mi patris domini Stephani, tit. S. Mariae Transtiberinae*".

[40] CASIMIRO 1744, "…*On the threshold of the door, one could read there, carved in marble with rough, almost worn away letters, the following memorial: ATA (?) D. STEHPA. VULTIS (?) ABBAT. REQUIESCIT IN PACE…*" p. 341.

[41] G. DIGARD and others, *Les registres de Boniface VIII*, Paris 1884-1935, III, p. 100 n. 4096.

64. S. Maria di Palazzolo, the so-called 'Sacristy' (early 20th century photograph): note the gothic structure emerging beneath the eighteenth-century stucco.

tii foris muros" – called S. Lorenzuolo and then St Philip Neri – came to Palazzolo after the Rector of the Tivoli church, a certain Nilo Palloni, returned it to the local ordinary who, in turn, granted it "*in usus proprios*" to the monks of Palazzolo[42].

The Benedictine monastery of S. Angelo in Valle Arcese, a site three miles beyond the S. Croce gate – reduced to a most desolate state of abandonment after its monks were driven out by the Bishop of Tivoli – was granted again by Boniface VIII with a Bull dated at Anagni 24 August 1302. The effective possession, however, is testified by another document a few years later, referring to an inquiry ordered by John XXII over the state of such an association. It in fact happened that, since the same Pope had, in 1318, assigned the Tivoli monastery to the Poor Clares of S. Lorenzo in Panisperna in Rome, the Cistercian monks living there had violently driven out those whose task it was to take possession of the property[43].

And yet there is a deed of sale, dated 3 March 1310, in which Abbot Benedict, always with the consent and order of the Abbot of Tre Fontane and the General Chapter of the Order at Cîteaux, sold some property (Torre del Vescovo, Rufelli, etc. ...) to the monastery of S. Maria della Rotonda in Albano for 152 gold florins in order to meet the many debts "*diversis, variis ac innumeris debitis fenerabilibus*"

---

[42] Cf. G. C. CROCCHIANTE, *L'Historia delle chiese della città di Tivoli*, Rome 1726, p. 213.

[43] G. MOLLAT, *Jean XXII (1316-1334). Lettres communes*, Paris 1921-1947, III, p. 13 n. 10417.

contracted by his predecessors who had squandered the assets of Palazzolo through bad administration. This situation of the erosion of assets – well known "*in totam contratam Maritimam*" – forced the Abbey of S. Maria di Palazzolo to allow even some precious church artefacts to be sold to meet debts, including two silver crosses, one of which was gilded, and all the vestments from a chapel, for 100 gold florins; not only that, but for 60 florins certain properties in Marino were sold, worth double what was received for them. The situation had reached such a point that, it being impossible to redeem these securities, due to the astronomical interest and the fact that it left hardly enough to provide for the governance and sustenance of the monastery, they were forced increasingly to sell the goods mentioned above[44].

S Maria di Palazzolo: from the Cistercians to the Observantines

Further decay at the Abbey of Palazzolo can be linked to the transfer of the Apostolic See to Avignon and the bewilderment that ensued. However, there is no shortage of documents that still testify to its vitality: there is one of 1368 in which an "*Abbas monasterii de Palazzola ord. Cisterc., diocesis albanens*" does not seem to have paid a particular tax[45]; another of 1383 mentions it in the list of Cistercian abbeys in Lazio which must pay the quota for the extraordinary benefit imposed some years before by Urban V[46]; and another of 3 January 1394 mentions the "*monasterium de Palazzolis prope Roccham de Papa*"[47].

Certainly, the schism that followed the "Avignon captivity" and – decisively – the institution of the benefice by Boniface IX (1389-1404) were so fatal to Palazzolo that the few remaining monks decided to abandon the abbey: in 1391, Knight Commander Tommaso Pierleoni, Bishop first of Ascoli and then of Jesi, wanted to build a residence for himself above the abbey but "the Cistercian fathers were so sickened, and largely because of the building begun by the Abbot Knight Commander on the arable land above (where the Villa is today) as if he wished to live there with them, that they in fact abandoned the abbey"[48].

Incidentally, the building started by Pierleoni, which provoked such a drastic reaction from the monks, was a modernisation of an older medieval tower to which the Knight Commander had added a building with mullioned windows (fig. 65).

It was in such situations that, aware of the condition the former Abbey of Palazzolo was in – that is, completely uninhabited and overrun by brushwood "*monasterium S. Mariae de Palazzolo, cistercensis ordinis, albanensis diocesis, ad praesens abbate et monachis caret omnino et spinis et vepribus est repletum*" – "the Carthusian Fathers, living at the moment in the monastery of Santa Croce in Gerusalemme, who were tormented by very serious illness, both because of the site, and of the new building of the monastery, [...] went to Boniface IX, so that he might grant them the monastery of Palazzola, where they have been able to take refuge in the summer, with

[44] F. NERINI, *De tempio et coenobio SS. Bonifacii et Alexii*, Rome 1752, pp. 484-486.
[45] Cf. *Monasticon Italiae* 1981, pp. 30 and 110.
[46] B. BEDINI, *Breve prospetto delle abbazie Cistercensi d'Italia*, Rome 1944, p. 143.
[47] TOMASSETTI, Vol. II, p. 201.
[48] Rome, Aracoeli Provincial Archives, henceforth A.P.A., (Palazzola File): *Memorie e fatti storico-cronologici del Monastero e della Badia Nullius di S. Maria di Palazzola nel Territorio Albanese*, 1737, pp. 3-4. ms.

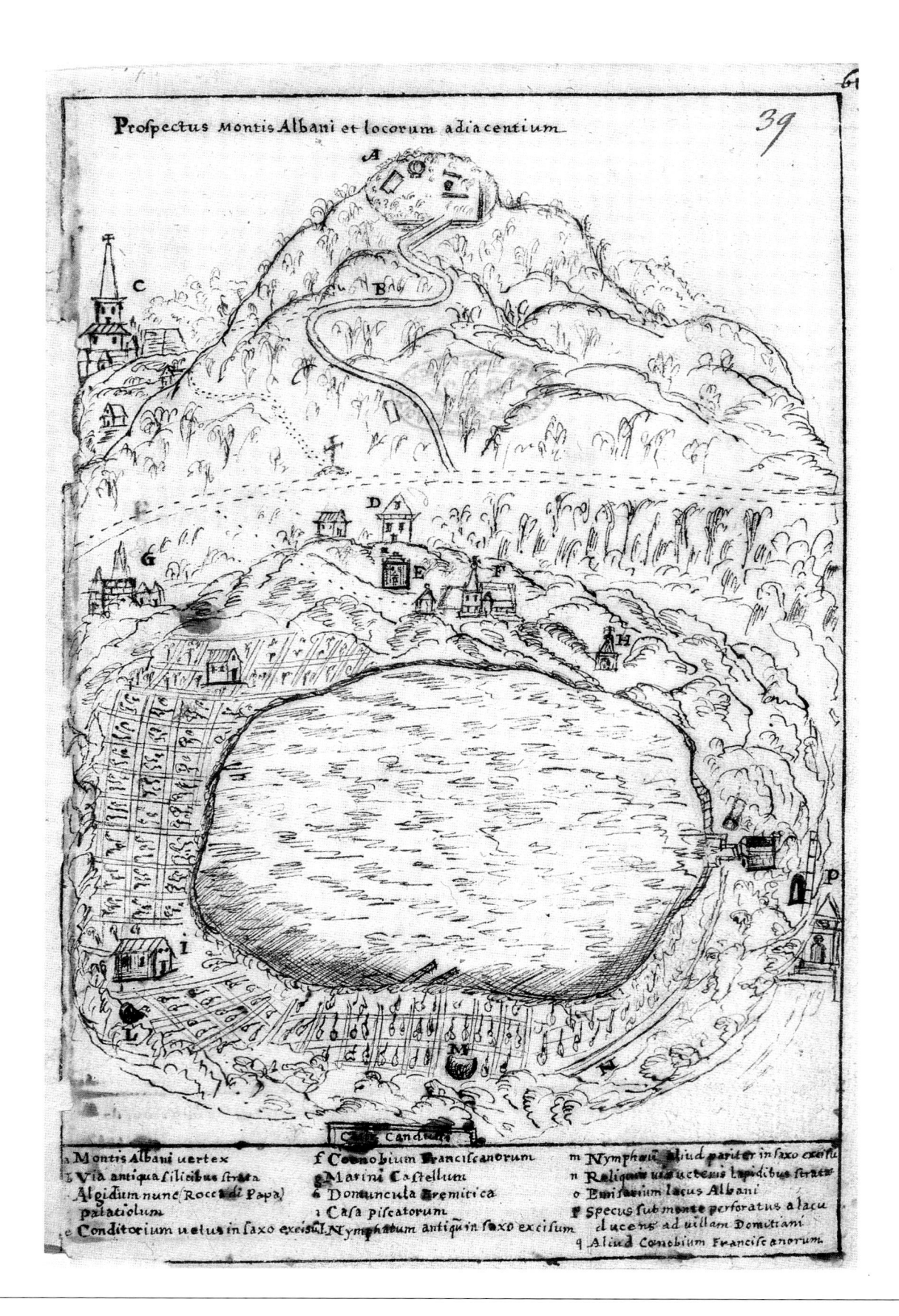

65. Cassiano Del Pozzo (1629), Prospectus Montis Albani et locorum adiacentium, B. A. V. Barb. Lat., 1871, f. 39.

66. S. Maria di Palazzolo, lunette with astylar cross, side entrance to the cloister.

the aim of fleeing from the path of this dangerous evil, which unfailingly was threatening not only priests, but also lay people, and all the families they are destined to serve"[49].

Thus, four months after its abandonment by the Cistercians, Boniface IX accepted the monks' request, through the intercession of the Count of Nola, Nicola Orsini, one of the promoters of the Carthusian settlement at S. Croce. With a Bull dated 21 October 1391, he united and incorporated the monastery of S. Maria di Palazzolo, "*cum suis aedificis, et curte, et horto ipsi monasterio cohaerentibus*", to the Roman monastery; all this without any prejudice to the benefice which followed, much to Pierleoni's delight.

Just like the Abbey of Tre Fontane, so the monks of St Bruno intended it to be a residence for the summer period.

With the arrival of the Carthusians there was a certain restructuring of the estate; for example, to them can be attributed the lunettes in which a diaconal or astylar cross is engraved, at the main and side entrances of the church (fig. 66). This is an unusual emblem in the Cistercian decorative repertoire, but very common among the emblems of the friars of St Bruno.

In the event, as we will see, the Carthusians' presence in the Alban Hills was short-lived.

We come to the papacy of Martin V (Colonna), who succeeded in extending the baronial domination of his family over a vast area of the Campagna and the Marittima: Marino passed to the Colonna family for 12,000 gold florins in 1423[50], while Rocca di Papa, in whose domain fell Palazzolo, became a Colonna fiefdom for 10,000 ducats in 1425[51].

Here it must be remembered that in the history of the Colonnas of Genazzano – the branch of the family which dominated these neighbourhoods of the Alban Hills – the territory of Marino and Rocca di Papa remained outside the fideicommissary patrimony instituted by Martin V in 1427 and was assigned to younger members: thus the Castelli fiefdom went to Cardinal Prospero Colonna and, on his death, to the children of Odoardo, first to Giordano, then to Giovanni, and then to Fabrizio[52].

This practice was to be institutionalised definitively by the Holy See in 1606 when the fiefdom of Marino and Rocca di Papa was erected into the Duchy of Marino and assigned to Cardinal Ascanio Colonna, recognised as head by the Colonese State deeds. Marino was to become the "*extra moenia*" Seat, alternating with Paliano which was the official baronial residence of the Grand High Constable and firstborn of the family[53].

This warlike Roman family was to participate actively in the events of Palazzolo for more than three centuries, interfering in its life in a more or less extraordinary way. The first evidence of this is the presence of Cardinal Prospero Colonna, the local magnate, who intervened in 1449 in the "transfer" from the Carthusians to the Franciscans of the Observance.

On 2 February 1449, a deed was drawn up by the lawyer Giovanni di Luca Francia between Brother Francesco of Viterbo, Guardian of S. Maria dell'Aracoeli, delegate of Brother Stefano of Rome, Vicar of the Roman Province of the Friars Minor of the Observance, and

[49] CASIMIRO 1744, p. 327.
[50] Subiaco, Colonna Archives, henceforth A.C., III B 4, 42.
[51] A. C., III B 29, 19.
[52] Cf. P. SCATIZZI, *I Colonna signori di Genazzano*, p. 29, in "A. BURECA (ed.), *Il castello Colonna a Genazzano*", Rome 2000.
[53] ibid., p. 30.

Brother Ludovico of Ferrara, Rector of the Monastery of S. Croce in Gerusalemme. Having run into economic difficulties in managing the Castelli property, and with it probably in need of restoration and maintenance, the Carthusians gave the Observantines "the church with its sacristy, the bell for ringing the hours (...*campanella ad pulsandum horas*...), the cloister and the house, the gardens which surround it, with a small vineyard adjacent to the garden, with its caves, and all the roads which lead to the monastery; the timber from the woods necessary for repairing the monastery, and the meadow above". They kept for themselves some personal property (chalices, vestments, etc.), some real estate (vineyard, fields, copse of chestnut trees) and the use of the monastery in summer periods as guests of the Franciscans who would welcome them – as the notary's deed specified – with all charity (...*Cum omni caritate*...)[54].

The agreement was drawn up in the home of Cardinal Colonna in the Trevi area of Rome, with the consent of Cardinal Capranica, Bishop of Fermo, Protector of the Carthusian Order, whose titular church was S. Croce in Gerusalemme; it was approved by Pope Nicholas V on 27 April 1449.

It was again through the Colonnas that Palazzolo received a remarkable visit. In May 1463, Pope Pius II, guest of Odoardo Colonna, was about to go up to Rocca di Papa and Monte Cavo and did not miss the opportunity to visit S. Maria di Palazzolo, leaving a clear description in his "Commentarii":

"The church is ancient, not very large, since it is has only one nave, and a vestibule supported on marble columns. Inside there are the monks' cells and convenient service quarters, although they are not very beautiful and broken down with age. The place overlooks Lake Albano. The rock has been cut away enough to provide the necessary space for the monastery and the garden. Caves have also been cut out, where abundant water gushes forth and the very clear springs fill the fishponds. In the summer heat it is delightful to see the cold and sparkling waters spurting high in the air from pipes and it suffices for all the monks' needs.

Behind the garden, which is splendidly cultivated, there is a cave, which is always shady up to midday and which is like a great hall, and several tables can be set out in it. Here, too, from an abundant spring, gush forth clear, never-failing waters that fill a nearby hatchery. Ruthenian Cardinal Isidore, when he sought shelter there from the summer heat, usually had lunch in this cave. The Carthusians used to live here, escaping from the Roman summer climate; now there are the monks of St Francis who have taken the name of Observantines. The approach to the monastery is very narrow and can be guarded by a small number of men. To the right sheer cliffs descend to the lake; to the left is a massive, very high rock, through which the ancients have cut a path..."[55].

And Piccolomini, having referred to the nymphaeum cave, the delight of Cardinal Isidore[56] (fig. 14), being the eminent humanist he was did not forget to describe the fascinating garden tomb at the side of the monastery (figs. 39, 56), ordering that it be cleared of the ivy suffocating it:

"Before entering the monastery, there is a high wall-like rock on

---

[54] CASIMIRO 1744, p. 334.

[55] E. S. PICCOLOMINI, *Commentarii rerum memorabilium*, Milan 1984, vol. II, book 11, pp. 2245-2247: "...*in itinere monasterium Sanctae Marie Palatioli cognominatm Ecclesia invisit ibiquemissarum solemnibus interfuit. Ecclesia est vetustis operis non magna uno contenta fornice, cujus vestibulum marmorei nitet columnis: in sunt monachorum habitacula, et officinae opportunae quamvis parum nitidae et vetustate corruptae. Imminet locus Albano lacui. Saxum excisum est ad tantum spatium, quantum monasterio necesse fuit et horto. Speluncae quoque suffossae sunt: aquarum vis magna hic scaturit et fontes perlucidi vivaria implent piscium. Delectabile est sub aestu frigidas et bullientes aquas cernere, quae, per fistulas emissae, sublime saliunt et ad omnia monachorum opera presto adsunt. Ultra hortum, quem pulcherrime excoluerunt, antrum est ante Meridiem sempre umbrosum, instar aulae in qua plures possint apparari mensae. Illinc quoque fons largus emanat perspicuae perennisque lymphae, quae iuxta piscinam implet. Isidorus cardinalis Rhutenus, cum per aestatis caumata eo profiigisset, in hoc antro plerumque prandium fecit. Olim Carthusienses inhabitarunt, aestivum Romae fugitantes aerem; nunc sancti Francisci monachi tenent, quibus observantia regular nomen dedit. Aditum ad monasterium perangustum pauci facile custidiant. A dextris altissima prae cipitia in lacum tendunt; a sinistris ingens ac sublime prominet saxum, in quo viam ferro excidit antiquitas...*".

[56] A. NIBBI, *Analisi storico-topografica-antiquaria della Carta de' dintorni di Roma*, Rome 1857, p 9: "...*Cardinal Isidore of Thessalonica, who died on 27 April 1463, had chosen one of these caves to dine in on feast days; today, however, the cave is flooded and without those sylvan decorations which made it such a delightful summer triclinium...*".

the left, on which have been engraved, according to the ancient custom, the fasces of the Roman consuls and twelve axes. Six of these were covered in ivy, six still visible. Pius ordered that the ivy be cut away, to honour the memory of antiquity."[57]

To return to the matter of Franciscans and Carthusians living together at Palazzolo – actually limited to the summer period – the serious difficulty of keeping to the agreement stipulated between them soon became obvious, with dissent, arguments and appeals; these events are documented in some detail by Father Casimiro of Rome in his *Memorie storiche*.

This unplesant situation, which lasted for forty years and which even Sixtus IV, a guest at Palazzolo in September 1475, was unable to do anything about, came to an end thanks to a Bull from Innocent VIII on 6 March 1489 and the consequent agreement drawn up on 16 March 1490 (Particappa Deed), in which the Carthusians were said to be right, but Palazzolo was in fact left to the Friars Minor of the Observance:

"After which the nominated Prior of S. Croce [P. Francesco of Capua], *that same day went to Palazzola, and there in the presence of the notary and witnesses"*[58] took possession of the church, the priory, the vineyard, garden, and the relative rights, which he did *"opening and closing the doors of the church and the said places, sitting down, walking everywhere, picking up some of the soil and putting it on his lap, ringing the bell and picking flowers and vegetables in the garden"*[59].

Thus, *"[T]his was the end of the story of the arguments, and together the start of perpetual harmony between the two parties; since they were satisfied by this glorious triumph, the Carthusians did not attempt to go to Palazzola any more, as they could have done, and would have been courteously welcomed, and politely treated. But with them remaining in the monastery of S. Croce, and we in that of Palazzola, in the future they both enjoyed an imperturbable peace..."*[60].

To conclude this historical digression about Palazzolo, let us recall a quick image from a later transcript and a comment on the documents quoted: *"...the convent was small and ancient, the number of monks who could stay there was reduced and the church very meagre and hardly suitable for divine worship..."*[61].

Restorations in the 1500s and the enigma of the tomb of Agnesina di Montefeltro

The resolution of the ten-year disagreement with the Carthusians and the effective possession of Palazzolo by the Observantines coincides with a whole phase of work – to which the Most Excellent Colonna family were not strangers – which lasted, more or less, up to the next century.

As if to ratify the Franciscan presence it was just after 1489 that a beautiful panel with a gold background, depicting the Virgin and Child, with Saints Francis and Anthony of Padua on either side (fig. 67), was completed and placed on the high altar. It was similar to a painting by Benozzo Gozzoli in the Paluzzi chapel of Aracoeli.

[57] PICCOLOMINI (1984 edition), p. 2246: "...*Priusquam monasterium in grediaris stat rupes alta pro muro sinistrae partis, in qua fasces consulum Romanorum et ducdecim secures pro veteri consuetudine sculptae fuerunt. Sex hedera cooperuit, sex adhuc visuntur. Pius hederam iussit amoveri, antiquitatis memoriae favens*".
[58] CASIMIRO 1744, p. 339.
[59] ibid., p. 340.
[60] ibid.
[61] Rome, Archives of S. Antonio de' Portoghesi, henceforth A. S. A. D. P., *Memoire, couvent et Eglise de ste Marie des Neiges a' Palazzola*, m., fasc. 36, 1, 1873.

67. ANTONIAZZO ROMANO, Virgin with Child between Saints Francis and Anthony, (post-1489). Tempera on wood. Formerly on the High Altar of the church of S. Maria di Palazzolo. Now in Rome, S. Antonio de' Portoghesi, second chapel on the left.

68. ANONYMOUS, Virgin enthroned with Child between two Saints (?13th century). Fresco. Apse of the church of S. Maria di Palazzolo.

The painting at Palazzolo, in tempera, was the work of Antoniazzo Romano and his school. It replaced for worship the 13th century fresco on the apse, representing the Virgin with the Child on her lap with two saints at either side, although these latter are difficult to identify (fig. 68). The central group of Romano's work faithfully followed an earlier (1487) panel of his, *The Virgin and Child between Saints Paul and Francis*, formerly housed in another Observantine monastery, S. Paolo at Poggio Nativo[62].

Between the end of the 15th century and the start of the 16th, two *Pietà* were added to the sides of the 13th century fresco. They were obtained from almost the same cartoon, with Christ supported by angels, and, in the background, a pavillion with open awnings (figs. 69-71); these paintings still bear something of the style of Antoniazzo Romano or his circle, and it is obviously a theme very dear to the Observantines.

This resumption of industry and restoration at Palazzolo is also shown by a variety of works, from the new dedication of the church – given the title of Our Lady of the Snows[63] – by Pius V (1567), to the opening (1576) of the so-called *Tomb of the Scipioni*, the garden tomb, the finding of treasure and its disappearance mentioned by Gonzaga, and the Bull of Sixtus V (1586), which approved the authenticity and legitimate possession of the goods of S. Maria di Palaz-

[62] This painting is now in the Ancient Art Gallery of the Palazzo Barberini in Rome.

[63] A. S. A. D. P. (Palazzola File) ANONYMOUS, *Palazzola ristrutturata ovvero descrizione dell'origine della chiesa e convento di S. Maria di Palazzola percorso di sette secoli*, unpublished, undated manuscript. The church at Palazzolo was given its title in reference to the "*image of the Most Blessed Virgin at present in the choir, behind the High Altar and copied, by a good hand, from that which is found in Saint Mary Major's*".

69. ANONYMOUS, Virgin enthroned with Child between two Saints (?13th century), and, at the sides, The Pietà (end of 15th – start of 16th century). Fresco. Apse of the church of S. Maria di Palazzolo.

70. ANONYMOUS, the Antoniazzo circle, detail of The Pietà (end of 15th – start of 16th century). Fresco. Apse of the church of S. Maria di Palazzolo.

71. ANONYMOUS, The Pietà, detail before the 1990s restoration.

72. ANONYMOUS, Coat of Arms of the Montefeltro-Colonna family, characteristic of Agnese Feltria di Montefeltro and Fabrizio Colonna. Marble (end of 15th century). Marino, S. Maria delle Grazie, High Altar.

[64] Frascati, Aldobrandini Archives, *Planta, et descriptio Status, ac Territorii Prioratus Albani*, in "Carte relativo al Priorato – vertenza del card. Gesualdo priore del Priorato ed il confine di Rocca di Papa per i confini del Priorato sud". Historic documents 35/147/2.

[65] A. S. A. D. P., fasc. 110, fasc. 106-14, M. SALUSTRI, *Stima dei fondi rustici e fabbricati di proprietà del Governo di Portogallo, posti nel territorio del Comune di Rocca di Papa, Mandamento di Frascati, Provincia di Roma*, 1880. Cf. CRIELESI 1995.

zolo. This put an end to disagreements with the nearby Abbey of St Paul (and the hermitage of S. Angelo in Lacu handed over as a fief), whose benefice was the concern of the Albano Priory of the Knights Hospitaller of St John of Jerusalem[64].

This emphasis on maintenance also affected the interior of the church: to this period belong the "marble bas-relief coats of arms of the Most Excellent Colonna Family" mentioned by Salustri in his *Stima*[65] and placed in the wall of the double façade above the "two bardiglio marble basins for holy water built into the wall"; and the repainting (1592) of the Antoniazzo high altar panel, already in need of restoration.

73. PIETRO DA CORTONA, The Resurrection of Christ and the resurrection of some members of the Colonna family (1623). Oil on canvas, formerly in the Cappella dei Depositi at S. Andrea di Paliano. Colonna Gallery, Rome.

THE ARTISTIC HISTORY OF CONVENTO DI PALAZZOLO 81

74. ALESSANDRO ALGARDI (in collaboration with the sculptors C. SPAGNA and G. RENZI), Cenotaph of Cardinal Girolamo Colonna (1652). Various marbles. Marino, Collegiate Church of S. Barnaba. Apse, left side. The monument was commissioned by the prelate himself while still alive. As the epigraph suggests, according to the Carthusian moral, he "died a Carthusian". Colonna was Protector of the Carthusian Order. In fact, his remains were buried in the Colonna Chapel in the Lateran Basilica.

But from an historical point of view – in that it shows in what high regard the church of S. Maria di Palazzolo was held – one of the most important testimonies of the time was the fact that, in the first decades of the century, the church was destined to become a Colonna family chapel, complete with tombs for some of its distinguished members: in 1486, Giulia Colonna di Stefano di Palestrina, first wife of Fabrizio Colonna[66], left a legacy of 200 ducats to the Madonna of Palazzolo; here were placed the tombs of, first, Federico Colonna and then his mother Agnesina, respectively the son and the second wife of Fabrizio.

[66] AC, III BB 20, 100 (format G. 53), Parchment Archive.

The tombstones, which remembered Agnese di Montefeltro and her firstborn, have their own history and particular mystery that is worth examining.

Even by Casimiro's time, the funeral monuments of these two Colonna family members had long been destroyed; the Franciscan himself confirms this in his work which, in mentioning the epigraphs[67], recalls a fragment, i.e. "a piece of marble on which some lines could be read, discovered in the new building of the priory in the year 1735" (i.e. during the Fonseca restoration).

Tomassetti, De Cupis[68] and other experts tried to answer the question of who removed the tombstones. Today we can provide the solution.

Agnese di Montefeltro, born in 1472, daughter of Federico, the Duke of Urbino, married Fabrizio Colonna (widower of Giulia) in 1488, and in January 1489 entered Marino: thus, the Colonna family had tied the destiny of its house to that of a prosperous and refined Italian Renaissance lordship, that of the Montefeltro family. It was more than necessary, given the burdensome economic conditions of the Colonnas after the Sistine wars of 1482-84. Seven children were to be born from this union: Federico, the famous poetess Vittoria, Ferdinando, Camillo, Ascanio, Beatrice and Sciarra.

The Colonna-Montefeltro court, to which people and workers from Urbino were certainly added, chose Marino as its usual residence; sadly, little remains there of the work ordered by Fabrizio and Agnese, apart from a delicate Urbino-made marble stand with the Colonna and Montefeltro coats of arms on the high altar of the church of S. Maria delle Grazie (fig. 72).

Fabrizio died in 1520, leaving his widow to protect the family name and benefit from the fiefdom of Marino as long as she might live. Agnese, wishing to fulfil a vow, wanted to go on pilgrimage to the Holy House of Loreto; but on the way back she was struck by a serious illness at Rocca di Mezzo, a town recovered from the Aragonese by Fabrizio Colonna in 1495. Here, on 1 April 1523 (?), as a guest of the heirs of Cardinal Agnifili, a native of the place, Agnese made her will[69], in which, among other things, she left a legacy of 150 ducats to the church at Palazzolo. She died a few days later.

Ascanio, her third child, heir and the only surviving male, commanded that she be buried at Palazzolo, as she had herself in fact ordered in her will. This was because S. Maria di Palazzolo already housed the tomb of her firstborn son, Federico, who had died at the age of 19 in 1516, shortly after being appointed General of the Cavalry by Emperor Maximilian I of Austria[70].

Contrary to what Casimiro asserts[71], followed then by Tomassetti and De Cupis, it is clear that there were two, very distinct inscriptions in the wall of the choir in the church at Palazzolo, as testified by two indisputable Colonna archive documents[72] and by the noted Colonna historian, De Santis[73].

One, therefore, for Federico, on the right hand wall, overlooking the common Colonna tomb, a marble memorial framed by heraldic elements painted on the wall:

---

[67] CASIMIRO 1744, pp. 341-343.

[68] DE CUPIS, p. 22: "...*and we know neither when not for what reason they were removed and taken out of the church, and hidden in an unknown place. We were unable to find any document or information about such a sacrilegious crime, and the reason for committing such an insulting offence to the memory of such an illustrious deceased person, and also damaging Italian history, since from that gravestone memorial we would have been able to verify somewhat better the precise date of Agnese Montefeltre's death...*".

[69] A. C., III BB Paper Archive, cart. 55, n. 20. "*Will of S.ra Agnesina Feltria di Colonna which installs Sig. Ascanio her son as heir and transfers to him the districts of Urbino. 1523*". Cf. Also III BB 54, 87 (format D. 401), Parchment Archive.

[70] A. COPPI, *Memorie Colonnesi compilate*, Rome 1855, pp. 269-271.

[71] CASIMIRO 1744, pp. 341-343. According to the Franciscan writer (who goes back to some none-too-precise passages from Jacovacci) and to Tomassetti, the marble memorial put up by Ascanio Colonna had only one, long inscription, the text of which incorporated memorials to both Agnese Feltria and her son, Federico.

[72] A. C., II A cart. 24 n. 62 "*Such inscriptions about the remains can be seen painted and described in the Choir of the Madonna of Palazzuolo a few miles from Marino*". Cf. Also AC, II A cart. 24 n. 56.

[73] D. DE SANCTIS, *Columnensium procerum imagines et memorias nonullas...*, Rome 1675. "*Inscriptiones Depositorum Columnensium. quae in Choro Ecclesiae B. Virginis de Palazzola proper Marinum inspiciuntur*", P. D, 2.

FRIDERICO COLVMNAE
FABRITII COLVMNAE SVMMI DVCIS PRIMOGENITO
RARAE
AC MIRAE INDOLIS ADOLESCENTI
QVI IAM DE
SE APVD EXTERAS ETIAM NATIONES EXPECTATIONEM
CONCITAVIT
VT CAESAR MAXIMILIANVS PRIMVS IMPERATOR
INGENTIBVS IN ITALIA INGRVENTIBVS BELLIS
OMNIS ITALICI EQVITATVS DVCEM VLTRO CONSTITVERIT
SED PROH DOLOR
VIX NONVM ET DECIMVM ANNVM INGRESSVM
IMMATVRA MORS ERIPVIT
TAM CERTO AC FIRMO PRAESIDIO ITALIAM EXPOLIAVIT
OBIIT ANNO MDXVI
ASCANIVS COLVMNA FRATRI P.

To Federico Colonna firstborn of the supreme commander (sic) *Fabrizio Colonna / a young man of rare and admirable temperament / who had already raised for himself* [great] *hopes / even among foreign nations / so much so that the Emperor Caesar Maximilian I / waging harsh wars in Italy promoted him commander / of the entire Italian cavalry. / But by misfortune / having just entered his nineteenth year / a premature death grasped him* [and] *deprived Italy of such a valid and sure defence. / He died in the year 1516 / Ascanio Colonna laid this for his brother.*

The other epigraph on the left, for Agnese, likewise set in decorations painted with the emblems of her house (a black eagle and cerulean bars) quartered with that of the Colonna family:

AGNETIS (sic) FELTRIAE
CVI PATER FRIDERICVS VRBINI DVX
CONIVX VERO FABRITIVS COLVMNA ROMANVS PRINCEPS
QVORVM INGENS GLORIA ORBEM PERVAGATVR
AST IPSA PIETATE IN DEVM
CHARITATE IN SVOS BONITATE IN OMNES
ATQ. ADEO PER SINGVLA SVMMA ET ADMIRABILIS
VT CVM QVAVIS ANTIQVA HEROIDE
MERITO CONFERRI POTVERIT
DVM EX SACRA AEDE LAVRETANA
QVAM VOTI CAVSA PETIERAT REDIT
IN ITINERE VTRIVSQ. PEREGRINATIONIS METAM IMPEGIT
OBIIT ANNO AETATIS QVINQVAGESIMO
MDXXII
....
CADVCVM ILLVD ET MORTALE IN HAC QVAM SIBI
DELEGIT ASCANIVS FIL. POSVIT STATIONE
VITALIS AVRAE REGRESSVM
PRAESTOLATVR

To Agnese Feltria / whose father was Federico Duke of Urbino / and husband Fabrizio Colonna Roman Prince / whose glory goes throughout the world. / She is famous rather for her piety towards God, / for charity towards those who are his, for goodness to everyone.

And in everything [she was] *so great and admirable / that with any ancient heroine / she could justifiably be compared. / When she was returning from the Holy House of Loreto / which she had visited to fulfil a vow / during the journey she reached halfway on the two pilgrimages. / She died at 50 years of age / in 1522. / In this resting place that she had chosen / her son Ascanio erected* [this monument] *fleeting and mortal /* [where she] *awaits the return of the living spirit. /*

It is worth noting that the inscriptions recalling Agnesina, both the one transcribed by Casimiro, quoted by De Sanctis, as well as the one in the Colonna archives, date the year of her death to 1522. Therefore, certain anachronisms – intentional or otherwise – present in the Will mentioned earlier, need to be pointed out. From the historical point of view, this is a very important document in which Agnesina institutes her son Ascanio as universal heir, making over to him, among other things, the much sought-after "districts" of Urbino, thus arousing suspicions of possible manipulation. For example, the date of the Will – 1 April 1523, a year after the death (sic) – is given as in the fourth indiction of the pontificate of Leo X. In that year Hadrian VI was actually on the throne of Peter, having succeeded the Medici Pope on 9 January 1522; another error is the name of "Giorgio Cardinal of this land (that is Rocca di Mezzo)" where Agnesina, returning from Loreto, was a guest in the house of his heirs: Cardinal Agnifili, in fact, who had died long ago in 1476, was called Amico.

The tombs with the Colonna remains were at Palazzolo for almost a century, until the High Constable Filippo I Colonna, on the strength of a Brief from Pope Paul V dated 8 October 1613, was authorised to take the bodies of his relations to Paliano.

So in 1616, after authorisation from the Spanish Father Antonio Marzer, then Provincial Minister of the Observantines, the remains of Agnesina and her son were exhumed[74].

On 11 June that year identification of the bodies began, in the presence of a notary, the Secretary of the High Constable, Cesare Leoncello di Cave, the Guardian of Palazzolo, Fr Aurelio of Rome, and Fr Teodoro of Rome from the same Priory. With the help of three experts, Nicolò Castiglia, smith and builder, Pellegrino, smith and carpenter, and Gaspare da Trevigliano, the Colonna tomb to the right of the choir in the church was excavated. The bodies of Federico and Agnesina were found, mixed up with the remains of five other people.

The remains were put into a wooden urn and given to Leoncello to be taken from Palazzolo to S. Andrea in Paliano, to the so-called 'Chapel of the Remains', which Filippo I Colonna had had extended in honour of his predecessors: great-great-grandfather Fabrizio, husband of Montefeltro; mother Anna Borromeo, sister of St Charles, whose body was brought, in 1616, from Palermo where she had died in 1580; wife Lucrezia Tomacelli, who died before him, and whose remains were moved in 1623 or 1622[75] from Genazzano; Ascanio and Giovanna

[74] A. C., III AA 193, 34. "*Consignment of the bodies of Sg. ri Don Federico Colonna and S. ra Donna Agnesina Feltria 1616*".
[75] G. TUCCI – SAVO – A. GIOVANNONI, *Paliano. Monografia Storica.* Tivoli 1933.

d'Aragona; Marcantonio, the hero of Lepanto, and his wife Felice Orsini; Marcantonio (IV), called the *Contestabilino*, who died in 1611 and was buried here in 1625. All the illustrious deceased of his direct line whom Filippo I wished to remember – including himself, still alive – were featured in an altarpiece of unusual iconography, a true genealogical tree, entitled *The Resurrection of Christ and the resurrection of some members of the Colonna Family*, commissioned in 1623 from Pietro da Cortona and destined for the mausoleum in Paliano[76] (fig. 73).

And so in the choir at S. Maria di Palazzolo there remained only the tombstones, mere cenotaphs, to remember for posterity Agnesina di Montefeltro and the unfortunate Federico.

But even at Paliano the Colonna remains did not find peace because in 1799, during the sacking undergone by this town of Ciociaria, even the 'Chapel of the Remains' was desecrated and the tombs of the Colonna ravaged, "to obtain lead from there to make ammunition"[77].

Cardinal Girolamo and Carlo (Dom Egidio) Colonna at Palazzolo

There is an important document dating back to the start of the seventeenth century: the recognition, in 1603, of the boundaries of the territory belonging to the Convento di Palazzolo sought by Costanza Colonna, Marchioness of Caravaggio and sister of Ascanio, first Duke of Marino. She had set in motion a lawsuit with someone whose property bordered that of the Franciscan Priory. The report shows that the territorial boundaries of the property surrounding Palazzolo had remained virtually unchanged since 1269, despite the fact that parts of Palazzolo's territory had been snatched or encroached upon in various ways[78].

The first decades of the seventeenth century also coincided with the great reforms of the religious Orders, and the Franciscan Order was not immune from this. In 1626, in the wake of the renewal which saw new Priories established *ex novo* in the area, at Frascati (S. Bonaventura) and Castel Gandolfo (S. Francesco), the fraternity of Palazzolo passed from the hands of the Friars Minor of the Observance to the Reformed Friars Minor, before returning, some decades later, in 1640, to the Observantines.

It was during this 14-year interlude under the Reformed Friars Minor – which also coincided with the passage of the Priory from the spiritual jurisdiction of the diocese of Albano to that of Frascati – that, in 1629, Girolamo Colonna (1604-1666) (fig. 74), second-born son of Filippo and Lucrezia Tomacelli, still fresh from his nomination to the Cardinalate, appealed to Pope Urban VIII for permission to continue to restore the remains of the "*Casino*" ("little house") of Knight Commander Pierleoni[79], overlooking the Priory. He wanted to build a country house there worthy of his rank and make use of the six *rubbie* of land surrounding the building, left neglected by the Reformed Friars Minor who professed the absolute poverty of the Rule.

"Cardinal Colonna provided the impetus for the building and payment for a tower above Convento di Palazzolo. It was falling apart and dilapidated to such an extent that all that remained were the four sur-

---

[76] Cf. E. A. SAFARIF (ed.), *Galleria Colonna in Rome*, 1998, pp. 104-105, inset n. 143. Cf. also A. LO BIANCO (ed.), *Pietro da Cortona 1597-1669*, Catalogue for the exhibition of the same name, Rome 1997, inset 11, pp. 296-297.

[77] G. BIZZARRI, *La Città di Paliano il castello di Zancati*, Rome 1915, pp. 34-35.

[78] A. C., III AA, 73, f. 349 r. v. *Termini del territorio del Convento di Palazzola*.

[79] A. P. A. (Palazzola File), ANONYMOUS, *Memorie e fatti storico-cronologici del Monastero*, pp. 3-4.

rounding walls without any floor, dividing wall, no roof. He thought that since it is separate from the said Priory it was part of the territory and jurisdiction of Rocca di Papa, but learned that the said tower is incorporated in and part of the Priory with five or six rubbie of land, which, while the Observantine Friars Minor governed the Priory, they benefitted from and put to good use. But afterwards the Reformed Friars Minor, who observed complete poverty, went to live in the Priory, and they left all the land uncultivated; so the Cardinal, having begun the building, wanted to improve it, and His Holiness, through a Brief, granted him the said tower, and land, with the water that is there (however, without depriving the Priory of water), with the caves that are there, so that he could, with greater taste, develop the building with the authority to do with it what he may wish after his death"[80].

Urban VIII agreed to the request and on 7 August that year sent a Brief "*datum Romae apud S. Mariam Majorem*" about the requested concession.

In this *Motu Proprio*, starting with the usual praises for Cardinal Girolamo for his merits and even more for his many favours on behalf of the Apostolic See, the Pope granted Cardinal Girolamo the semi-ruined building and the surrounding six *rubbie* of land:

"*tibi nonullas aedes, seu muros, majori ex parte dirutos, ac circa illos existentis, partem territorii inculti mensurae sex rubbiorm circiter ad Domum Regularem B. Mariae Virginis F. rum Ordinis Minorum S. Francisci de Observantia Reformaturum nuncupatorum Loci Palazzola Albanem Dioecesis...*"[81].

This concession was also made in favour of the Cardinal's future heirs, i.e. for life, with the authority to rebuild or restore all that was necessary and opportune, turning the neglected land surrounding Pierleoni's former house into a garden, and granting use of the nearby caves, with possession of the water for servicing the building and irrigating the land, on condition that all this caused no damage or lack of water to the Friars Minor.

The building of this villa, whose history is linked to that of the former Priory below it, can be placed in the context of the increase in value of this district of the Alban Hills that blossomed on Urban VIII's accession to the papacy.

As a Cardinal, the Barberini Pope had overseen the start of a modest construction near the ancient rock of Castel Gandolfo. From the year after his election in 1624 the summer presence of the Pontiffs in that little town in the Alban Hills, apart from an occasional interlude, was to become customary.

Under the Barberini Pope work began on the Apostolic Palace at Castel Gandolfo. As is known, the work was entrusted to Maderno, helped by Bartolomeo Breccioli and Domenico Castelli[82]. Urban VIII also planned another villa, as an alternative to the papal residence at Castel Gandolfo, to be built just a short distance from Palazzolo in the level space next to the ruined castle of Malaffitto. This plan never came to fruition. The project is dated 1631 and the designs are by Luigi Arrigucci: a building with a great portico and two side wings with a vast terrace overlooking the lake; behind the palace, a garden of three hectares di-

[80] A. C., Misc. Storica II A, 71, n. 28.
[81] A. C., III BB 19, 4; ibid III BB 15, 37; Cf. also: III AA 73. f. 343; ibid III KB, 6, 24.
[82] Cf. F. BONOMELLI, *I papi in campagna*, Rome 1953, pp. 41ff.

75. Vicomte De Senonnes (1820), Vue d'un Casin près du Lac d'Albano. Etching. The Villa del Cardinale at Palazzolo here appears realistically in its original 17th century aspect.

Vue d'un Casin près du Lac d'Albano.

vided into four parts, with a central fountain and a long avenue that linked up with the then *Via di Napoli*[83] (fig. 24, 27).

Contemporaneous to these buildings designed for the papal court – both expansions and new buildings – there are other constructions in the vicinity of the lake: the Villa of the Prince and Prefect Taddeo Barberini, married to Anna Colonna, which was begun in 1625 and almost finished in 1635, and, of course, that of Cardinal Colonna at Palazzolo (fig. 75), whose architectural authorship could be attributed to one of the workers active during this period in the other Colonna "*factories*" in the area.

This last construction, at least in its architectural structure, was more or less finished in 1631, as proven by Arrigucci's drawing in the Vatican Library[84] (fig. 76).

The illustrious prelate did not benefit from this pleasant Castelli residence for too long. About ten years later, following a request about the matter, in his first Will dated 21 February 1643 he ratified the earlier grant he had made of it to his own sister, Anna.

From the Will we know that Cardinal Girolamo granted Anna the right of temporary possession and revenue, as well as residence, of the

[83] Vatican City, Vatican Apostolic Library, henceforth B. A. V., *Disegni e Piante diverse*, Chigiani Manuscript, P. VII, 12. *Pianta del Castello sud fatto da Luigi Arrigucci*, fol. 3. Bonomelli 1953, p. 69, note 24.

[84] B. A. V., *Disegni e Piante diverse*, Chigiani Manuscript, P. VII, 12. *Territorio di Castel Gandolfo, con sue strade, Palazzuolo, Casini e strade diverse con il Lago dove Papa Urbano hebbe disegno di fare un Castello, et il disegno lo fece Luigi Arrigucci*, fol. 2.

76. LUIGI ARRIGUCCI (1631), The territory of Castel Gandolfo with its streets, Palazzuolo, lodges and various streets with the Lake where Pope Urban wanted to build a Castle, B. A. V., Disegni e Piante diverse, Chigiani Manuscript, P. VII, 12. Detail with a view of the complex of S. Maria di Palazzolo and the Villa Colonna (Villa del Cardinale) above.

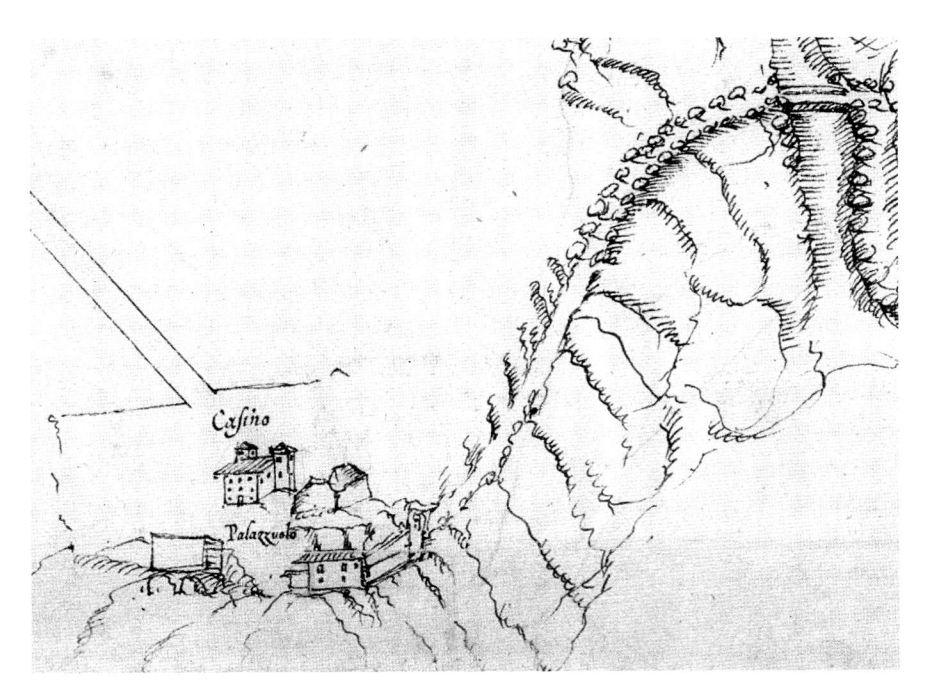

Villa of Palazzolo itself – the *haeremo*, as it is defined – situated, as the notary's document recalls, "in the diocese of Albano or Frascati" (sic).

According to the Will this was all granted on condition that the use and benefit was only during the natural lifetime of the *Prefettessa* and that any work or improvement must be to the benefit of the property, without any obligation of repayment. Furthermore, the beneficiary was obliged to preserve and improve both the Villa and its land, ensuring necessary planting was carried out. If this was not done then the concessions and use of the Villa would be annulled[85].

It is worth recalling that, in order to guarantee the future ownership of the Villa, and with the building almost finished, on 4 January 1631 Cardinal Girolamo Colonna had been appointed Protector of the Priory of Palazzolo[86] by Urban VIII, an appointment which was confirmed by the same Barberini Pope on 2 June 1640 and the privilege extended to the Cardinal's successors in perpetuity[87].

But the Prefect's wife Anna Colonna certainly had no way of enjoying the *haeremo* of Palazzolo. With the death of Urban VIII and Innocent X Pamphilj ascent to the throne the Barberini were forced to leave Rome, not to return until 1653; but she wanted to remain in the city, far from all clamour and worldliness. She withdrew to the Regina Coeli Convent of the Discalced Carmelites she had had built according to Contini's plan, and died there on 31 October 1658.

The Villa Palazzolo was used by her brother, Dom Egidio Colonna – alias Carlo – Archbishop of Amasia (fig. 77), whose presence in the Castelli retreat is testfied from 1652, according to correspondence sent from there to Girolamo and a manuscript of Domenico Jacovacci a little before 1658. Two of the seven watercolour illustrations attached to the latter show the building on the lake with the words: "*Casino di Mons. Egidio Colonna*" (plate 1C), and, "*Casino de Monsg. Colonna*" (plate 1E)[88] (figs. 31-32).

[85] A. C., III AA 73, 343. The Will was drawn up in the Palazzo Colonna, and on 28 February ratified by the Capitoline Judge, Pietro Paolo Cavalletti.

[86] A. C., III BB 773, 15, 32.

[87] A. C., III BB 15, 106. Cf. CASIMIRO 1744, p. 345-6.

[88] Ariccia, Palazzo Chigi Library, D. JACOVACCI: *Notitie /di / Castel Candolfo, di Albano/ della Riccia, di Genzano, e/ di Nemi. / Con una tavola delle cose in esso contenute. / Al / santissimo Padre/ Alessandro VII. / Date dal suo Vassallo e Servitore / Domenico Jacovacci*. It is worth noting that Castel Gandolfo (Plate 1 D) is shown prior to the Bernini transformations, begun after April 1658 with the laying of the foundation stone of the church of S. Tommaso. Cf. F. PETRUCCI in "L'Ariccia del Bernini", Catalogue for the exhibition of the same name. Ariccia 10 October – 31 December 1998, pp. 45-47.

Born on 20 December 1606, Carlo, Duke of Marsi, third son of Filippo I Colonna and Lucrezia Tomacelli, and brother, therefore, of Cardinal Girolamo, was a person whose story seems to call to mind that Manzoni figure Ludovico-P. Cristoforo.

His military career began brilliantly in the Neapolitan army, where he reached the rank of Captain in the Armoured Corps, and then that of Field Commander of a regiment during the siege of Casale in May 1630[89], as documented by, among other things, a painting, *The siege of Casale di Monferrato*, in the Colonna Gallery[90]. At this rank he fought against the Swedish forces in Germany, commanded by Gustavus Adolphus, took part in the defence of Franchendal, and fought in the battle of Spira, before returning to Rome[91].

And here, on 1 September 1634,

"...there was a solemn feast in the church of S. Egidio, in the Borgo S. Pietro, and in those days it was customary to be driven by carriage through the district of S. Egidio. The coachman of the Caetani dukes was taking two children of that family, along with others from the Cesarini [family], and tried to overtake the coach that was carrying D. Carlo Colonna. But the latter got suddenly angry and ordered his own staff to block the right of way of the Caetani coach at all costs, pushing the horses backwards, and this was done along part of the street, while Colonna shouted "This is what you do to people with no manners".

In those days theseizing of right of way for a carriage by the arrogant driving of the coachman was considered the greatest of insults, and no one could tolerate it.

The next day Carlo Colonna left his palace in the P. dei SS. Apostoli by carriage, along with Lorenzo Mutini and the brothers Francesco and Papirio Capizucchi with Guilio Bufalini.

Shortly afterwards, Gaspare Caetani, Knight of Malta, and uncle of the two Caetani children already mentioned, also left from the former Rucellai palace in Via Fontanella di Borghese. He ordered his coachman to head for Piazza Colonna, since he had been told about the intervention of Colonna in Via del Corso, and that consequently Colonna voluntarily wanted to meet him. This happened precisely at the place called Arco di Portogallo. He immediately called to the coachman to stop and, getting down from the carriage, went towards D. Carlo Colonna, saying "I am coming so that you can give me an explanation for your impertinence towards my nephews yesterday". In retort Colonna denied this, got down from his carriage, and took up his sword. Six friends rushed to the help of Caetani, while Colonna was defended only by the Capizucchi brothers, who were armed with swords, and shortly afterwards Bufalini and Mutini were provided with swords, too.

Caetani, being an able swordsman, struck Colonna in the chest several times, but since Colonna was wearing a jacket, the strikes were in vain, and he was wounded only on a finger on the right hand. Finally, Bargello and the police intervened, but a carter, who was passing along the Corso with his cart, butted in, too. That suspended the fight between the parties.

Caetani, having seen that Colonna was wounded on the hand, turned his back to walk away, but was stopped by the cart. So Bufalini,

[89] Cf. P. Litta, *Famiglie celebri d'Italia*, 2, IX, Milan 1837.

[90] Cf. E. A. Safarif (ed.), *Galleria Colonna in Roma*, 1998, p. 75, table n. 91.

[91] Coppi 1855, p. 384. Cf. A. C., Misc. Stor. II A 4, 74 cc. 509-513., 19, 23; 19, 26, 71, 20. Cf. also: De Cupis, p. 29; Scatizzi 2000, p. 70, note 234.

77. P. P. RUBENS (copy of), Portrait of Carlo Colonna, Duke of Marsi (then Dom Egidio, Archbishop of Amasia). Oil on canvas (pre-1638), formerly at the Colonna Palace at Genazzano. Colonna Gallery, Rome.

in a rage wounded him from behind with the sword, piercing him through from one side to another. Caetani took a few steps and fell to the ground: they took him immediately to his palace, but shortly afterwards, having had only just enough time to confess..." [92].

Colonna, wounded, immediately took refuge in the Palazzo Theodoli, near the monastery for women penitents; any form of revolt was avoided and calm was restored thanks to the mediation of the authorities and, largely, the families themselves.

Once recovered Carlo Colonna returned to military life and in 1636 was involved in the taking of Corbiè in Picardy.

But just a few years later, still troubled in conscience, Carlo Colonna wanted to retreat from the world and decided to become a monk at S. Scolastica at Subiaco. He made his profession on 4 December 1638, taking the name of Egidio, out of devotion to the good 13th century fam-

[92] DE CUPIS, p. 30.

ily member who bore that name and in honour of the Saint on whose feast the fateful duel had taken place[93].

Subsequently, he was ordained priest and in 1643 appointed Archbishop of Amasia, a title to which, at the end, in 1672, he added that of Patriarch of Jerusalem, which had formerly belonged to another of his brothers, Giovan Battista[94].

The Colonna Archives contain some of the contemporary correspondence between Girolamo and Egidio Colonna. In April 1662, while the Cardinal was holidaying in Marino, the Archbishop of Amasia wrote to him from Palazzolo, recommending him to send the gardener and another worker as soon as possible, in order to trim the hazelnut trees along the Villa's avenue, since he understood that the Pontiff wanted to visit there again. Therefore, he deemed it absolutely necessary to widen and clean up the avenue leading to the Villa:

"Your Eminence Most Reverend Lord
Would you command the gardener to come with his helper to trim the avenue of hazels which have not come up, because if the Pope comes he will come by the said avenue. I beg you to order him to come immediately so that he can gain access. Also, I beg you with all my heart to let him bring me four flasks since it would give me great pleasure to let him drink some red wine. I am sorry for the inconvenience I cause you; I humbly kiss your hand.

Egidio Archbishop of Amasia
Palazzola 23 April 1662" [95].

It is worth noting that the request for red wine is often repeated in other correspondence examined in the Archives, and this is because the Palazzolo Villa did not have a little vineyard.

On 27 April, only four days after the above letter was sent, Archbishop Egidio Colonna wrote again to the Cardinal, informing him that Pope Alexander VII had been brought to Palazzolo and he had received him with as much dignity and honour as possible. After dining, the Pope had wished to see again the new covered spiral staircase, the so-called *Passaggio del Cardinale* – today impassable – which led from the Villa to the back of the Convento di Palazzolo.

In the same letter Archbishop Egidio Colonna did not forget his usual request for two flasks of red wine...and another four of white wine, too:

"Your Eminence Most Reverend Lord
With specific regard to certain favours of mine, I am sending with this letter six empty bottles so that Your Eminence may, from his store, fill them with Pantanelle red wine, and four with that beautiful white wine. I hope this is alright.
The Pope, the same day that he came here, after dining went out to see the new staircase above the new road near to the church" [96].

Furthermore, the same document contains some important information about the church of the Assumption in Ariccia. In fact, the Arch-

[93] COPPI 1855, pp. 384ff.
[94] ibid.
[95] A. C., II A 19, n. 24.
[96] A. C., II A 19, n. 4.

bishop states that he has learned that on the following Sunday – 31 April 1662 – the Pope was to lay the foundation stone of the church of the Assumption in Ariccia, and since as Cardinal Chigi he had done this for the church at Castel Gandolfo, he wanted to do the same for the *Rotonda*, even though there were to be some unforeseen circumstances and notable absenteés:

> "...*they say that on Sunday 31 they want to lay the first stone at the church of Riccia, although the Lord Cardinal is absent, and even though the Pope wants to lay it at Riccia the Lady Principessa Chigi [will be absent] due to her pregnancy [...].*
> Egidio Archbishop of Amasia
> Palazzola 27 April 1662"[97].

Cardinal Girolamo Colonna, the *princeps, dux et nihil*, as he had himself described on his cenotaph, died on 4 September 1666 in Finale Ligure[98] and his remains were temporarily buried in the chapel of S. Vincenzo in the church of St Catherine the martyr, attached to the Dominican Convent[99]. Six years later, the body was moved to Rome and buried in the Colonna Chapel – the so-called *winter choir* – in the Lateran Basilica (fig. 74).

In his second Will, dated 15 October 1664[100], among many provisions the deceased Cardinal ordered that 3500 Masses be celebrated for the repose of his soul, dividing the celebrations between the Basilica of the Holy Apostles, as his parish church, St John Lateran's, St Peter's at the Vatican, St Paul's, St Mary Major's, and S. Carlo ai Catinari. He also wished that another 1500 Masses be celebrated in other churches in Rome, while in the parishes and churches linked to the Colonna church estate another 4000 Masses be celebrated, including "...500 to be said in the church of S. Maria at Palazzola"[101].

Perhaps to satisfy his old passion for horses, his brother Archbishop Egidio Colonna was left "the best country carriage, which upon my death will be found with a second team of six and their harnesses, and the framed head of St Peter In Tears by Guido. [Guido Reni?]"[102].

In addition, the Archbishop would have tenancy of the Villa in his natural lifetime "allowing also my heir [Don Lorenzo Onofrio Colonna] to enjoy it during his life, enjoy the fruit of my Villa of Palazzola"[103] (fig. 79).

It is worth noting here that, thanks to the presence of Archbishop Egidio Colonna in his Villa at Palazzolo, many embellishments were made, such as the pictorial decoration that adorned the ground floor room of the building. According to Tomassetti, on the largest walls were views of two coastal towns; according to De Cupis one of these was the town of Marino as an imaginary seaport, in which the Pope's *Capitana* – the papal galley which the Barbareschi had captured on 11 May 1560, during the unhappy naval battle at Gerbe in the Tunisian Gulf and later salvaged by Marcantonio Colonna in the battle of Lepanto in 1571 – was floating, thus recalling for posterity one of the most glorious adventures of Colonna splendour. But more likely it was a representation of the lake below in all its glory and the well-known mock sea battle decreed by Alexander VII in May 1656.

78. S. Maria di Palazzolo. Plaque recalling the opening and closure of the Holy Door in 1650. It was an office delegated to Cardinal Girolamo Colonna: the inlaid marble cross, as the epigraphs below it note, is – contrary to what is stated by Tomassetti and De Cupis – the one placed into the Holy Door at St. John Lateran's by Colonna at the closure of the 1650 Jubilee; it was recovered at the opening of the next Jubilee Year, in 1675, and embedded into the wall at Palazzolo.

[97] ibid.
[98] A. C., II C A, 27, 17.
[99] ibid.
[100] A. C., III A A 73ff. 265r-270v.
[101] ibid., f. 265 r.
[102] A. C., III A A 73. f. 265 r.
[103] ibid.

79. Palazzolo, Villa Colonna (Villa del Cardinale), entrance to the former stables. Weather-beaten coat of arms of the Cardinal's hat of Girolamo Colonna, formerly at the entrance of the Villa. Travertine.

The paintings adorning the room today – the result of 'strong' repainting by Gattoni (1933) during the De Cupis restoration – provide a panoramic view of the Palazzolo complex with the Villa Colonna above (fig. 80) as it would have appeared in the second half of the 17th century, including the famous cave, once a delight of Cardinal Isidore, the Malaffitto ruins and those of the hermitage of S. Angelo in Lacu, Rocca di Papa, the ridge on which Castel Gandolfo was to be built and beyond to the sea.

Again, it is to Archbishop Egidio that we owe the short flight of steps, the Passaggio del Cardinale, which already existed in April 1662, as is shown by Colonna's letter quoted above. This work, which was probably carried out with the agreement and under the direction of Friar Giorgio Marziale, can be attributed to the time of the many restorations and improvements planned by Antonio the Great (1625-1671), active at this time in Palazzo Colonna, at Rocca di Papa[104], in Marino, and in Genazzano[105], etc.

Credit is also due to the Archbishop of Amasia for planting the much-desired vineyard that resolved the problem of the chronic lack of good wine (red or white) on his table:

"...Some years previously, Mgr. Egidio Colonna had had a small vineyard planted at Palazzolo with the aim of leisurely enjoying its produce, which due to its aspect should always be excellent. From a topographical indication compiled by the agronomist Carlo Qualeatti, it seems that the said vineyard was, according to the agricultural measurement of the time, of only six-and-a-half Roman chains – about three hectares – and, beyond the wood cultivated to the high trunk, around the little Colonna palace, and near the Priory, it extended as far as the place called 'Tre Ione', bordering on the hermitage of S. Angelo above the lake, with a total surface area of 17 roman rubbie, Ea 31 . 423 hectares" [106].

On the death of Archbishop Egidio Colonna, the good neighbourly relations between the Villa Colonna and the Friars from the Priory below were broken. The Villa, hastily emptied of all furnishings by his heirs in January 1687, then became a farmhouse given over to sharecropping. A disagreement arose among the farmers who had started the deforestation of the scrubland, to which the Francscian community, armed with ancient documents, boasted of rights that it did not intend to renounce[107] (figs. 81-82).

The dispute that began in 1690 was only resolved in 1772, as testified by the numerous Chronicles written about this matter by the Guardians of Palazzolo and kept in the Archives at San Francesco a Ripa and at Aracoeli. The history of the Villa Colonna transformed into a humble agricultural store, would drag on, with appeals and petitions against lease-holders and defaulting tenants, into the first decades of this century.

And it was as a semi-abandoned farmhouse that Tomasetti found it, upset by the squalor and decadence into which the noble dwelling had fallen.

Sold by the Colonnas and bought by the Venerable English College[108] in the years 1920-21, the property was then sold in 1924 to Gui-

---

[104] C. M. GUARINONI, *Le chiese Parrocchiali di Rocca di Papa*, Rocca di Papa 1998, pp. 31-38.

[105] Cf. M. CAMPISI, *Architettura e storia della Fabbrica*, pp. 103ff. in "A. BURECA (ed.), *Il castello Colonna a Genazzano*", Rome 2000.

[106] DE CUPIS, p. 54. Cf. A. C., AA 73, f. 342, [Qualeatti survey 6 April 1656].

[107] DE CUPIS, pp. 20, 54, 63.

[108] Rome, Venerable English College Archives, henceforth V. E. C., Pal. 3., 23.

80. EMILIO GATTONI (?1933) View of Lake Albano and its surroundings, as it would have appeared in the 17th century. Detail of the Priory with the Villa Colonna above. Palazzolo: Villa Colonna (Villa del Cardinale), former billiard-room. The re-painting done by Gattoni during the De Cupis restoration altered the seventeenth-century wall decorations.

do De Cupis who carried out a radical restoration. On his death in 1938 the property passed to the Redemptorist Fathers who owned it until 1970. It then passed on to other owners and then fell into a state of neglect up to the present time, when a breath of revival seems to suggest a better future (figs. 83-84).

Around about 1674, as he neared his final days, Archbishop Egidio Colonna left the pleasantness of the hermitage at Palazzolo and retired to S. Callisto in Trastevere, to a little palace which formerly belonged to Cardinal Moroni, property of the Cassinese Benedictines to whose Congregation the Subiaco monasteries of S. Scolastica and S. Speco had belonged from 1514. Here, at over eighty years old, he gave up his impetuous soul to God on 18 October 1686.

Colonna had been a son of the Subiaco monastic family, a fact he remembered even in his Will. To the monastery of S. Scolastica he left all his furnishings and holy artefacts, decreeing also that his body be buried there, and to S. Speco he left the princely sum of 8,000 scudi, for the upkeep of four monks at that Sanctuary, just as the Congregation of Bishops and Regulars had proposed in 1654 after a visit there had found the place to be semi-deserted[109].

Sadly, his executors – or rather his relations – did not respect his pro-

[109] G. P. CAROSI, *Badia di Subiaco*, Subiaco 1970, pp. 89-90.

81. Palazzolo, Villa Colonna (Villa del Cardinale), façade of the little church on the entrance path. Travertine boundary stone of the Colonna family property.

visions: Sacro Speco received nothing left to it by Dom Egidio and remained in a desolate state, and his own body was buried instead at S. Callisto with an epigraph that thus remembered him in posterity[110]:

> D. O. M.
> AEGIDI COLVMNAE
> MONACHI CASSINENSIS
> AMASIAE PRIMVM ARCHIEPISCOPI
> HIEROSOLIMITANI DEINDE PATRIARCHAE
> OCTVAGENARII AETERNITATIS METAM ATTINGENTIS
> OSSIBVS ET CINERIBVS
> . . . .
> OBIIT ANNO D. NI MDCLXXXVI XIV KAL.
> NOVEMBRIS

Friar Giorgio Marziale, Minorite architect, and the seventeenth-century work

In 1655 the death of the Pamphilj Pope Innocent X was followed by an 80-day conclave which elected Cardinal Fabio Chigi, who took the name Alexander VII.

The Chigi Cardinal's acclaimed accession to the throne of Peter resulted, with renewed splendour, in the resurgence of the famous family which, after the Renaissance magnificence of the banker Agostino the Magnificent, patron of Raffaello, Giulio Romano and del Peruzzi, had disappeared from the political and financial Roman scene, withdrawing to its native Siena.

Following the stagnation of the Pamphilj pontificate, with the Chigi Pope the genius Gian Lorenzo Bernini returned to rule the papal court.

Bernini's presence in the Alban Hills was certainly not new: already, in 1633, during the Barberini Pontificate, he had been summoned to Castel Gandolfo for a series of works at the Apostolic Palace and in the nearby villa of Taddeo Barberini, as well as for other undertakings in various Castelli localities.

So, in 1656, together with Bernini, responsible for a number of artistic enterprises in the Castelli, there appears at Palazzolo and as Director of works in the most important of these, the figure of the Minorite architect Friar Giorgio Marziale, or Marziali, "a native of Ponzano della Marca di Fermo, clothed in the Roman Province"[111]. Until now he had almost been forgotten or not even mentioned.

The Friar (whose original name was Giorgio di Cesare di Giorgio?) was born into a family of local landowners in the small town of Ponzano in Fermano. When he left the town he took the Franciscan grey of the Friars Minor of the Observance of the Roman Province, based at Aracoeli, with the name Friar Giorgio of Fermo. The name Giorgio was common in his family in honour of the co-patron Saint of Ponzano to whom a little church was dedicated in the small village in the Marches.

Little is known about the friar's architectural formation, although the possibility should not be excluded that he had already learned the craft from following the master Lombard masons, present in Ponzano[112]; it was

82. Palazzolo, Villa Colonna (Villa del Cardinale), façade of the little church facing the entrance path. Travertine boundary stone with the property of S. Maria di Palazzolo.

[110] COPPI 1855, pp. 385ff.
[111] A. CRIELESI, *Fra Giorgio Marziale di Ponzano*, in "Atti del Convegno Ponzano di Fermo tra Medioevo e Rinascimento", Ponzano 19 July 1998, henceforth CRIELESI, July 1998, pp. 20-33.
[112] F. SCOCCIA, *Ponzano nel Cinquecento*, Monte Ottone 1995, pp. 94-99.

83. Palazzolo, Villa Colonna (Villa del Cardinale), detail of the main façade, as it appears following the De Cupis restoration in the 1920s.

84. Palazzolo, Villa Colonna (Villa del Cardinale), detail of the tower as it appears today after the 1920s De Cupis restoration. Just above the sundial can be seen Pope Alexander VII's coat of arms, in marble, formerly on the main garden gate (1662), designed by Friar Giorgio Marziale from the Priory below.

an experience which, according to some of his fellow brothers, the Franciscan Minor quickly put to use in the service of the Order's many houses in Lazio, as noted in the Annals.

In fact in 1650 he was Guardian of the Priory of S. Maria del Giglio at Bolsena, where he repaired the church roof, and the following year, having moved perhaps as Guardian to the community of S. Francesco di Tarquinia, here too he restored the roof of the old conventual church: "*P. Georgius Firmanus tecta renovat sui conventus Cornetani ad S. Franciscum, sicut anno praecedenti, dum erat Guardianus ad S. Mariam de Lilio Bulsinii, tectum refecerat ecclesiae*"[113].

In 1654, appointed Guardian of the Toscanella priory – modern-day Tuscania – he had the walls of the cloister built, this too an enterprise worthy of a mention in the Annals:

"*...Ad historiam nunc nostrarum procedimus domorum P. Georgius a Firmo, Guardianus conventus Tuscanellae in Provincia observante clausura muraria vallat ipsum coenobium cum prato atque silva, magna ex partis rogatis expensis a D. Jacobo Betti, Patrimonio S. Petri doganario*"[114].

Finally, in 1656, and probably in combination with Alexander VII's presence in the summer residence in the Alban Hills, Friar Giorgio was at the Priory of S. Maria di Palazzolo, with the job of supervising the construction of the Bernini building of Castel Gandolfo.

Here it is right to ask who introduced this Friar, already esteemed in his art, into the Chigi papal court and succeeded in getting him into such high positions of responsibility.

At the time when he was presiding over the work at Palazzolo, Friar Giorgio was so zealously helping those infected during the raging bubonic plague epidemic, from May 1656 to August 1657[115], that, as a sign of gratitude the Provincial Chapter held at Aracoeli appointed him Provincial Assessor:

"*In conventu Aracoelitano mense maio celebratur capitulum Provinciae Romanae, praesidente in eo Generali Ministro Michelangelo a Sambuca, nuper ex Hispania et Gallia reverso Provinciae minister deligitur P. Archangelus Romanus, P. generalis familiaris. In quo capitulo publici juris facta sunt nonnulla apostolica privilegia in favorem religiosorum qui pestiferis curam praestiterant, inter quos erat P. Georgius a Firmo, qui actu praesidebat, fabricae apostolicae Castri Gandulphi, qua ratione electus quoque est Provinciae Definitor*"[116].

From this time, Marziale's presence at Palazzolo is also linked to the friendship he had made with his neighbour, Archbishop Egidio Colonna, who, as has been noted, had become a permanent guest in the Villa above.

Pope Alexander VII's love for the Alban Hills is fairly well known, an admiration which also showed itself in personal comments and a special care for the beauty of the area. Testimony to this is the fact that, having initiated an extensive restoration of the summer residence at Castel Gandolfo (it had been modestly cleaned up with some general painting)[117], he had already begun to go there for a holiday in spring 1656,

---

[113] L. WADDING, *Annales Minorum seu Trium Ordium a S. Francisco Institutorum*, vol. XXX (1651-1660). Quaracchi 1931, tomus XXX (1651-1660), p. 23.

[114] ibid., p. 253. Cf. also *De Conventibus Provinciae Romanae Obs.*

[115] Cf. also: P. A. CASTRO, *Pestis Neapolitana, Romana, et Genuensis, annorum 1656 et 1657*, Verona 1567. G. BALESTRA DA LORETO, *Gli accidenti più gravi del mal contagioso osservati nel lazzaretto all'Isola*. Rome 1657.

[116] WADDING 1931, tomus XXX (1651-1660), p. 483. Cf. A.P.A., O. DA CASABASCIANA, *Memorie di avvenimenti appartenenti alla Provincia Romana dei frati minori osservanti incominciando dall'anno 1612...*Ms. 8, folio 87 s.

[117] BONOMELLI 1953, p. 71 and note 3 p. 99.

thus reviving the custom begun by Urban VIII and interrupted for about ten years by his successor Innocent X.

On 17 May that year, with his family who had come especially from Siena as guests, the Chigi Pope held the aforementioned mock sea-battle on Lake Albano. It simulated a battle, with many bombardiers, between the Knights of Malta and the Turks, and for the occasion he used a brigantine and six feluccas, the latter hired[118] and especially transported from the port of Ripa Grande on the Tiber.

Alexander VII was inclined to lengthy meditations and was a lover of the silences that the fertile lake offered. He used to go for walks along the lake, on Monte Cavo, and visited the nearby sanctuary of Galloro and Palazzolo.

Here, he was always the welcome guest of Friar Marziale and Archbishop Colonna. For example, he called in on 21 May 1656, at 9.00 p.m., when "he went down from Palazzolo of Cardinal Colonna into the Friars' Priory and so to the church whence, after a short walk in the cloister and the garden, he returned to the said palace; where there was produced a sumptuous reception of 12 large bowls full of various sweet things"[119].

Friar Giorgio Marziale's presence at Palazzolo is also testified by a series of restorations and expansions undertaken by him in the Priory beginning in 1660. These were all sponsored by the generosity of the Chigi Pope, or, to be more precise, by his *Elemosineria Secreta* (*Secret Alms*), as shown by some receipts, one from 20 July that year:

"*...Most Illustrious Monsignor Ferrini, paying to Sig. Biagio Tintisona 90 scudi in cash which is the price and payment for one hundred and twenty-seven loads of lime, transported by horse, equal to the sum of six hundred and fifteen pounds per load and so agrees with the amount of lime ordered by His Lordship for the work to be done, which will be a good price of 8 Giuli [giulio, a coin first minted by Pope Julius II, 1503-1513]. The weight makes the total of 90 scudi cash.*
Fra Giorgio Martiali..."[120].

And the other dated 31 August 1660:

"*I have received from the Most Illustrious Mgr. Ferrino, responsible for the Secret Alms of His Holiness Alexander VII, seventy-five scudi in cash for the bill of the aforesaid one hundred and twenty-seven loads of lime [...] which was brought to me at the Priory of the Observantine Fathers at Palazzolo of Castel Gandolfo through the charity that His Holiness offers for the maintenance to be done in this priory and in faith of this. 31 August 1660.*
Biagio Tintisona"[121].

And it was then, in the picturesque Priory clinging to the lower slopes of Monte Cavo, that "two wells for snow" were built for the convenience of the nearby Apostolic Palace. The Priory itself was extended with other rooms and, by knocking down peperino walls of the overhanging rock, a further span was added in the south-east corner where the library was built.

[118] *Battaglie navali a Castelgandolfo*, in "Castelli Romani" anno X n. 8, October 1965 p. 72, (from G. Del Pinto, *Notizie seicentesche sui Castelli Romani*, in "Roma" February 1924): "31 May 1656 – 33 scudi and 70 baiocchi cash paid on the order of the Most Illustrious Monsignor the Treasurer to Pasquale Amorosi for his expenses, that is 8:70 scudi for his expenses in the mock naval battle on the lake of Castel Gandolfo and 25 scudi in recognition of himself and his other bombardier companions"; "1 June 1656 – On 1st June the sum of one hundred and twenty scudi cash on the order of the State administration paid to Costanzo Panzieri as reimbursement for others he had paid and to six owners of feluccas, hired and taken to the lake at Castel Gandolfo for the mock battle on the occasion of the sojourn of Our Master".

[119] Casimiro 1744, p. 324.

[120] B. A. V., Arch. Chigi, n° 3652. "*Castello Gandolfo e Ariccia – Per Fabriche – 1659 al 1666*". Document 60 r.

[121] ibid., Documents 60 r. and 60 v.

[122] CRIELESI, July 1998, pp. 24-25.
[123] B. A. V., *Disegni e Piante diversi*, Chigiani Manuscript, P. VII, 12.
[124] Rome State Archives, henceforth A. S. R., Giustificazioni di Tesoreria e dai Mandati Camerali, "[16 May 1661] *extent and estimate of the work to the land done by Giuseppe Buccimazza, street builder, for making two wells, one for storing snow, the other for ice, along with other restoration work on the new path, which goes from Castel Gandolfo to the Franciscan Priory at Palazzolo, done at the behest of His Holiness Our Lord Pope Alexander VII on the order of the Most Illustrious Monsignor Boncompagni, Majordomo of His Holiness, as well as the planting of trees along the said path and elsewhere, measured and estimated by us the undersigned* [Gian Lorenzo Bernini and the surveyors of the Apostolic Chamber G. M. Bolini and Mattia de Rossi]". Cf. CRIELESI, July 1998, pp. 24-25. Cf. R. LEFEVRE, *Strade castellane del 600*, in "Autostrade", 1959, n. 12 (reprinted in R. LEFEVRE, *Storia e storie dell'antichissima Ariccia*, Ariccia 1996, pp. 154-161).
[125] CRIELESI, July 1998, pp. 24-25. In 1662, on the occasion of the Pope's visit to Palazzolo, Buccimazza, the builder involved in the opening and maintenance of paths, indicated the restored path opened by himself on behalf of Friar Giorgio: so in the account we see the sum of 1.7 scudi and 20 baiocchi "*for having cleaned and tidied the new path from the gardens of the Palace at Castel Gandolfo up to Palazzola, on the occasion of the visit of His Holiness in the said month of May, removing earth, stones and mud*": the work was repeated in May 1663.
[126] A.S.R., Giustificazioni di Tesoreria e dai Mandati Camerali. Cf. CRIELESI 1998, p. 25.

Marziale's seventeenth-century structure at Palazzolo can still be glimpsed in the later eighteenth-century structure commissioned by Fonseca.

With the disappearance of the great main entrance to the garden – whose Chigi coat of arms now adorns the tower of the Villa Colonna (fig. 85) – among the few pieces of evidence of Friar Giorgio Marziale's work at Palazzolo left to us there is the little niche – once a fountain – placed in front of a large square. Like the main entrance it was decorated with the emblem of the Chigi Pope[122] (figs. 10-11) and, like the mysterious rock tomb at the side of the Priory, was framed by pillars supporting spheres: this was because the monuments were linked and were part of the various embellishments which flanked the path[123] from Castel Gandolfo to Palazzolo[124] (fig. 33), made accessible for carriages by the Chigi Pope and designed by Marziale.

It is worth remembering here that this road was part of a much vaster road network, planned or in part restored by the Papal Household through the mastery of Bernini. It was the so-called Via Alessandrina (after the Pope), in those days winding through the dense woods. From Castel Gandolfo, following the "Upper Path" of Urban VIII, it reached the Capuchins at Albano, and then divided to Ariccia and Palazzolo[125], whence it continued around the lake up to the road to Marino (fig. 86).

Just out of curiosity, it is worth noting that the opening of this road to Palazzolo meant a careful and vast programme of re-forestation and tree-planting: 22 scudi and 50 baiocchi "[in May 1663] *for planting 60 elms along the path*" and then 417 and 24 baiocchi "*for planting 1098 trees in the above-mentioned new street, providing wooden supports for them and clearing around them at 38 baiocchi each, as agreed with most illustrious Mgr. Majordomo in keeping with his instructions, providing living plant for three years beginning in March 1661 for the foreseeable future*"[126].

But to return to Bernini. With the conclusion of the first phase of the restoration and extension of the papal residence at Castel Gandolfo, in 1658 the famous architect was entrusted with the planning and construction of the church of S. Tommaso da Villanova, which the Chigi Pope wanted to dedicate to a Blessed, the Archbishop of Valencia, canonized by him in November that year.

The church (finished in 1661) was built next to the Apostolic Palace, knocking down a pre-existing oratory, S. Nicola, erected by the community of Castel Gandolfo in the first years of the 17th century. Bernini's collaborators included Antonio Raggi, who did the stucco of the vault, Giacinto Gimignani, Guglielmo Cortese (the Borgognone) and Pietro da Cortona for the paintings, while the architect who directed the work was again Friar Giorgio (fig. 87).

From 1661, the focus of Friar Giorgio's work, like that of Bernini, moved from Castel Gandolfo to the nearby town of Ariccia, which, through the generosity of Alexander VII, had passed from the Savelli family to the Chigis. The fiefdom deed of sale, already planned from 1659, bears the date 20 July 1661 and was drawn up by Prince Don

85. Palazzolo, Villa Colonna (Villa del Cardinale). Detail of the tower with the marble coat of arms of Alexander VII, formerly on the main garden gate of the Priory below.

86. ANONYMOUS (1662-1663), Map of the properties around Lake Albano attached to a report about a dispute between the community of Castel Gandolfo and the Abbey of St. Paul's. Note the "Upper Path", the elm-tree avenue desired by Urban VIII, which went from Castel Gandolfo to the Capuchins at Albano, before branching towards Palazzolo along the new "paved road" – in the document it is still not tree-lined – designed by Friar Giorgio Marziale. The date of the map is suggested, among other things, by the wording "copse of the Chigi", and is therefore just a little before the passage of the Ariccia fiefdom from the Savelli to the relatives of Alexander VII. Rome, State Archives, Camerale III

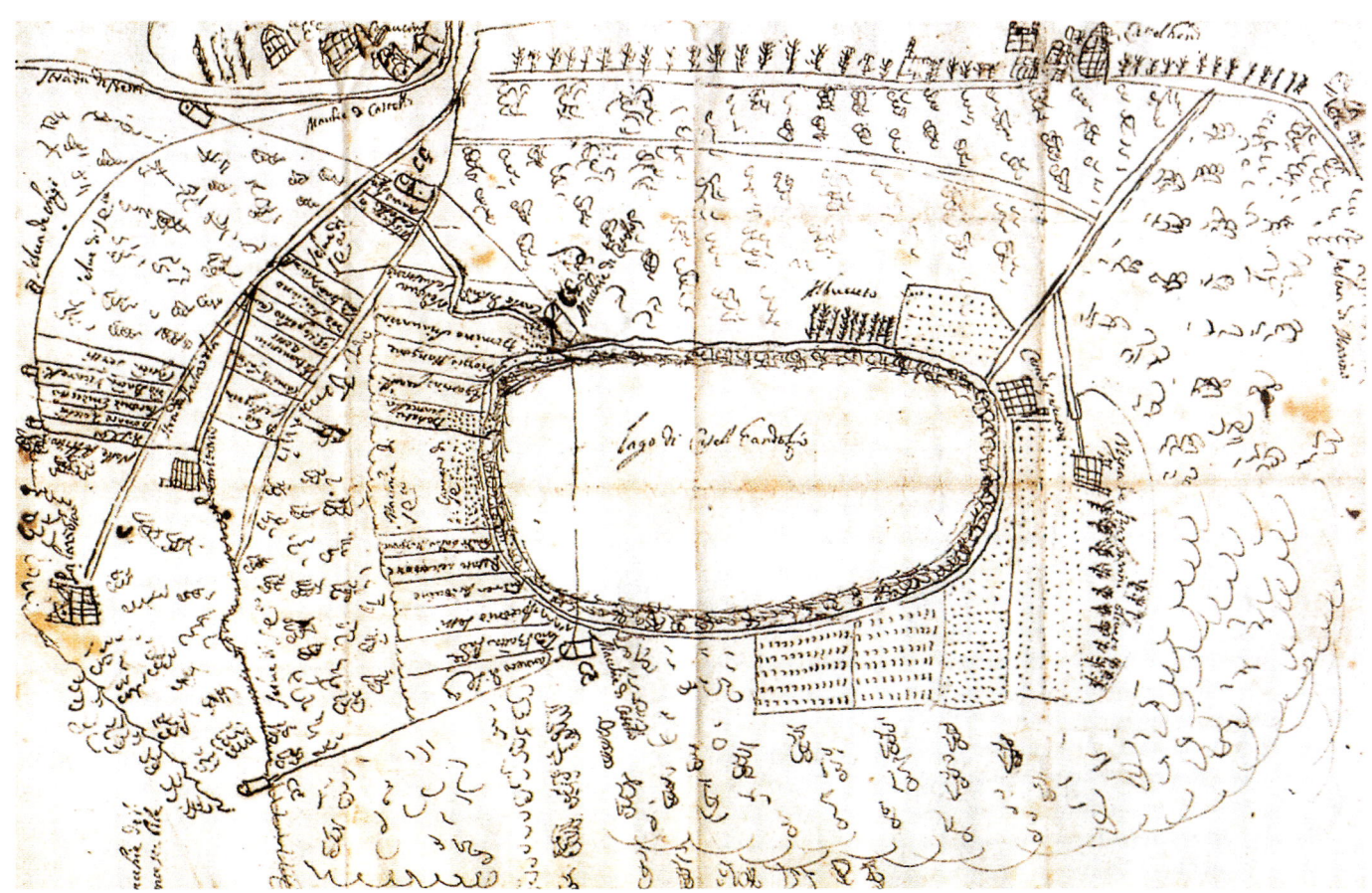

Giulio Savelli and the buyers, Mario, Agostino and Cardinal Flavio Chigi[127], respectively the brother and nephews of the reigning Pontiff.

Under the Chigis the Ariccian fiefdom underwent a series of urban and architectural improvements entrusted to the direction of Bernini or his close circle[128].

However, a distinction must be made between the works carried out directly at the expense of the Apostolic See and those financed by

[127] A.S.R., Not. Ac. Tommaso Paluzzi, 1661, vol. 4982, ff. 237ff.

[128] For the work of Bernini and his circle in Ariccia cf: *L'Ariccia del Bernini*, Ariccia 1998, Catalogue of the exhibition of the same name, Ariccia 10 October – 31 December 1998.

87. G. Lorenzo Bernini, S. Tommaso da Villanova, Castel Gandolfo.

Agostino Chigi and in part by Cardinal Flavio, obviously also helped by the lavish generosity of Alexander VII.

The first works – Galloro and S. Maria Assunta – were undertaken completely by Bernini, with the help of Mattia De' Rossi (draughtsman and surveyor), the Ticinese Giovanni Maria Bolini (surveyor) and Friar Giorgio Marziale as director of works.

The second – largely concerning the real Chigi patrimony at Ariccia, such as the baronial Palace, the Park, etc., - were instead planned and directed mainly by Carlo Fontana and Giovan Battista Contini, even if, as in the Assunta, Luigi Bernini, Felice della Grecia and other minor figures were also involved.

In chronological order, one of the first Bernini workshops to open in the Ariccia area was that of S. Maria di Galloro in 1662 – standardis-

88. G. Lorenzo Bernini, S. Maria di Galloro, Ariccia.

ation of book-keeping Mattia De' Rossi and Bernini, with Friar Marziale as director of the workshop – where important restoration work was undertaken, with the completion of the first two chapels, of S. Tommaso da Villanova and S. Franceso di Sales. These had been left incomplete after the previous work planned and directed by another papal architect, the Capuchin Friar Michele da Bergamo (+ 1641), previously active in the Villa Barberini and in the Pontifical Palace at Castel Gandolfo (fig. 88).

At Galloro, among other things, the dome was restored, replacing the guttered roof tiles with lead, and the present façade was built with its square in front.

In 1662, Friar Giorgio was entrusted with the supervision of another successful building, the Assunta, once again following a Bernini idea. In fact from spring 1662 to April 1665, the Friar issued regular receipts, for his provision of six scudi a month, in his role as director of the *Rotonda* workshop, the collegiate church of S. Maria Assunta:

"...I, the undermentioned Friar Giorgio Marziale, from the Most Illustrious Monsignor Ferrini, responsible for the Secret Alms of His Holiness, [received] 18 scudi cash, as alms for my board for the month of April, May, and June of the present year 1662, with regard to my hard work in building the new edifice of the new church of Riccia, 22 June 1662..."[129].

Here also is one of his signed letters dated 28 May 1662, in which Marziale provides, in flavoured Italian, a panorama of the workshops he directs. It was sent from Palazzolo[130], but the addressee is unknown – maybe even Bernini himself, but probably the person responsible for the "Secret Alms", Monsignor Ferrini:

"Most Illustrious Lord
The Master tinsmith Giovanni, having already used half the lead which I brought from Rome, 40 sheets, has only covered a third of the dome and is still in need of a great quantity of lead, as you will hear from him himself, since he will be in Rome for these festivities.
The façade is already levelled as far as the capitals, too, so that after the holidays the cornice can be put on.
The two little houses were already neglected so a prison won't have to be built; on Friday he started again and continues to work now.
The Rotonda Church towards Albano is 18 hands high above the foundations, it is not possible to go round it yet, the area needs to be levelled, but with three or four days in the coming week it will be possible to do the foundations.
From Wednesday up to this evening 528 loads of lime have come from Giuliano, with more to follow until supplies run out.
153 loads of bricks came from Pradica. It is very good material and next week I will send for all these containers which carry the lime to be loaded so that it is all brought here. It can be done as quickly as possible because I have other places to go to and plenty of people working here. Between artisans and workman it rises to 108, 30 scudi a day is not enough, and furthermore there are 40 donkeys from Riccia who carry the pozzolana in carts, and this is 10 scudi a day. There are also eight carts carrying stones, and that is not enough. To carry everything it is necessary to use other beasts, and to pay for all of these 300 scudi a week would not be enough, along with the provisions that have be paid for, such as lime and bricks. I leave the matter for the consideration of your Illustrious Holiness.
It is right to hurry along with the dimensions of the Castello Church, and to provide a vault, with the duty of adjusting it on one side and the other. I cannot be wrong if after five years of tired work I still have been able to finish it, hence the little matter of the favour, which I requested.
Honourable, Most Illustrious Holiness, with no tasks to be done or work that delays me in words, I will be in Rome hoping to see the end of it for next week, and I sweetly kiss your hand from Palazzola 28 May 1662.

Your Illustrious Holiness, *Affection always*
　　　　　　　　　　　　　　　　　　　　　　Friar Giorgio Martiali"

---

[129] B.A.V., Arch. Chigi, "*Castello Gandolfo e Ariccia. Per Fabriche. 1659 al 1666*" n. 3652, Document 730 r. Cf. also: Documents 728, 729, 731.

[130] ibid., Document 630 r. Cf. G. INCISA DELLA ROCCHETTA, *Notizie sulla fabbrica della chiesa collegiata di Ariccia (1662-1664)*, in "Rivista del R. Istituto d'Archeologia e Storia dell'Arte", I, Rome 1929-30, pp. 349-392. Cf. also: CRIELESI, July 1998, p. 27.

89. G. LORENZO BERNINI, Church of the Assumption, Ariccia.

The first paragraph almost certainly refers to the lead covering of the dome at the Galloro sanctuary, the second to the façade of the same church. The "two little houses" are rather those at the sides of the *Rotonda* in Ariccia, one destined to become the seat of the Governor with the appropriate gaols, the other, towards Albano, the residence of the Secretary of the Chigi family.

On the side facing Albano, the church wall, according to Marziale, was already 18 hands high above the foundations, while elsewhere it was still not as high. He also mentions the town of Giuliano (today Giulianello, not far from Velletri), where the lime came from, and Pratica di Mare, a Borghese fiefdom, where an oven produced bricks for the workshop. The letter concludes with a reference to the church at Castel Gandolfo and a mysterious "favour" which Marziale had "requested" and the answer to which he awaited anxiously.

The *Rotonda* was consecrated in May 1664 by Alexander VII (fig. 89).

As regards privileges and favours, Friar Giorgio certainly did not neglect social relations and his justified career aspirations. This can be noted in a signed plea to His Holiness dated 28 April 1662, in which he tries to pressurise him so that he might be promoted to *Permanent Assessor* and therefore, in the future Chapter, be raised to Minister Provincial of the Minors[131].

Pope Alexander VII kindly accepted the request concerning the job of Permanent Assessor of the Roman Province of the Friars Minor of the Observance, presented by Monsignor Nepalini on 2 June 1662, and the appointment was made in a Brief dated 9 June the same year[132].

But if Friar Giorgio's aspirations to become Permanent Assessor were fulfilled, it was not so with his ambition to become Minister Provincial. We do not know by what tricks of fate a certain Fr Alessio of Rome was elected instead of Friar Giorgio at the Observantines' Chapter held in the Priory of S. Francesco in Tivoli in 1665.

In the meantime, still a guest at S. Maria di Palazzolo, Marziale car-

[131] "...*To His Holiness Our Lord Pope Alexander VII*
Most Holy Father
Friar Giorgio Martiali Assessor of the Roman Province of Observant Minors humbly called to the buildings of Castel Gandolfo, most humble child of His Holiness, begs you to deign to enumerate him among the good perpetual Fathers of the Order in the Roman Province, that is, among those who have been Generals or General Administrators, and in the next future Chapter soon to be celebrated for this Roman Province to declare him Minister Provincial, which lasts for three years. According to God's will". Cf. A.S.V.Secret. Brevium vol. 1257, f. 533v.: "...*28 April 1662. Friar Giorgio Martiali, Assessor of the Roman Province of the Friars Minor of the Observance, called to the buildings of Castel Gandolfo. By grace enumerated among the good Perpetual Fathers of the said Province, that is those who have been Generals or General Administrators, and are declared Minister Provincial at the next future Chapter of his Province...*".

[132] "*Dilectio filio Giorgio Martiale Ordinis Fratrum Minorum S. Francisci de Observantia. Pro P. Georgio Martiali, definitor Obs. Provinciae Romanae, qui "aedeficiis Arcis nostrae Gandulphi, Albanensis diocesis, operam navas [...] commemoratio inter definitores perpetuos suae Provinciae nempe eos qui ministri generalis vel commissarii ordinis muneribus functi sunt: Religionis zelus, 9 iunii 1662*". Ibid., ff. 531 r and 531 v. Cf. WADDING 1931, tomus XXXI (1661-1670), p. 93. CRIELESI, July 1998, p. 29.

ried on with the restoration of the Priory and various adornments such as, before 1667, the building of a thick holding wall for the square in front of the church entrance:

"...Measurements of the wall that must be built at Palazzola Priory. [author's note, handwritten by Friar Giorgio].
The wall which His Holiness of Our Lord wishes to put in front of the church of Palazzola is 110 handbreadths long and 23 handbreadths high and 5 thick which must contain soil, which makes 63 canne [canna, *a measurement of length] and 25 handbreadths of wall of appropriate stone at 24 giuli per canna, which makes the sum total of 2 scudi 51-80 in cash. The wall will be filled by the Friars as exercise and entertainment..."*[133].

In reading this document carefully it is worth noting how Friar Marziale, good workshop director and follower of religious rules that he was, had, with the help of the *"exercise and entertainment"* of the Friars, saved on labour!

On 22 May 1667, the death of Pope Alexander VII meant the architect Friar had lost a strong supporter. Consequently, this led to a decrease in assignments, even if work continued all the same at Palazzolo, as is shown by this receipt of 22 April 1668 for 25 scudi to finish off the square in front of the church:

"I, the undersigned Friar Giorgio Marziale, [acknowledge] that I have received from the Most Illustrious Lord Ferrini, responsible for the Secret Alms of Our Holiness, twenty-five scudi cash, which His Holiness himself ordered that I be paid as alms, given by His Holiness to Palazzola Priory to do the wall in front of the Priory church. In faith this 22nd day of April 1668.
Friar Giorgio Martiali in his own hand..."[134].

Also in Friar Marziale's "own hand" is a 1670 memoir – formerly at Palazzolo but now kept in the Archives of S. Francesco a Ripa in Rome – in which he tells the story of the Priory of S. Maria di Palazzolo up to that year.

This precious manuscript, knowledge of which would have avoided some unnecessarily detailed analyses by past historians (such as, for example, one on the hypothetical extension of the church at Galloro by Bernini), bears the title: *"Description of the Palazzola Priory by P. re Frà Giorgio Martiale Permanent Assessor of the Observantine Minor Province. 1670"*[135].

Here are some excerpts from it in which, among other things, he mentions, with not just a little pride, not just his work at Palazzolo but also his hand in the direction of the Bernini "workshops" in the Alban Hills:

"...and in 1662, P. re Friar Giorgio Martiali, a native of Ponzano della Marca di Fermo, having taken the habit in the Roman Province, was declared Permanent Assessor by Alexander VII of happy memory for his honourable work and assistance given for ten continuous years

---

[133] B. A. V. Arch. Chigi n° 3652, Document 55 r. Cf. CRIELESI, July 1998, p. 29.

[134] ibid., Document 727 r.

[135] S. Francesco a Ripa Archives, henceforth A. F. R., (Palazzola File I), *"Descrittionne del Convento di Palazzola fatta dal P. re Frà Giorgio Martiale Definitore Perpetuo della Provincia Minore Osservante. Anno 1670"*, Ms. p. 9. Cf. CRIELESI 1997, pp. 16-18.

as architect in the new Church of Castel Gandolfo, built from its foundations to the sumptuous dome; and the other church of Riccia, likewise erected from its foundations with a dome; and that of the Madonna, so-called, of Galloro in that land [where] he did the façade from the foundations and the square in front with the two sumptuous chapels inside; perfected and restored that church and also levelled other streets at the behest of the said… P. re Friar Giorgio Martiale, in the happy memory of Alexander VII, made the path from Castel Gandolfo as far as the Priory of Palazzola for carriages and the first carriage to pass along that path, a carriage and six, was that of the Excellency Mgr. Egidio Colonna Archbishop of Amasia, a prelate who, with the help of the same Friar Giorgio, often relaxed and entertained Cardinals, Prelates, Chancellors and other people from the court of His Holiness. They remained to dine in the Palazzino of the said Prelate at his convenience[136] [where he entertained] with great soul and great generosity and magnanimity as was his wont, and held by all on the occasion that His Holiness himself took recreation, and heard Mass in the said Priory, where to give better entertainment to His Holiness the aforementioned Friar Giorgio often held forth in recounting his interests and the jurisdiction of the said Priory.

Now following the cut of the path, cutting through woods, demolishing stones and boulders for greater convenience, he made the peperino benches half a mile from each other, from where in wonderful comfort one can enjoy the pleasantness of the Campagna, the hills, the seas, woods and sails which plough the sea and the little boats on the lake, and P. re Friar Giorgio, at the end of the path, as an entrance into the Palazzola garden, had built a large gate with beautiful symmetry and architecture of the same Father with the Pontifical Arms and other embellishments, in front of which there is a most fresh fountain in a beautiful piazza with a continuous green swathe of trees; adjacent he had also built two wells to store the snow and the Palace of His Holiness used this in the past when he went to sojourn at Castel Gandolfo. He also restored the church, in front of which he put up a great wall in order to make a piazza for the carriages. He did much restoration in the Priory for better comfort and had built (sic) new rooms and apartments. Such major work required the use of cutting machines and breaking up huge blocks of peperino stone, to the great taste of His Holiness, who occasionally set fire to the mines of stones which Pius II mentions in the eleventh book of his history: Imminens locus Albani lacui saxum [...] fuit extorto"[137].

Shortly after finishing at Palazzolo Friar Giorgio passed away. He had returned to the Aracoeli Priory in Rome – now not just the General Curia of the Friars Minor but also the seat of the Observantine Provincial – and died in autumn 1672, as the Necrologium laconically notes: "*26. Sexto Kalendas Octobris* [...] *Aracoeli. R. P. Georgius a Firmo Architectus celebris 1672*"[138].

Friar Giorgio had gone, but towards the end of the 17th century there was still some restoration work going on. Inside the church, two altars were constructed along the nave, as Casimiro recalls, one dedicated to the Virgin Mary and the other to St James della Marca.

[136] A.F.R. (Palazzola File I). "*Descrittione del Convento*" p. 11.
[137] A.F.R. (Palazzola File I). "*Descrittione del Convento*", pp. 12-13. CRIELESI 1998, pp. 30-31.
[138] A.P.A., *Necrologium sive Mortilogium Almae Observantis Provinciae Romanae a P. Gratiano M. a a Verulis transcriptum ex Necrologio S. Mariae Virginia Tyburis, ex commissione adm. H. P. Mauritii a Subloco eiusdem Provinciae Ministri Anno Domini MDCCCLXXXXIV*. Ms. n. 30, p. 539.

90. Priory of S. Maria di Palazzolo. Garden, marble washbasin with the date inscribed MDCXCIII (1693).

This second altar, dedicated to one of the promoters of the Observantines, is linked to the canonization of the saint which took place in 1690, an event that had great repercussions at the heart of the Order. Also of that period is a fresco, formerly on the left going into the church, depicting Saints Lucy, Clare and Elizabeth[139].

To this restoration phase must also be ascribed the removal of the memorial stones – by now just recalling empty tombs – of Agnesina and Federico Colonna which adorned the walls of the church choir. This was perhaps due to a different internal layout or, more probably, following the Colonnas' estrangement from and disinterest in Palazzolo, meaning that consequently the Friars were no longer paid the offerings arranged through the various legacies of this noble Roman family.

As far as innovations or modifications made to the Priory are concerned, some notable marble artefacts indicate activity which, if not construction was at least decoration and maintenance. There is an ornamental fragment of local stone inscribed with the date 1696, formerly in the garden, and two washbowls in white marble bearing the inscription of the year MDCXCIII (1693). The first little fountain is decorated with two eight-point stars (fig. 90), which fortuitously recall the similar heraldic symbol present in the Chigi coat of arms; the second, in the sacristy, again with a star (ten-point) in the basin. During the renovations carried out under Fra' Josè Maria de Fonseca this washbowl was set in a stupendous little stucco niche stamped with one of the heraldic emblems of the Portuguese Friar: this, too, a star but with five points. (fig. 91).

[139] C. RICCI, *Rocca di Papa, appunti d'Arte e Storia*, Rome 1927, p. 29: "…in a niche, on the left as you enter, behind the statue of the Sacred Heart, remains part of a seventeenth century fresco, with Saints Lucy, Clare and Elisabeth…".

91. Priory of S. Maria di Palazzolo. Marble washbasin, with the date inscribed MDCXCIII (1693), framed with stucco and heraldic motifs belonging to Fonseca (1735-39). It is in the corridor near the sacristy and vestry.

The 1700s and the Fonseca restorations

The most important architectural events concerning the Palazzolo complex down the centuries took place in the first half of the eighteenth century. Up until then, the appearance of the Priory can be deduced from a series of documents, since the period from the third decade of the seventeenth century to 1730 is, in fact, well-documented: there are the accounts of the Pastoral Visits of 17 December 1636 and 17 June 1660, the so-called *Relazione Innocenziana* of 1652, the description of the work carried out by Marziale at the time of Pope Alexander VII Chigi, as well as various pictorial testimonies. Among these, the two maps (March 1588) preserved in the Aldobrandini Archives[140] (figs. 23, 92) show the territory concerned in a reproduction of the Palazzolo com-

[140] Frascati, Aldobrandini Archives, *Planta, et descriptio Status, ac Territorii Prioratus Albani*, in "Carte relative al Priorato – vertenza del card. Gesualdo priore del Priorato ed il confine di Rocca di Papa per i confini del Priorato sud". Historic documents 35/147/2.

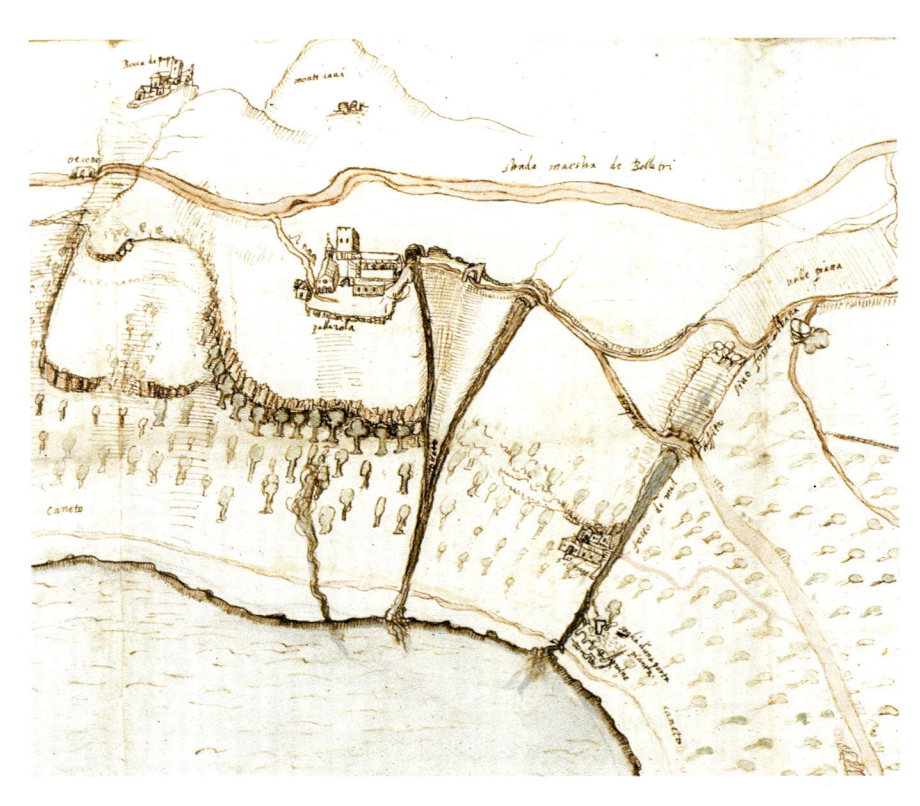

92. ANONYMOUS, Planta, et descriptio Status, ac Territorii, March 1588. Frascati, Aldobrandini Archives. Detail with a view of the Palazzolo complex before the major work carried out by Friar Giorgio Marziale.

plex even before the restorations of Friar Giorgio. In these, the Priory, to the right of the church, appears to be built along the two wings overlooking the rock and the lake, while the side closest to the present garden is surrounded by a wall; an arch not far from the Priory prevented access to the enclosure.

Two drawings in the Vatican Library present a similar picture: the one already mentioned by Arrigucci (1631)[141] (fig. 76) and one by Cassiano dal Pozzo (1629)[142]. In the latter, high up, above the Priory – small, enclosed by a wall and surrounded by scrub – one can see *Palatiolum*, or, to be precise, the unfinished building of the Pierleoni *Casino* which was about to be transformed into a Villa by Cardinal Girolamo Colonna (fig. 93).

In the 1636 Pastoral Visit this graphic description of the Priory is confirmed: it is "*recte constructum et cum suo peristilio et Porticu et omnibus officinis recte constructis in parte inferiori, in superiori vero adsunt cellae n. 20 circiter*"[143].

The *Relazione Innocenziana* of 1652 states: "*the Priory is built with a cloister, Refectory, foodstore, cellar, kitchen, cave, storage, stable, barn and another room. Above there are two dormitories with eighteen* (sic) *habitable rooms, and the community laundry*"[144].

In the subsequent 1660 pastoral visit the cloister is "*in antiqua forma constructum cum pluribus columnettis marmoreis in totum reclusum cum porta bene clausa*"[145].

There are other invaluable documents: the Pastoral Visit of 1703[146] and some watercolour maps by the architect Giandomenico Navone (from October 1733 and August 1739), kept in the archives of S.

[141] B.A.V., *Disegni e Piante diverse*, Chigiani Manuscript, P. VII, 12. fol. 2.
[142] B.A.V., CASSIANO DAL POZZO, Barb. Lat., 1871, f. 39.
[143] Tuscolano Episcopal Archives, henceforth A.V.T., IOANNEM BAPTISTAM DE' ALTERIS, *Acta Apostolicae, ac Generalis Visitationis Tusculanem episcopatus ac Diocesis* [...] *anno Domini 1636*. ms, ad annos 1636-1640, ms., f. 254.
[144] A.S.V., Sacr. Cong. Stat. Regul., *Relationes 39, Osservanti F4*, ms., ff. 95-97, 1650.
[145] A.V.T., D. ATONIUM SEVEROLUM, *Acta Apostolice, ac Generalis Visitationis Tusculanem episcopatus ac Diocesis* [...] *anno Domini 1660*, ms. f. 118.
[146] A.V.T., FRANCISCUS MARIA DE ASTE, *Visitationes Civitatis et Diocesis Tusculanae.*, ms. ad annum 1703, ff. 1001-1019.

110 CHAPTER III

93. CASSIANO DEL POZZO (1629), Prospectus Montis Albani et locorum adiacentium, B. A. V., Barb. Lat., f. 39. Detail with a view of Palazzolo, the rock tomb and Palatiolum (the lodge started by Pierleoni) standing above.

Francesco a Ripa, showing the territory of the Priory of S. Maria di Palazzolo: in one it is worth noting the church façade as it was before the now imminent work of Fonseca (figs. 94-95).

The 1703 Visitation – strangely enough still carried out by the Ordinary of Frascati even though Palazzolo, following the decree of the Sacred Congregation of Bishops in 1678, was re-united to the diocese of Albano and reconfirmed as being under the parochial jurisdiction of S. Barnaba at Marino[147] – begins with a description of the church, with three altars, a high altar and two others, one dedicated to Our Lady and the other to St James della Marca. The choir, lower than the principal nave, had seats for the monks. It was all covered by a vault with pointed buckle arches.

The measurements of the church are also given: 72 hands long (about 16 metres), 35 hands wide (about 8 metres) corresponding to the actual measurements; the choir was 32 hands wide and 39 long. Detailed descriptions are given of the entrance hall and the lower and upper sacristies, with an inventory of the objects contained therein.

Finally there is a description of the cloister: "...*visitavit* [...] *claustrum ad quod patet aditus a pluribus locis nempé a Choro* [...] *a viridario proximo, et a via prope Ecclesiae atrius; est* [...] *stratum lapidibus sectis longit. p. 98* (21.89 metres = actual measurement) *lat. p. 84 latitue p. 13* (2.90 metres corresponding to the actual distance) [...] *et duplice ordine parvularum columnarum de marmore substentatum, et partim discopertum, quod est in medio...*"[148]. The portico of the cloister was partly covered by a roof supported by small, coupled-columns, partly uncovered. At the centre of the cloister there was the "*Viridarius claustro*".

According to the descriptions quoted and the pictorial evidence, the

[147] GALIETI 1948, pp. 50-51, note 196.
[148] ibid., ff. 1014-1015.

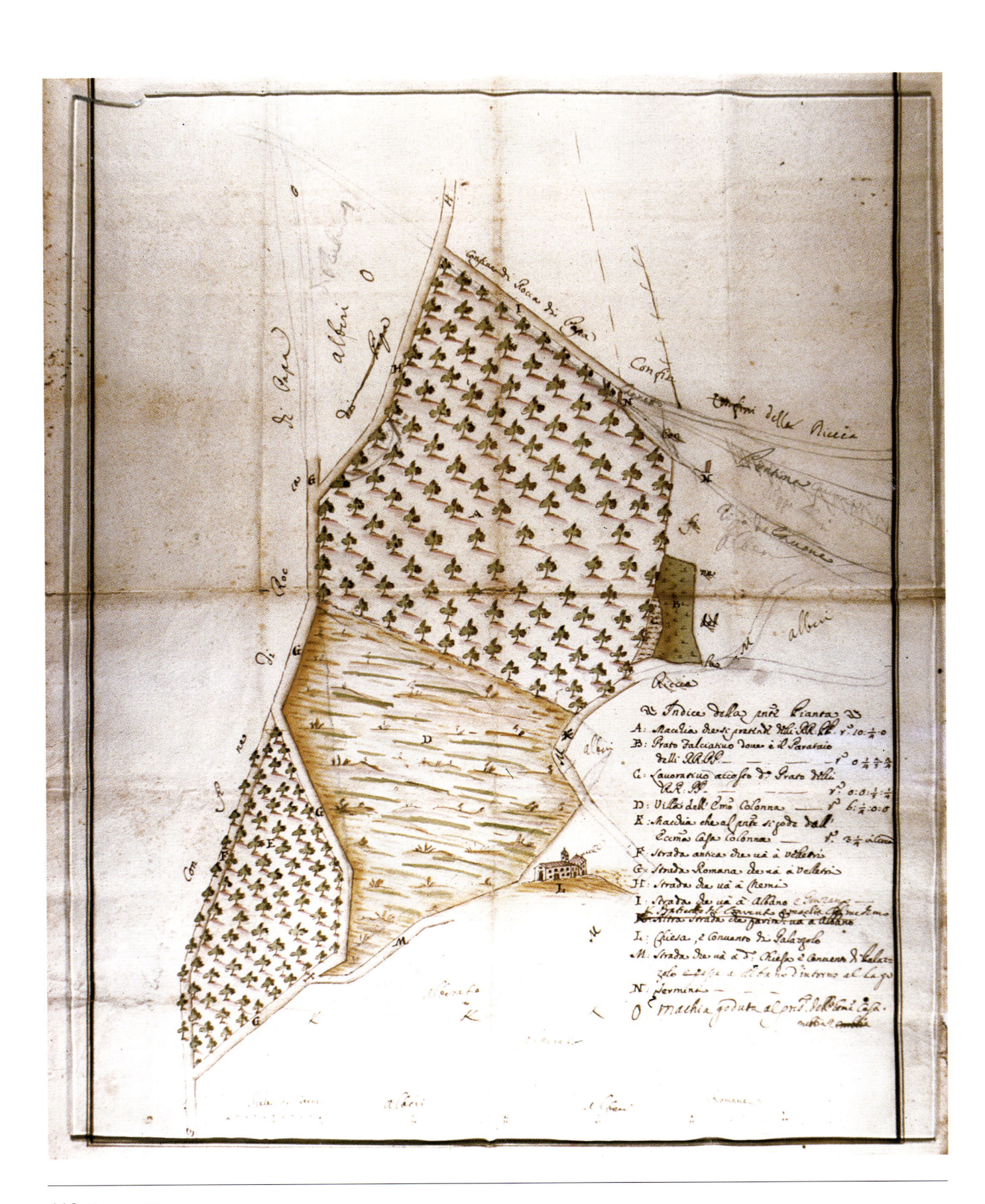

94. GIANDOMENICO NAVONE (August 1739), watercolour map of the land belonging to the Priory of S. Maria di Palazzolo. Rome, S. Francesco a Ripa Archives.

95. GIANDOMENICO NAVONE (August 1739), watercolour map of the land belonging to the Priory of S. Maria di Palazzolo. Rome, S. Francesco a Ripa Archives. This map shows in detail the Priory garden and the church façade, the latter as it was some years before Fonseca's restoration. It also shows the Villa del Cardinale (Colonna).

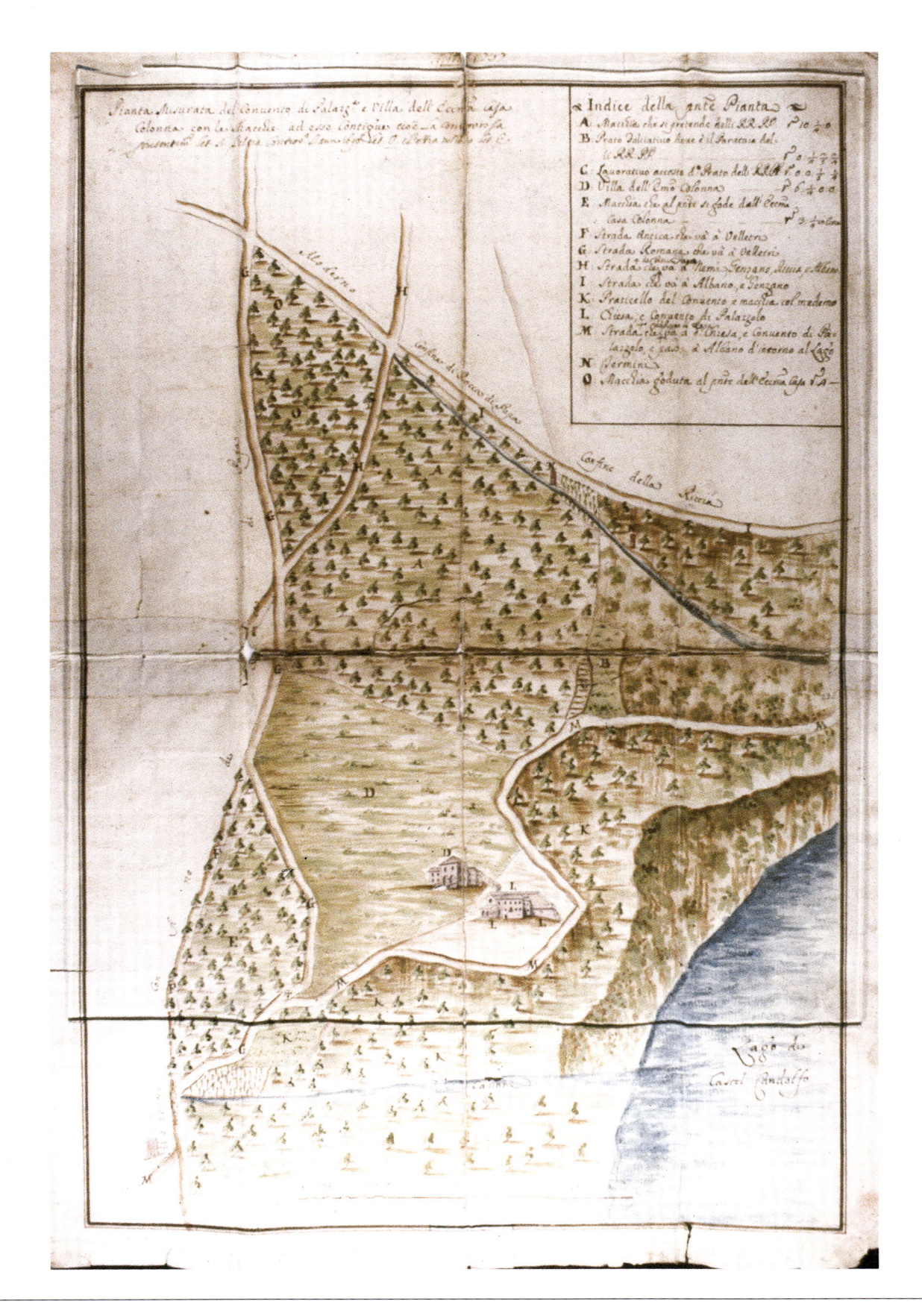

96. GIORGIO DOMENICO DUPRÀ, Portrait of P. José Maria de Fonseca of Evora, (1733), formerly at S. Maria di Palazzolo. Oil on canvas. Rome, Istituto di S. Antonio de' Portoghesi.

95b. GIANDOMENICO NAVONE (August 1739), detail from a watercolour map of the land belonging to the Priory of S. Maria di Palazzolo. Rome, S. Francesco a Ripa Archives.

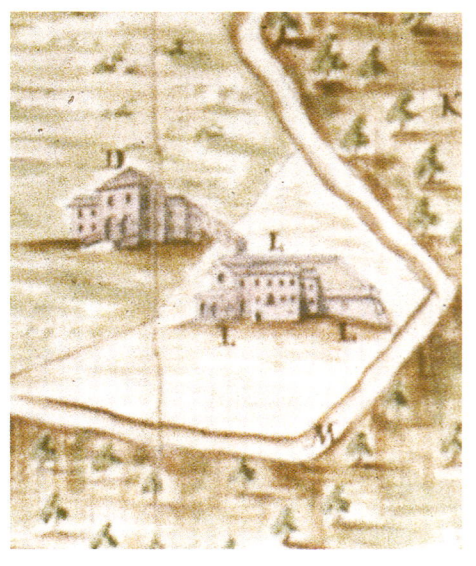

external façade of the church was simple, in peperino ashlars, brought to life by the multi-foil rose window in white marble. There was an atrium supported by columns, and the sides were pronounced by buttresses into which mullioned lancet windows opened. The roof was sloping and the belfry was not a tower.

The Priory, which largely followed closely the typical Cistercian plan, was completely to the right of the church, with a floor above looking towards the lake. This had undergone various transformations and enlargements in distinct phases. The first, when it belonged to the Cistercians and "three monks and a lay brother" lived there; the second, up to the pontificate of Alexander VI, when the Priory had up to 18 monastic cells; the third, between 1655 and 1667, in the reign of Alexander VII, when the works described by Friar Giorgio Marziale were carried out.

The first phase should correspond to the first three spans, in the second the Priory was raised by one floor with the cells and extended to seven spans; in the third the spans became nine, and the last two are slightly withdrawn compared to the main front.

114 CHAPTER III

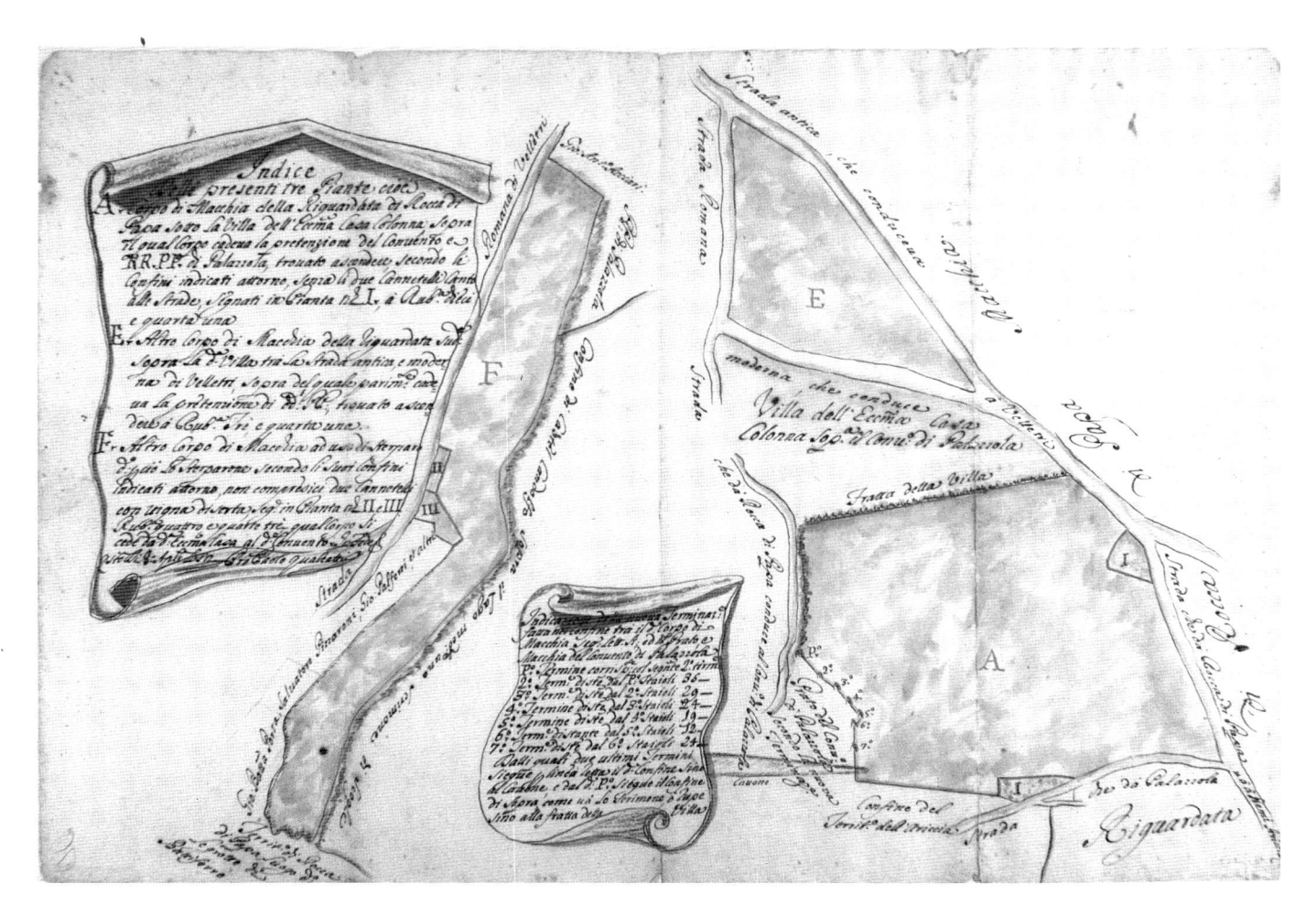

97. GIANDOMENICO NAVONE (August 1739), map of the boundaries of the landed property of the Priory of S. Maria di Palazzolo. Rome, S. Francesco a Ripa Archives.

Under Alexander VII, or, to be precise, at the time of Friar Marziale, between 1661-62, the Priory was enlarged by the span at the south-east corner when the library – not mentioned in the pastoral visits of 1636 and 1660 – was built, along with the *Passaggio del Cardinale* between the Villa and the Priory. This covered staircase – which had its purpose as long as the Villa was the residence of Girolamo and then Egidio Colonna – in fact abutted the first floor of the Priory.

To the north the complex was bounded by the rock face and to the east by the boundary wall. The whole seventeenth-century structure differed from the eighteenth-century one which followed by the reduced size of the rooms, the lower vaults and the different size of the window frames. The old refectory, the one large room on the south side, with nearby kitchen and appendages are all recognisable. The old Priory developed on two levels in the south-east corner, corresponding to the entire area of the present mezzanine. Successive additions in the north-east area brought the ground-floor vaults to the same height as the mezzanine vaults in such a way that the new dormitory cells were at the same level as the old ones.

To end this rapid summary of evidence, there are two curiosities to note: a painting by Gherardo delle Notti (1618), commissioned by Flaminia Colonna-Gonzaga for the high altar of the Capuchins at Albano,

98. ZACCARIA FARINELLI (from October 1733), Land registry Map (from an original by the architect Giandomenico Navone) of the landed property of the Priory of Palazzolo; note in the background some architectural plans by Navone himself which can be identified as the actual entrances to the Priory facing the garden. Rome, S. Francesco a Ripa Archives.

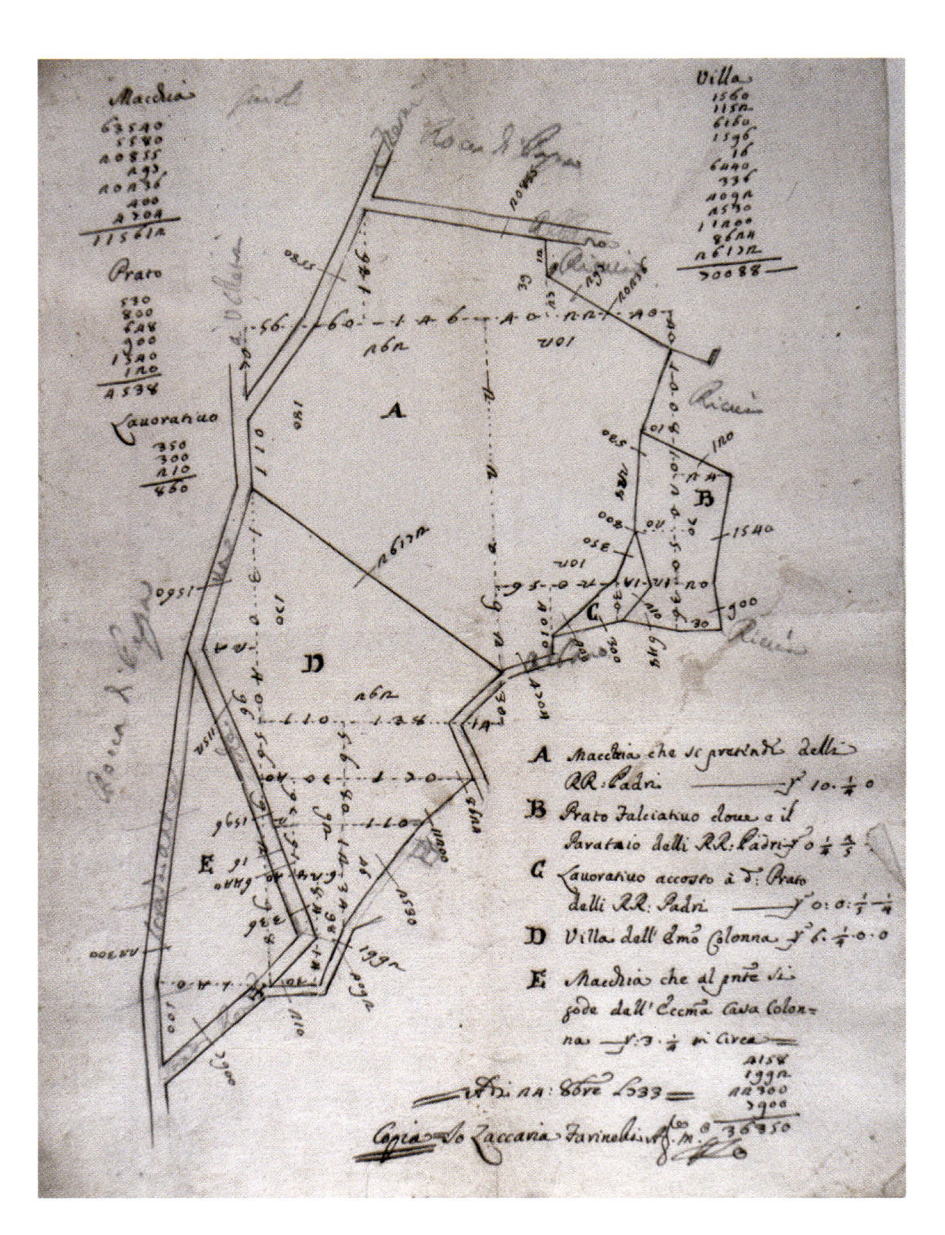

and one by Gaspar Van Wittel (1710), which belonged to the Colonna family and shows "*The Monastery of San Paolo at Albano*"[149]. In the background of both there is a place of honour for the Palazzolo Priory and Dom Egidio's Villa. To the left of the church in Van Wittel's painting there is a little two-storied palace, already pictured differently in earlier paintings: it is the same building which, twenty-five years later, Fonseca was to set apart for guest rooms.

The 18th century began with the previously mentioned Pastoral Visit in 1703 and with two "quick visits" to the Castelli Priory by Clement XI Albani, a guest at Castel Gandolfo. The first was on 23 June 1711, and on that occasion the Pope "...after celebrating Mass at the high altar, kindly allowed the religious to kiss his feet in the chapel named after St Didacus [Spanish *Diego*], situated in the cloister [the present-day Common

[149] Florence, Palazzo Pitti, state rooms, inv. 9291.

99. ANONYMOUS, Portrait of the architect Gian Domenico Navone. Oil on canvas 18th century. Rome, Galleria Accademia di S. Luca.

Room], and attended by their Eminences Paulucci and Gozzadini..."[150]; the second visit was on 18 June 1713, and after Mass the Pontiff wanted to visit the nearby hermitage of S. Angelo, rebuilt in 1636.

In 1733, as reported by Wadding[151], the restoration and extension of Palazzolo began under the direction of the distinguished Franciscan P. Josè M. de Fonseca of Evora, one of the most important people in the artistic and cultural life of Rome in that period[152] (fig. 96).

There was a general rumour that he was a natural son of John V of Portugal[153]. Fonseca, whose original name was Josè de Ribeiro Fonseca Figuiredo o Sousa da Evora, was born at Evora on 10 December 1690. He was clothed in the Priory of Varatojo on 14 May 1711 and came to Italy in the retinue of the Marquis de Fontes. He was professed in the Priory of S. Bernardino of Orte (8 December 1712); and until 1740 his residence in Rome was the Aracoeli.

[150] Cf. CASIMIRO 1744, p. 346.
[151] WADDING 1931, Vol. XII, p. 40: "*P. Josè Maria de Fonseca Eborensis ad illud, non modo reparandum, sed etiam ingenti sumptu amplificandum adjecit animum. Itaque interiorem conventij area, quod claustrum appellant, porticus marmoreis pileis, et fornicibus circuì undique instructo ornandum curavit. Refecti a fondamentis parietes, fratrum nova cubicola edificata, cum diversos recipiendos advenas; atque aditus ut commodior esset, novus parieter ordo scalarum extructus est. Dormitoria con camerata, et in quadratum deduca: quod ut fieret, confragosum montem, qui ex latere orientali imminet, ad vertice ad planitiem usque domus incidi necesse fuit. Recentes et meliores officine opportunior, atque amplior locus biblioteque datij. Denique coenobium non instauratum dixeris, sed ad integre per partes singulas aedificatum: atque tam provide et feliciter, ut eodem in loco 1733*".
[152] CF. CRIELESI *L'eredita del Fonseca a S. Maria ad Nives di Palazzolo*, in "Castelli Romani", a. XXXV, Monograph 1995, pp. 16-19.
[153] G. MORONI, *Dizionario di erudizione storica-ecclesiastica*. Venice 1840/1861, vol. IV, p. 232: "*...This is the famous little Portuguese [man], a natural descendant of John V*".

100. Giandomenico Navone, S. Maria di Palazzolo, the garden with the fountain (fish-pond).

He was Procurator General (1727-28), Commissioner for the Roman Curia, General Minister of the Order of Friars Minor, Permanent Assessor, Member of the Supreme Roman Inquisition, Examiner of Bishops, Consultant to various Congregations, Ecclessiastical Adviser to Emperor Charles VII, Roman Senator for life, member of the Councils of the King of Sardinia and the King of Portugal, a Noble of Venice, Plenipotentiary Minister of John V of Portugal, and Ambassador to Clement XII in Rome (1733).

Furthermore, he became a member of various literary and scientific Societies in Europe, including the Arcadia (1726), with the name Garaste; the Etruscan Academy of Cortona (1736), in which he was known as Lucumone; the Portuguese Royal Academy, and so on.

On 11 February 1739, Pope Corsini, under pressure from the King of Portugal, who was grateful for Fonseca's help in resolving some delicate diplomatic problems, appointed Fonseca Bishop of Porto. He left Rome in October 1740 to begin the work to which he was officially appointed on 12 March the following year; his solemn entry to the diocese was in May 1743 and he remained in charge until his death on 16 June 1752.

101. GIANDOMENICO NAVONE, S. Maria di Palazzolo, the main entrance of the so-called "Citrus Garden" in front of the cave-nymphaeum used by Cardinal Isidore of Thessalonica.

He was the founder of the Aracoeli Library (1732), "the second in Rome in terms of its vastness, size, beauty, abundance". The Italian State took possession of it in 1883 and it formed the nucleus of the National Library (the Fondo Eborense).

Within the Order and the Roman Province, a number of works must be credited to this outstanding personality. These include the new dormitories, the re-modelling of the cloisters, the infirmary, and the chapel of St. Francis at S. Maria dell'Aracoeli (1719-1723); the entire Priory of S. Liberata at S. Angelo Romano (begun in 1737); the high altar, cloister, and new well in the Priory of S. Lorenzo at Velletri (1735); the Seminary in the Viterban Priory of Paradiso (1738); the extension of the Priory of S. Michele at Montecelio (1727); the rebulding of the Priories at Nemi, at Giulianello, at Caprarola; the building of a bell-tower at S. Francesco a Ripa, and so on.

But the Priory that benefitted most from the generosity of the man from Evora was that of Our Lady of the Snows at Palazzolo, to such an extent that, in an account printed in Rome for the 1740 General Chapter at Valladolid, it is in fact called "Palazzevora"[154].

The famous prelate enlarged and rebuilt it in order to create pleas-

[154] A.P.A., (Palazzola File): "*List, and summary of the expenses, and noteworthy work done and directed by Most Reverend P. re Friar Josè Maria De Fonseca D'Evora, starting in the year 1715, up to the present, for the benefit of the whole Religion, but also for the comfort, use and honour of the Roman Observantine Province, in which he was clothed as a Religious in 1712*". CF. CRIELESI 1997, pp. 26ff.

THE ARTISTIC HISTORY OF CONVENTO DI PALAZZOLO

102. Agostino Masucci, The Glory of St Didacus, formerly in the vault of the room of the same name at Convento di Palazzolo (Foto Moscioni 1915-19. Photographic Archive of the Vatican Museums). The present whereabouts of the picture is unknown.

ant accommodation worthy of the Portuguese diplomatic service at the papal court at Castel Gandolfo, to host the General Curia of the Order and to hold the General Chapters there (figs. 97-98).

As a 1735 plaque recalls[155], the work started with the building of a massive supporting wall. Five hundred hands long and 100 high, looking towards the south-west side of the garden, it followed the construction of a terrace garden, with the fountain, the vegetable garden, the orchard, and an appropriate system for the interception and distribution[156] of the spring waters. From the evidence provided by a contentious legal process entered into with the neighbouring Barberini[157], it seems that it was all planned by Giandomenico Navone (fig. 99), helped by two Roman architects, Lorenzo Santinovi and Francesco Fiori. The vegetable-garden was divided into squares intersected by little paths; between these there were some peperino slabs with appropriate stools, or so it would seem from an 1810 inventory. The real garden was the south garden with the fountain (figs. 100-101).

In 1739 the work had not been completely finished, so the attempt to enclose the large cave within the Priory's property failed because of the contentious legal process with the Barberini. Nor was the plan carried out to build a large entrance from which the garden of the famous cave would have opened along the path to Albano.

The Priory, too, underwent restoration. Apart from the Friars' rooms, two "apartments" were also made for Fonseca, along with a large room, named after S. Didacus (fig. 102), and the billiard room, "all that is necessary for sixty guests, including lay people", furnished and with a magnificent collection of *azulejos*, paintings and prints[158], including the portraits of the founder and one of his illustrious ancestors, Cardinal Pietro de Fonseca, called 'the Portuguese', killed accidentally at S. Cosimato near Vicovaro in 1422[159].

Some rooms were decorated by the Bolognese painter Ippolito Sconzani[160], who had already worked in Vienna and Melk. He died, in fact, at Palazzolo in May 1739 and was buried there in the centre of the church[161].

The dilapidated and crumbling medieval cloister was completely rebuilt according to a plan already tried out in other Priories belonging to the Friars Minor[162]: the old small marble columns were in part stored in the garden (up until 1810), or used as supports for the dining room tables, or used to adorn the parapet of the well (fig. 103). A large refectory, with walnut benches and a painting of the Wedding Feast at Cana, opened on to the corridor, while a first-floor library, near the monks' cells, housed a modest collection of books[163].

To the left of the church, on a pre-existing construction, a small palace was built for guests, and attached to it a "house for their families"[164] (figs. 104-105). On the ground floor, it consisted of two sheds, two stables, oven, etc., and then there were various rooms on the first floor, including a "large room" furnished with "eight large Maps and six canvas paintings"[165].

In 1739, as the plaque formerly on the double façade says[166], the restoration of the church was finished. The floor had been renewed "with square bricks and squaring of irregular marble"[167], the inside was painted half tints and the high altar re-built. It had "two marble steps to go

[155] The text reads: "*Imminentes rupi hortos / ob loci asperutatem / disiecto muro saepe collapos / ne deicenps ruerunt / qua exciso monte qua aggesta humo / superne complanatos / ingentisque operis substructione fulcitos / novo a fundamentis excitato muro / cinxit subiectamque viam abrupto adversi lateris margine / olim impeditam / circumducto aggere / ac leni mollitam declivio / expedivit fr. Iosephus M. Fonseca Eborensis Lusitanus / ord. min. / Iohannis V Lusitaniae Regis / apud S. Sedem minister plenipotentiarius / anno r. s. MDCCXXXV*".

[156] A.P.A. (Palazzola File) "Nota, e resumo delle spese...": "*43. In the great garden wall 500 handbreadths long and 100 high done first, and in the other two done afterwards to support the path, and the villa above, as on the mountainside about two thousand, and more handbreaths; planted on the new roads are gardens, (fruit) orchards, fountains, pools, and all that is associated with them, as indicated in the (current) accounts and set-aside accounts,from number 322 to number 350. Sc. 27910*".

[157] A.F.R. (Palazzola File I), Depositiones, in causa vertente PP Min. Conv. Palazzola Barberinos: "*...examinati fuerunt* [...] *Ill. Eques Dominicus Navona fili bo. me., F. ci Antonij Romanus, et etatis sua annor 52 circ.* [...] *et D. Laurentius Santinovi* [...] *et Frans. Fiori* [...] *in urbe architecti...*".

120 Chapter III

103. Giandomenico Navone, S. Maria di Palazzolo, cloister. (Foto Moscioni 1915-19. Photographic Archive of the Vatican Museums).

up and two for candlesticks with the ciborium at the centre and a wooden predella" flanked by two doors "with marble displays in the jambs and unframed tympanum architraves and surmounted by plinths holding busts of St Francis and St Anthony"[168].

On the back wall of the choir was placed "another altar with a fur altar frontal [*sic*] as in the descriptions, with three marble steps to ascend and two for candlesticks," and above this a "stucco frame with moulded borders and surrounded by angels' heads and by two angels on the clouds in an act of prayer"[169]. Here, along with a decorative scroll, was set the beautiful Antoniazzo panel (fig. 106); a canvas painting of the Crucifixion was placed in the apse, thus covering the medieval fresco previously mentioned.

In the nave, "on each of the side walls", two other altars were erected "with marble steps and coloured fur [*sic*] altar frontals [*sic*] and a canvas painting in a frame"; the one on the right, dedicated to St Joseph, the other, on the left, to SS. Anne and Joachim, with paintings by Agostino Masucci (1691-1768). "The facing of each altar is decorated with pillars, stucco capitals and tympanum pediments".

Two choirs and a pulpit in walnut were built while a balustrade "of marble pillars and balustrades, with a decorated base, unframed moulding and a step for the feet"[170] separated the sanctuary from the rest of a nave furnished with at least fifteen pictures apart from those of the Stations of the Cross.

To the left of the sanctuary, in the two medieval rooms, the sacristy was restored with a beautiful *Preparatorio*, and, in the small corridor, that

Cf. P. Roccasecca, *Il Giardino del Convento di S. Maria della Neve a Palazzola e i lavori di padre de Fonseca ed Evora*, in "Giovanni V e la cultura romana del suo tempo", Rome 1995, pp. 185-186.

[158] A.P.A. (Palazzola File), "Nota, e resumo delle spese...": "*41. In the Apartment, and lower guest rooms within the cloister, pictures, furniture, fittings for wardrobe, sideboard, and kitchen apart, all necessary for sixty guests, secular, too, as in the set-aside Account, and from number 291 up to 308 of this. Sc. 8200*".

[159] The two paintings of the Fonsecas are in Rome, at S. Antonio de' Portoghesi. About the Cardinal cf. A. Crielesi, *Il Complesso conventuale di S. Cosimato*, Rome 1995, pp. 59-60.

[160] S. J. De Pasqueira, *Palazzola (Um convento portguez na Italia)*, Porto 1904, doc. XV, p. 237: "*...the rooms, corridors and stairs indicated above are covered in real vaults, part cross vaults, part arched roof, part barrel vaults. The walls and vaults are fixed and painted in half-tint, while those of the lounge and the rooms on to the path are painted floridly and with landscapes...*". Ibid., p. 241: "*...the first areas with walls and real vaults and fixed barrel vaults, [...] with paintings in the same vein and landscapes in the vaults and the walls...*". Ibid.: "*...two entrance doorways to two rooms with walls covered from the lunette barrel vault and painted with frescoes of rustic scenes...*".

[161] Casimiro 1744, p. 344.

[162] M. Brancia Di Apricena, *Le committenze di padre Josè Maria de Fonseca ed Evora a Roma e nel territorio*, in "Giovanni V e la cultura romana del suo tempo", Rome 1995, pp. 153-184.

[163] A.P.A. (Palazzola File), "Nota, e resumo delle spese": "*40. Expenditure in the building of the new Priory, and the comforts for the General Curia and to celebrate there the Provincial Chapters, and as follows etc., the Offices, the Enclosure, Cistern, Stairs, furniture, and everything else, as in the set-aside account and from number 282 of this present account up to number 290. Sc 20860*". Cf. also: A.F.R., (Palazzola File I): "*...Inventario del 22 giugno 1810...*".

[164] A.P.A. (Palazzola File), "Nota, e resumo delle spese...": "*44. In the little Palace for noble guests outside the Priory with the attached Casino for their Families completely decorated inside, with two stables, and two coach houses, and likewise room for the fodder, little courtyards, and storage for the Animals necessary for Vacations etc., to be used also by the Portuguese Ambassadors when the Popes will be resident at Castel Gandolfo, etc., as in the set-aside Account, and from number 351 up to number 363 of this. Sc. 11077*".

104. GIANDOMENICO NAVONE, S. Maria di Palazzolo, entrance to the "Little guest house" with the two marble Coats of arms of Fonseca, formerly on the church façade.

105. GIANDOMENICO NAVONE, S. Maria di Palazzolo, internal courtyard.

[165] Cf. CRIELESI 1997, "*Inventario delle robe e suppellettili [...] 12 novembre 1752*", pp. 55-69.

[166] The text is: "*In honorem deiparae Virginis / templum vetustate fatiscens ac situ sordens / instauratis exornatisque fornce ac parietibus / extructis odeis pavimento starto / marmoreis excitatis aris / fronte ac vestibulo exeterius renovatis / in splendiorem formam restituit / fr. Ioseph. M. Eboren. Lusitan. / ord. Min. / Iohannis V Lusitaniae Regis / apud S. Sedem minister plenipotentiarius / et electus episcopus Portuen. / anno r. S. MDC-CXXXIX*".

[167] DE PASQUEIRA 1904, p. 244.
[168] Ibid.
[169] Ibid.
[170] Ibid.

delightful stucco niche, bearing the Fonseca heraldry, crowning the seventeenth-century marble lavabo: fortunately, all of this escaped the twentieth-century restorations (figs. 64, 91).

Externally, on the façade – decorated with the coats of arms of John V of Braganza and Fonseca in their boldest versions (figs. 107-108-109) – a floor was built above the portico to hold the tribune, the choir and the organ, thus eliminating the gothic rose window which

122 CHAPTER III

106. GIANDOMENICO NAVONE, the Antoniazzo panel following its arrangement on the High Altar during the Fonseca restorations (Photo I. C. C. D., early years of the 20th century).

was then stored in the garden. Then, two twin bell-towers were placed either side of the façade, one with three bells, the other with a clock[171]. As can be seen from a 1762 engraving by Piranesi[172] the two towers – at least before the necessary repair work following an earthquake in 1806 and the stripping of the roofs for lead by French troops[173] – culminated in fantastic spires which revealed the cultural Borromini background of their originator, the architect Giandomenico Navone (an impression also found in the similar manuscript of S. Maria dei Miracoli) (fig. 110).

It was in fact this famous academic from S. Luca who, besides the garden, restored the church and modernized the Priory at Palazzolo. Equally, it was often from the same Giadomenico Navone that the generous Franciscan commissioned many of the works which made him magnanimous in the eyes of his descendants: the Aracoeli Library, the church of S. Liberata at S. Angelo Romano, S. Lorenzo at Velletri, and so on[174]: the '*Portoghesino*' commanded such esteem that he most certainly would not have been an unworthy recipient of entering the honorary circle of the Knights of the Order of Christ!

When all the work was done, total expenditure at Palazzolo amounted to 79,447 Roman scudi.

In the Bull *Exsponi Nobis* dated 9 April 1738, Clement XII gave Fonseca permission to stay outside the Priory enclosure, granting him, for the length of his natural life, the use and convenience – but not the ownership – of the guest quarters. Following the death of the distinguished prelate, they became a lodge for Priory guests, apart from women, with a prohibition on any members of the Franciscan community staying there.

Further testimony to Fonseca's presence at Palazzolo comes from a valuable little booklet which lists not just the costs paid in advance by the Franciscan community but financed by P. Josè Fonseca of Evora in 1738, but also the various detailed expenditure for his holidays[175]; it is also worth noting payments for the gardeners and for the garden furnishings, such as the citrus flowerpots from the Cibo park at Castel Gandolfo.

Of course, the splendour of Palazzolo also had its critics, even within the community itself, so much so that it was described by one of the brothers as "...a theatre of the noisiest luxurious cheerfulness in the world..."[176] (fig. 112).

As already indicated, Fonseca left Rome and Italy in 1740. His destination was the Episcopal See assigned to him, Porto, in Portugal; hence, he was unable to complete some of his projects, like that of S. Liberata at S. Angelo Romano, nor was he present for the visit of Benedict XIV who made his way to Palazzolo by carriage on 28 October 1741. Here, just like his predecessors, the Pontiff prayed in the church and then went into the Priory to receive the homage of the Friars. It was on this exceptional occassion he gave special permission to the Dowager Contessa Colonna, Princess Caterina Maria Zeffirina Salviati, wife of Fabrizio, to enter the chapel of St Didacus within the enclosure.

[171] A.P.A. (Palazzola File) "Nota, e resumo delle spese": "*42 [...] Expenditure in the church, a new façade, two choirs carved in walnut, an organ, marble altars, Confessionals, Paintings, and two bell towers with larger bells, a clock with three bells and, in the Sacristy, a new Preparatorio, and in different rooms, furniture in them with three loggia, etc., as in the Account and from number 309 up to number 321. Sc. 11400*".

[172] G.B. PIRANESI, *Sepolcro Regio o Consolare, inciso nella rupe del Monte Albano o nel conv. to de' PP. Franscescani a Palazzuolo...*, from "Le antichità di Albano e di Castel Gandolfo descritte ed incise da Giovanbattista Piranesi", Rome 1762-64.

[173] A.F.R. (Palazzola File), letter from the Guardian of the Priory, 19th century: "...*the vaults of the cloister which, as the ancients said, formed an open gallery paved with lead like the vault of the church [...] were ravaged in the Napoleonic suppression...*".

[174] The now-demolished (1937) church of S. Lorenzo *in Piscibus* or degli Armellini (S. Lorenzuolo) in the Borgo area of Rome, where the artist was born in 1687, was also Navone's. His architectural style was elegant and simple. Cf. R. BATTAGLIA, *Due architetti borrominiani in S. Lorenzo in Piscibus di Roma*, in "Bollettino D'Arte", XXXI, III, 1938. pp. 370-275.

[175] A.F.R. 124, "*Spese della Fabrica Del Vn. ble Convento di Palazzola fatte dal R. mo Evora l'anno 1738*", ms. 1738.

[176] M. BRANCIA DI APRICENA, *Il Complesso dell'Aracoeli sul Colle Capitolino*, Rome 2000, p. 228.

107. GIANDOMENICO NAVONE, façade of the church and Priory of S. Maria di Palazzolo, before the post-war restorations (Foto Moscioni 1915-19, Photographic Archives of the Vatican Museums).

108. S. Maria di Palazzolo, marble coat of arms (1739-40) of Friar José Maria Fonseca of Evora, complete with royal crown.

109. S. Maria di Palazzolo, marble coat of arms (1739-40) of Friar José Maria Fonseca of Evora, Bishop of Oporto, complete with episcopal hat and the emblem of the Franciscan Order.

Palazzolo in the 19th and 20th centuries

With the coming of the French Revolution and the establishment of the Roman Republic in 1798 Palazzolo suffered a great deal.

22 June 1810 saw the Napoleonic suppression with the confiscation of all goods which, once listed, were given over to the safe-keeping of the Priory Guardian Fr Giuseppe da Cavrago[177] by "Antonio Volpi delegated commissioner of Sig. Francesco Giarletti" and by the Mayor of the Commune of Rocca di Papa, Gentilini.

Even the bells and the clock on the bell-towers were sold as State property; the first went to the Commune of Marino, the second to that of Rocca di Papa. Even the organ, built under Fonseca and decorated with the coat of arms of the King of Portugal and which had cost 1,000 scudi, "was sacrilegiously sold by the so-called State Property Office of Albano to certain Jews for the vile price of 80 scudi, and the Jews then gave it to the community at Genzano for 84 scudi" where it was destined to adorn the "new Church".

It is highly likely that the Priory remained uninhabited for some time, so that it became a den for drifters and wanted people, as was the case with Lorenzo Mazzoleni "..the famous Jacobin who took part in the scaling of the Quirinal in 1809 and the capture of the Pope; at the restoration he was exiled from Rome by Pius VII and found refuge in the Priory of Palazzolo, still not re-inhabited by the Friars, where he moved about freely. And this was until 1814 when Mazzoleni was arrested by the Chief Constable of Albano, in October 1814..."[178].

On their return to Palazzolo, the Franciscans found the Priory in a disastrous state. Furthermore, their pleas to have the organ back at the cost of "...restoring to the same Community at Genzano the sum of forty-four scudi, which they said they had given to the first Jewish buyers" were in vain, as can be ascertained from a request made by the Guardian

---

[177] A.F.R. (Palazzola File): *"Inventory of 22 June 1810": "...I, the undersigned, promise to undertake to jealously safeguard everything in so far as I can. P. Giuseppe da Cavrago..."*. CRIELESI 1997, pp. 39-41.

[178] B.A.V., Vat. Lat. n. 9896, f. 115 (Memoirs of Mgr. Gregorio Speroni). Cf. BONOMELLI 1953, pp. 188-189.

110. G. B. PIRANESI, Royal or Consular Tomb, cut into the rock of Monte Albano, now in the Franciscan priory at Palazzuolo..., from: "Le antichità di Albano e di Castel Gandolfo descritte ed incise da Giovanbattista Piranesi", Rome 1762-64.

of the Priory to the then Portuguese Plenipotentiary Minister to the Holy See, Luiz Pinto, in November 1817[179].

With the return to "normality", Palazzolo once again became a place of prayer and contemplation, but also one of the favourite destinations of those romantic spirits from beyond the Alps who, descending in droves upon Italy, found, in the Eternal City and its surroundings – with its nature, folklore, history and millenial cultures – a continual source of inspiration. The Danish scholar Andersen – as his *Diaries* recall – wanted to visit the Alban Hills, along with Albert Küchler, the poet Ludwig Bødtcher, Ditlev Blunck, the Norwegian artist, Thomas Fearnley, and others: it was 26 October 1833 when, to complete their usual visit, the group of Scandinavian artists wanted to climb the "holiest" of the peaks, that of Monte Cavo, "where even the clouds are among the grazing flocks". On the way they came across the former Priory of S. Maria di Palazzolo, clinging to the grey peperino rocks into which Cardinal Isidore's cave opened: "...we rode the little donkey along the slope of Lake Albano, the wood was multicoloured, an enormous natural cave covered in ivy lay at the side of the ancient Priory..."[180].

[179] A.S.A.D.P. (Palazzola File): "...*since every representation made by those same poor religious to those communists* [of the Genzano Commune] *had been fruitless, they therefore placed all their trust in the well-known mercy of Your Holiness in order that....*".

[180] H.C. ANDERSEN, *Dagbøger, 1825-1875*, (edited by R. Olsen and H. Topsøe-Jensen), København 1971-1976. Vol. I, pp. 220-24. CF. A. CRIELESI, *Il pittore Fra Pietro da Copenhagen al secolo Albert Küchler*. Rome 1999, p. 28.

111. Priory of S. Maria di Palazzolo. Niche for a small fountain with a marble coat of arms (1739-40) of Friar José Maria Fonseca of Evora, Bishop of Oporto, adorned with episcopal hat and the emblem of the Franciscan Order.

[181] A. DA ROCCA DI PAPA, *Sunto storico dei Conventi Case e Monasteri appartenenti all'antica Provincia Romana dell'Ordine dei Minori*, Rome 1898, pp. 26-28.

[182] A.F.R. (Palazzola File II): Letter from Friar Mariano of Velletri, Provincial Minister of the Observantine Minors, to Antonio, Count of Thomar, Minister to the Holy See (post-1870): *"And so it is for the reasons outlined above that the religious making up the actual family of Palazzola faithfully beg Your Excellency to take it upon yourself to request the Government of His Most Faithful Majesty, so that we may be placed under the protection of Portugal, so that in case of suppression the same religious might not be troubled"*. A.F.R. (Palazzola File II), letter of P. Luigi da Caprarola O.F.M., Guardian of Palazzola, dated 13 July 1873, to the Count of Thomar: *"furthermore, I let him know* [the Mayor of Rocca di Papa] *that we are simply custodians of everything in the Priory of Palazzola, the owner being His Majesty the King of Portugal"*.

[183] A.S.A.D.P., fasc. 110, fasc. 106-14, M. SALUSTRI, *Stima dei fondi rustici e fabbricati di proprietà del Governo di Portogallo, posti nel territorio del Comune di Rocca di Papa, Mandamento di Frascati, Provincia di Roma*. 1880.

[184] A.P.A. (Palazzola File): Various Papers; letter from P. Nazareno Paris, Guardian of Palazzola Priory, to Cardinal Antonio Agliardi, Bishop of Albano – 16 September 1907.

As far as visits to Palazzolo are concerned, mention must also be made of two by other Popes during the traditional holiday at Castel Gandolfo. They are both recorded in the memorials painted in the *sala di S. Diego* [Chapel of St Didacus]: in 1831 Gregory XVI, who as Cardinal had already been a guest of the Franciscans in 1824, and Pius IX, on 15 September 1852.

And who knows if these Pontiffs were able to note the curious scroll which today still stands out in the refectory, inviting the table companions to:

EAT SLOWLY
AND CHEW WELL

The authority of the Papal States was to come to an end with "the capture of Rome" in 1870. As a consequence of that, and more damaging to S. Maria di Palazzolo (and not just to Palazzolo, in fact) even than the Napoleonic invasion, was the so-called Italian suppression: the Friars Minor, hoping to avoid the consequences of the confiscation decree of 29 June 1873, resorted to a trick, as testified to by Fr Andrea Basili from Rocca di Papa[181]: "...in order not to lose this Priory [they] begged for protection from Portugal. What? By giving to Italy the famous Aracoeli Library, work of the same Portoghesino, they obtained from the State the Priory of Palazzolo and at the same time appropriated the woods, acknowledging for us, as a great favour, sole free use of the Priory and garden..."[182].

In fact, on 7 June 1880 the S. Maria di Palazzolo complex – excluding "some grottoes and caves which are supposed to have been Nymphaeum, the Consular Tomb attributed to Gnaeus Cornelius Scipio Hispalus, the great vertical cuts straight into the stone which it is believed were done to improve the defence of the Albano Citadel, the quarries, reduced to conserving water, the path chiselled through the peperino" – was sold by the Portuguese Government Director Generalate of Funds for Worship, as can be seen from an agreement between the lawyer responsible for Portuguese Affairs, Bernardino Antonio Faria Gentil, and the Director of the Funds, Vittorio Grimaldi (deeds. Egidio Serafini, 25 June 1880). With the property having passed from the Director Generalate of Funds for Worship, the Portuguese Government entrusted the Albano architect Mariano Salustri with the task of drawing up an evaluation for the place (29 October 1880)[183].

In 1896, Alfredo de Monteverde, Secretary of the Portuguese Royal Legation to the Quirinal, "...attracted, who knows how, if by the view of the place, or by other particular motives of his own, had the guest house restored, wishing it to be ready for the use and convenience of the Portuguese Minister and his personnel resident in Rome (but in fact the one who has lived there and still lives there for the greater part of the year is the above-mentioned Secretary)..."[184].

Furthermore, in July 1903, the Portuguese authorities made the Franciscan community give up part of the Priory to be used for holidays by the guests of the S. Antonio de' Portoghesi Institute, the college in Rome for Portuguese theology and fine arts students.

Not even this managed to save the Priory. With the outbreak of the

112. Agostino Masucci, Portrait of Cardinals Neri Corsini, Gentili, Passeri with Friar José Maria de Fonseca of Evora, c. 1738, formerly in the Library at S. Maria dell'Aracoeli. Rome, Biblioteca Nazionale Centrale di Roma.

Portuguese Revolution in 1910 and the proclamation of the suppression of religious Orders and the consequent confiscation of their goods, the Republican Government took possession of the Priory, deeming it to be patrimony of the deposed Portuguese Crown.

It is from this period that we have the gloomy description of Palazzolo left to us by Voss in his book, *Du mein Italien*: "...I looked to the right in a dark and plain church, and to the left into a long room where some old friars were walking up and down reading worn out books..." and again "...on one side the high cliff rising straight up was covered by luxuriant vegetation; on the other there was a low parapet, and beneath it just emptiness. The garden, then, is a forest of flower beds, little vegetable gardens, areas planted with fruit trees, of avenues with laurels, cypresses and lemon trees [...]. A Roman tomb is used as a water receptacle; the whole garden is full of antiquities and capitals used as seats, we found a bust of Venus dressed in roses..."[185] (fig. 113).

Despite furiously having defended their rights, the Friars were forced to leave the Priory after centuries of almost uninterrupted presence. In 1912, as emerges from a letter and inventory drawn up on 10

[185] R. Voss, *Du mein Italien*, 1910, translated by V. D'Onofrio, *Visioni d'Italia*, Lanciano 1912, p. 41.

113. FELICE GIANI (circle of), View of the Palazzolo Garden with the Villa Colonna above (first decades of the 19th century). Rome, Gab. Naz. le Disegni e Stampe.

March by a certain Caporilli[186] on behalf of the lawyer Lambertini Pinto Josè, Attaché for Portuguese Affairs, the Priory was further stripped of its furnishings, among which were eight paintings which had been in the church, including an altar piece of the Virgin and Saints Francis and Benedict which Tomassetti had noted banished at that time to the sacristy[187]; the furnishings were loaded onto a cart and sent to Rome and collected on 2 June 1912[188].

The Antoniazzo panel remained at Palazzolo, along with the oil-painting of the unfortunate Cardinal Pietro Fonseca, the marble lunette with the *Mystical Lamb* (fig. 58), the canvas of *S. Didacus in glory*, and 24 other pictures which, for the most part, were devotional.

The Priory was then leased, first of all, on 28 November the same year, to a lawyer, a certain Giuseppe Marchesano, for accommodation and the seat of a curious institute, *The Universal Lay Monastery*. Then in 1915 it was sold (deeds. D. Filodoro, Frascati 14 October 1915), along with other attached and neighbouring property (the *Macchia*, a house at Marino, etc.), for the sum of 63,000 lire to a certain Professor Carlo Arnaldi, "scientist, artist, philanthropist" (sic) who transformed it into a health farm, *Cenobio di Cura e Profilassi*. Here it is worth remembering that Arnaldi had the idea of returning the whole complex

[186] A.S.D.P. Fondo Palazzola, *Various papers*.
[187] TOMASSETTI, Vol. II, pp. 196f.
[188] A.S.D.P., Fondo Palazzola, *Various papers*.

"to its pristine gothic-roman architecture", and to do this he had promised himself (he was a doctor) "to cut out, with a firm hand, the gangrene of ugly baroque from the medieval frame"[189].

But Arnaldi had not chosen the right moment for his curative plan. Palazzolo did not receive the crowd of patients (for the most part committed to the Carso trenches) he was banking on and the *Cenobio di Cura e Profilassi* was forced to shut up shop. By a deed drawn up on 6 April 1920 the former Minorite Priory changed hands once again. It was bought for 260,000 lire by the Venerable English College, based in Rome, which wanted to turn it into a summer residence, as had been its relentless destiny for centuries.

Restoration work began on the church in 1929 with the pretext, as had already been Arnaldi's intention, of wishing to return to the original Gothic-Cistercian structure. The two towers were knocked down, the façade demolished and rebuilt using white marble and peperino with the addition of two lancet windows at the sides of the restored Cistercian rose window. Inside, the side altars were removed, along with the high altar with its stuccos, the other altar against the apse, and the marble balustrade; in fact, all the mouldings and artefacts of the Fonseca period went.

It was during this period of restoration (1935) that the fragments of the apse frescoes of the *Virgin Enthroned* and the two "*Pietà*" came to light once again.

Meanwhile, the final stripping: the painting of Cardinal Pietro Fonseca and the Antoniazzo panel, which up to now had both been kept in a Priory storehouse, left Palazzolo on 17 November 1936 and were "returned" to the S. Antonio de' Portoghesi Institute in Rome. The first adorns one of the rooms, the second, the tempera by Antoniazzo, after restoration by Pico Cellini, found its place in the church of the same name, in the first chapel on the left (1937).

The English were left with the Masucci paintings and some others, as documented by a Venerable English College inventory drawn up in 1920 when the complex was bought[190].

The restoration begun with such alacrity by the Rector, Mcmillan, was interrupted by the war and it was precisely during this forced pause that, under the dim light of its walls, Palazzolo received a certain individual, a renowned fugitive, one of the greatest performers in that great farce which was transformed into tragedy and which was now drawing to its conclusion: Giuseppe Bottai. The party official, survivor of 25 July 1943 when the Great Fascist Council had put Mussolini in the minority and prepared his fall, had been condemned to death in his absence by the Verona tribunal of the Italian Socialist Republic.

Hunted by fascists and Germans, he saved himself by going from hiding place to hiding place. This took him, among other places, to Palazzolo, thanks to the interest taken by Cardinal Pizzardo and Monsignors Tardini and Montini, with the *nulla osta* of Pius XII.

On the night of 28 October 1943 a car with Vatican number plates (S.C.V.) arrived at Palazzolo and out stepped Cardinals Pizzardo and Canali, President of the Pontifical Commission for the State, Commander Bonomelli and Giuseppe Bottai.

The College caretaker took Bottai into safe-keeping, having being

[189] V. Misserville, *Il dott. Arnaldi a Palazzolo*, in "Castelli Romani", a. VII, n. 9, September 1962, pp. 74-75.

[190] For the inventory of the furnishings at Palazzolo (Archive of the V.E.C.. Palazzola File 6A), cf. Crielesi 1997, p. 52, note 68.

114. S. Maria di Palazzolo, view of the cloister and the side of the church. Photo after the 20th century restorations.

assured by his eminent companions that he was a priest and person of high regard within the Spanish Embassy.

Through recommendations and various promises the same custodian also received a "Special Safe-conduct" pass to go to Castel Gandolfo twice a week to collect provisions and pick up the post.

The esteemed guest was given the Rector's apartment, situated at the centre of the monumental façade of the building directly up from the lake, the same apartment that had belonged to Fonseca.

Attached to the College at Palazzolo is a building which served as the accommodation of the Italian Elisabettine Sisters [now St Edward's wing], to which many other religious sisters often came during this period. Bottai only spoke with one of them, at length, and often emotionally and affectionately: it was his wife. Early on, after she left the Ricciarelli family where she had fled, she went to find the renowned fugitive.

Unfortunately, Notebook XVI of Bottai's *Diari* (which goes from 28 October 1943 to 13 January 1944) was lost by the person to whom it was entrusted. It was specifically about the time spent at Palazzolo and was densely written, like all those of this type of writing, in a note-book with squared paper to save paper and space. Most of the contents were probably a gloss on the trial at Verona about which we are left a note about at the start of Notebook XVII (which goes from 14 January to 9 May 1944). In his reflections the author allows a glimpse, an indirect picture of Palazzolo, its silence and peace which pushed him, a despairing unbeliever, to draw closer again to God, to the eternal wisdom of the Creator.

"15 January – I see my soul, surprised by the crystal clear, bright peace into which it has fallen, after the violent psychological blow, albeit brief, of the announcement of the death sentence. I ask myself how has this peace come about, these pleasant and identical days pass by, without even

115. S. Maria di Palazzolo, present-day cloister.

one of my life habits disturbed in this refuge: Mass, in the morning, at first light, the long hours of reading in the sun, when there is, in the gathered half-light of these cells, rosary and benediction at sunset, and even every evening a little card game with the priest and the sisters, with much happiness and discreet tricks. I have made my rule ever more severe, renouncing also the furtive and cautious walks in the garden, and suspending all corrrespondence with my family. Thus I have taken steps to make all traces of my own presence here disappear, increasing every possible precaution.

But apart from this, all is as before. Once again there is that interior peace where before there was more a shaking nervous tension. Death, which as a potential threat was so legally precise, works in me according to its virtue, which is purifying..."[191].

There, the silence, the stillness – not the fear – of death!

That same fascination struck all the famous people who loved this place: Colonna, Fonseca, Mazzoleni, Monteverde, and so on, all satisfied by that "indefinable sense of calm, and of mysticism [which] is all around in the air...".

Half way through January, given that events were pressing, time was running out and it would have been dangerous to remain, Bottai left Palazzolo to return to the heart of Rome, the Ghetto, to an Institute of

[191] G. BOTTAI, *Diario 1935-1944* (Ed. B. Guerri), Milan 2000, p. 488.

the Oblates of S. Maria del Pianto. From there he went to a Jesuit house near Piazza Sant'Ignazio, from February 1944 until 4 June 1944, the day of Rome's liberation. In July 1944 he enrolled in the Foreign Legion and then, in the Roman silence, he sought deliverance from history.

But to return to Palazzolo. On 7 February 1944 the profound and beatific silence that reigned was broken by a group of German soldiers who occupied the whole of the first floor of the College, just at the time when the most pressing and furious carpet-bombing was taking place over Marino, Albano, Rocca di Papa and "in the woods on the opposite side of the lake and on the slopes of Monte Cavo, where the Germans were hiding with their machines and artillery".

There were "sights, which leave every human soul filled with dismay...To those who see with anguish the palace vanish beneath the fire of the explosions, and then to find apparently intact the known outlines of Rocca di Papa, Grottaferrata, Marino, Palazzola, Albano, it almost seems a miracle"[192].

A few days later the Germans fled in small groups, followed closely by Anglo-American troops coming from Artemisio along the Via dei Laghi.

On 2 June, Palazzolo and Monte Cavo were at the centre of a desperate and awful fire. Most of the Germans had left Palazzolo and only a group of seventeen, hidden in the nearby caves, gave themselves up to the Americans.

The fleeing Germans took with them an artistic bell, which for centuries had been at the Priory's main entrance, and in return they left some obscene graffiti showing Bacchus and Venus, drawings of nude women, and various coats of arms.

The English religious returned to Palazzolo that summer and removed the titillating scenes from the dining room walls, just leaving the coats of arms of the anonymous soldier-artist.

With the end of the war, restoration work at Palazzolo began again and continued up until a few years ago, thus arriving at the present restoration (fig. 114).

For whoever enters Palazzolo now there is no point in looking for Sconzani's paintings and the other decorations which, in some rooms, reproduced, by a *trompe l'oeil* effect, the insides of the Palazzolo caves, with virtual glimpses towards the lake below and the solemn Roman countryside: they have sunk into oblivion. A more generous future – if still hidden under the dullness of the plaster – will certainly restore them to history (fig. 115).

[192] BONOMELLI 1953. p. 454.

IV. The restoration
Marina Cogotti

The Project: problems and solutions

Compared to the spiritual and religious significance of the Jubilee Year, the work at Palazzolo might seem somewhat marginal. Nevertheless, it is important in its own right, above all with regard to cultural heritage. Perhaps more so than on other occasions, the financial quota entrusted to the Ministry for Fine Arts and Cultural Activities, which worked through its own branches, provided concrete and visible results with respect to the timescale foreseen by law. The work plan financed under Law 651/96 also allowed investment to be extended to some monuments in the province of Rome, thus encouraging the recovery and restoration of monumental complexes which would usually be difficult to carry out in the general planning of the resources granted to Fine Arts. The work on the church and Priory at Palazzolo came under the programme of works entrusted to and carried out by the Department for the Environmental and Architectural Properties of Lazio. This work included the reclamation, strengthening and restoration of twenty monuments located in the province of Rome[1]. The area of the Castelli hill towns, within which lies the papal residence at Castel Gandolfo, was affected by a number of works carried out by different institutional bodies, including the Department[2]. The actual finance did not always correspond to the necessary requests submitted at the preparatory planning stage; therefore, in the initial planning stage, strategic priorities had to be chosen which would allow both the identified aims and those common to the whole Jubilee programme to be reached. The recovery, benefit, improvement of access and service, in relation both to the economic resources made available and the timescale imposed by the law, were not subject to any exceptions.

Convento di Palazzolo benefitted from a financial package of two thousand million lire, corresponding to a net amount for works of just under 1,700,000,000 lire [*c*.£6 million]. It was decided to spend most of this money on external work, focussing on both the fabric of the building and the terrace garden. In fact, it should be stated immediately that the state of preservation within Palazzolo was not good, largely due to lack of maintenance. A series of concurrent factors can, in part, justify this state of affairs, above all the size and dimensions of the site; the close relationship with the local environment which at times lacks any type of continuity; the relatively isolated position; and the particular micro-climatic conditions.

The problem of maintenance and safeguarding is found constantly throughout Palazzolo's history, often described as being in ruins and infested by briars. Following the "restoration" concluded in the 1930s, the next decades saw the Venerable English College[3], owner of the estate since 1920, concentrate its efforts, understandably, on work inside the building to improve living standards, in order to continue its use as a summer residence for the seminarians and, increasingly, as a place available for spiritual activities. However, perhaps those who were materially concerned with the preservation of the buildings, the surrounding area and the garden lacked the necessary cultural expertise and care of those who should take charge of such

---

[1] For a concise review of the work undertaken by the Department for the Environmental and Architectural Properties of Lazio, cf. CANCELLIERI and R. CIPOLLONE (eds.), *Il Giubileo 2000 alle porte di Roma – Monumenti ritrovati nel Lazio*, Rome 1999.

[2] Ibid., cf. articles: M. COGOTTI, *Il Convento di S. Francesco a Velletri*, pp. 26-29; M. COGOTTI, *La Cattedrale di S. Clemente I Papa a Velletri*, pp. 30, 31; G. FATICA, *L'Abbazia di S. Nilo a Grottaferrata*, pp. 32,33; M. COGOTTI, *Il Convento di Palazzola*, pp. 62-64.

[3] The Venerable English College, based in Rome at Via Monserrato 45, boasts a long-standing presence in Italy, dating back to its origins in 1361, when the Community and Guild of the English in Rome bought the first house in Via Monserrato. The College took over Palazzolo as a summer residence in 1920, thus replacing their former villa at Monte Porzio Catone.

116. Changing rooms built for the swimming-pool; behind them can be seen the mouth of the cave with a massive rock in front, which fell in 1930.

work. On the part of the institution, a certain aversion to openness to the external institutional organisations has probably limited attitudes of dialogue and comparison which would have fostered an awareness of the value of the architectural heritage and the consequent need to respect it, safeguarding not just its integrity but also its decorum.

While not underestimating the burden of maintaining a property such as Palazzolo, it remains my strong conviction that the problem is, above all, cultural. After all, many of the losses suffered are not simply due to the processes of decline that inevitably accompany the ageing process, but are the fruits of definite, deliberate acts. These are attributable, in part, to the twentieth-century restorations, and in part had already happened during the course of the nineteenth century. They began with the plunder following the institution of the Roman Republic in 1798, and the Napoleonic suppression which followed in 1810, and continued up until that delicate moment when the Franciscans, in an attempt to save the property from confiscation by the Italian State following the 1873 decree of confiscation, linked to the Italian laws of suppression, indirectly supported its transfer to Portugal in 1880.

Even if the fact that the most substantial losses can be attributed to the twentieth-century restorations remains an indisputable assertion, it is right and proper to place these restorations not just in the context of the purchaser's Anglo-Saxon sensitivity, but equally in that of a common theoretical understanding of restoration as a return to the original *facies* of a monument. This idea is not, in fact, foreign to us, and terrible losses suffered by the national architectural heritage can be ascribed to it[4].

It is also interesting to note that, at the same time as the eighteenth-century restorations in the Priory were being wiped out by the demolition of the bell-towers and the church façade, an "interpretative" rebuilding was taking place in the Villa Colonna above under the

[4] One can think of restoration work done throughout Italy in the last years of the nineteenth century and the first years of the twentieth, such as that at S. Maria in Cosmedin in Rome, where the work of Giovenale resulted in the destruction of Sardi's 18th century façade; or the work of the architects Nava and Cesa-Bianchi at S. Babila in Milan. To them is due the loss of the 17th century façade, the demolition of the little bell towers of the Pantheon, and numerous works involving stripping plaster, still being carried out in the first fifty years of the twentieth century, etc. Cf. C. Ceschi, *Teoria e storia del restauro*, Rome 1970.

56.05   3.35
11.10   10.90

119. VICOMTE DE SENONNES, Vue d'une Grotte à Palazzola, from *"Choix de vues pittoresques"*, 1820.

120. Plan of the Priory, drawn up by M. Salustri for the Portuguese Government in 1880 (Rome, S. Antonio dei Portoghesi Archives).

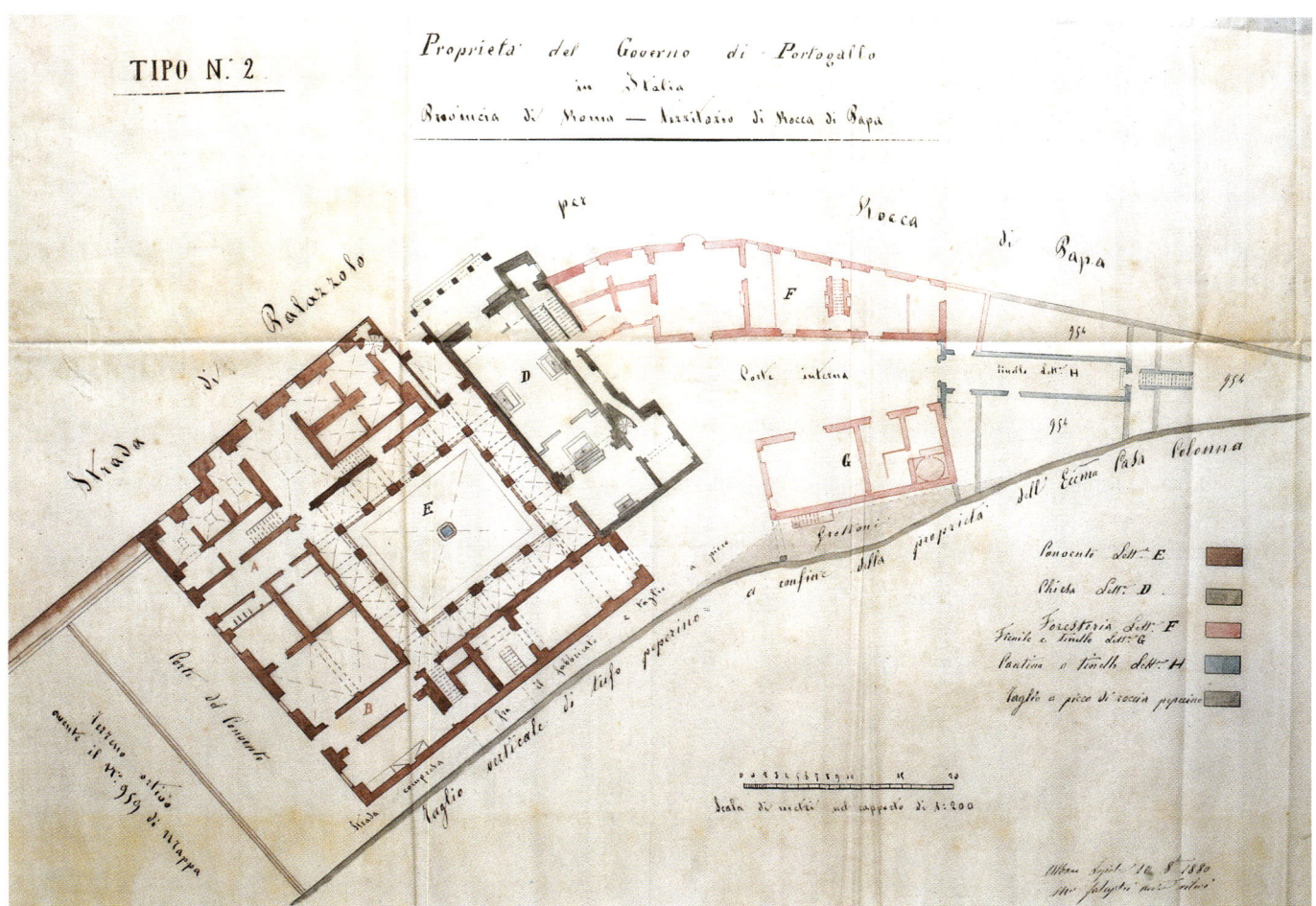

136 CHAPTER IV

117. Area of restoration: West elevation.
118. Area of restoration: South elevation.

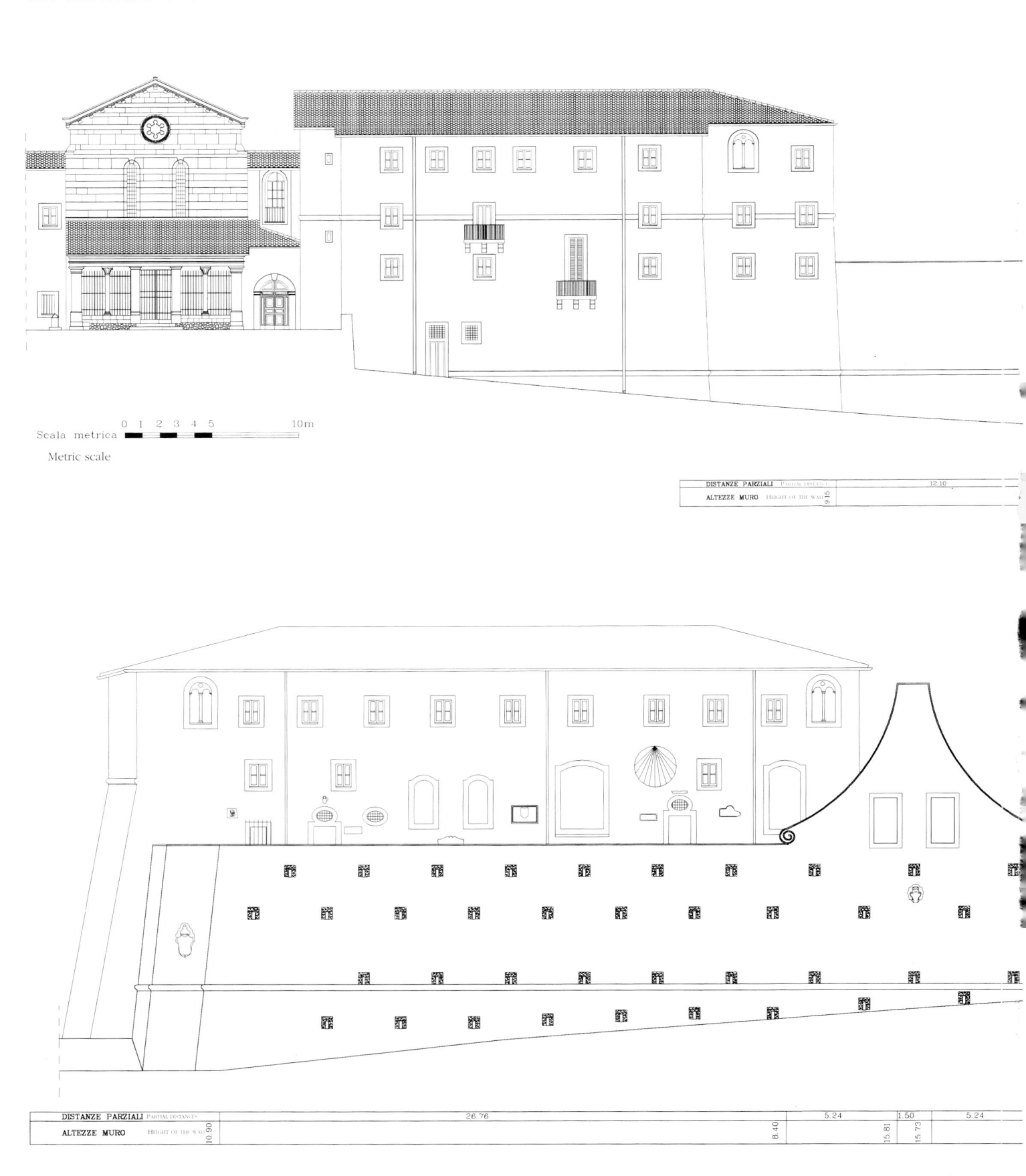

3.40　　　　　　　　　　35.10

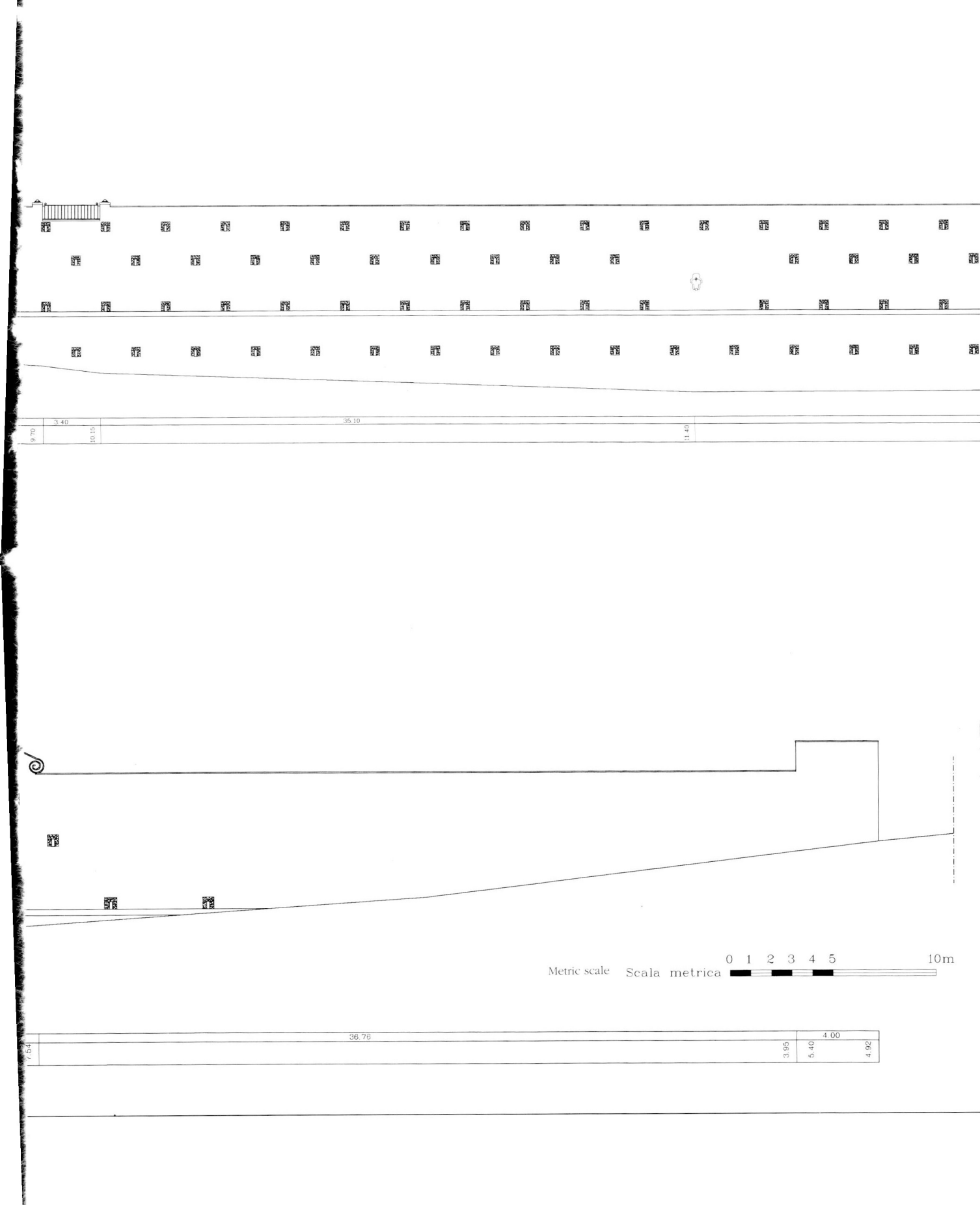

Metric scale　Scala metrica　0 1 2 3 4 5　10m

36.76　　　4.00

work of De Cupis[5]. The aim was more a re-creation of the setting of the seventeenth-century villa than its literary reconstruction. In the report drawn up in 1924 by Ing. Filippo Sneider at the request of the Rector of the English College, the building was described as "in ruins", in the worst possible conditions, "not only from the point of maintenance but also stability", with the roofs almost completely caved in. But the Villa was "recontextualised", with the arrangement of findings from various sources and provenances (coats of arms, friezes, etc) and decorated with murals (fig. 80) which, in some way, represent the development of a planned idea and at the same time a sort of legitimisation of the work carried out. There was a clear aim, too, of bestowing on the newly acquired property, reduced to such a state, echoes of its noble past[6].

Less "natural" choices were then made over the decades, like that of having a swimming-pool, with changing-rooms attached, on the site of the old orchard (fig. 116). It is in front of the large cave whose praises were so often sung in the ancient chronicles and which features in the drawings and paintings of artist-travellers. To be fair to history, mention must be made of the fall of an enormous lump of rock on 20 May 1930, which partially blocked, if not the entrance, certainly the view of the cave. This episode, preceded by "serious cracks in the cave, on the vaults which are badly supported by pillars"[7], and by partial collapses that already had taken place in the summer of 1928, also caused the loss of the ancient little public fountain, served by the waters from the spring on Villa Colonna property. It can often be seen in engravings and paintings (figs. 14, 119).

The current culture of preservation further removes the risk of sacrificing the historic moment on the altar of aesthetics. Certainly, no-one today would see eighteenth-century changes or additions as excesses to be eliminated in order to pursue a theoretical search for the purity of the work. Today perhaps, the greatest risks come from negligence, abandonment, unsuitable use and an exclusively functional relationship with the building. Here, credit must be given to the management of the Venerable English College for the committment it has shown in setting out a course of action in harmony with the results achieved through the restoration.

Within the more general aims proposed by the plan for the work for the Great Jubilee of 2000, the more specific objectives proposed in the restoration plan drawn up by the Department for the Environmental and Architectural Properties of Lazio[8] for Convento di Palazzolo aimed to face the physical structural decline and attempt a formal recovery of the image of Palazzolo. The poor state of preservation of some parts of the complex, besides constituting a risk to the very preservation of the building, distorted the appreciation of its aesthetic qualities. Even if the solution to technical problems was unable to exhaust the vision behind the restoration, nevertheless it contributed in a substantial way to the definition of the choices made, just as the degenerative processes of the materials used in the work had, in their own way, contributed in time to a progressive modification of the picture of Palazzolo itself. It is enough, for example, to think of the imposing wall lying romantically in ruins in the dense vegeta-

[5] From the time of its construction by Cardinal Girolamo, the Villa and its territory had belonged to the Colonna family. In 1922 it was sold for 85,000 lire to the Venerable English College by Donna Vittoria Colonna, a Sforza-Cesarini widow (Deed No. 17988, drawn up on 4 July 1922 by the notary Girolamo Buttaoni); after various offers from Guido De Cupis, the Rector, Arthur Hinsley, requested and obtained permission (15 July 1924) from the Sacred Congregation for Seminaries and University Education to sell the property, on condition that the proceeds be used for the restoration of Convento di Palazzolo. V.E.C., *Palazzola*, 97. 4.

[6] In this context, it is symptomatic to point out that until today these murals were believed to be contemporary with the building of the Villa, and, therefore, were a precious iconographic witness to the order of Palazzolo in the 17th century. The possibility of seeing the paintings and archival documents sheds light on the dates of these, placing them in the 1930s restoration.

[7] V.E.C., *Palazzola*, 97. 5.

[8] The work on Convento di Palazzolo benefitted from two seperate fundings under Law n. 651/1996 "Jubilee 2000". The general Project, which I drew up with geometer Danilo Mattei and the collaboration of architect Marco Dolce, was divided into two executive lots, apportioned to the two specific fundings.

tion, which, obviously, posed the question of what image it should be restored to, in a context where the changes which took place slowly over the centuries, and the re-appropriation by natural materials, compared to artificial ones, represent a constant reality.

The identification of what was the original *facies* at Palazzolo was not a matter of simply consulting a manual; from the year 1000, layers of history have built up over the primitive settlement, often adding, sometimes eliminating, sometimes modifying, culminating with Fonseca's great eighteenth-century restoration[9]. Not only do the last major additions date back to this era, but Fonseca's restoration was also the last redefinition of the formal and stylistic characteristics of the complex. Up until then it was still substantially Cistercian; but from that time it assumed baroque connotations.

The work of the high-ranking Portuguese prelate represents the height of splendour in Palazzolo's history. Only a few decades later, with the establishment of the Roman Republic, as has already been said, damage and plundering diminished the structure. In part abandoned, it became a refuge for fugitives. It was the start of a decline which, through the confused events that followed, was to see the estate pass through private hands before being bought, in 1920, by the Venerable English College, which fortunately preserved its historic use.

In the years immediately preceding the acquistion by the English College, Palazzolo had been taken over by Carlo Arnaldi, that curious doctor and self-defined "hygienist". He restructured the place in order to adapt it to its new role as a 'Nursing Home'. The work from 1916 to 1919, by the firm of Luigi Santangeli, following plans by the architect Raimondo Angeletti, merits a mention since the relevant documentation, besides providing useful information on the state of Palazzolo at the time, also allows us to date correctly some restorations and modifications that were thought to have been subsequently undertaken by the English College[10]. It was under Arnaldi, in fact, that the arches in the cloister, filled in in the nineteenth-century, were re-opened, and the architectural mouldings of the pillars reconstructed (fig. 103); on this occasion, too, the marble lavabo situated "in the room under the stairs near the kitchen door" was moved and remounted on the façade of the Priory facing the garden, with the substitution of one piece (fig. 90); again, the two side altars of the church, still visible in the plan drawn up for the Portuguese by Salustri about forty years earlier (fig. 120), were deconsecrated, removed and sold to the Convent at Rocca di Papa. The massive wall supporting the garden[11] was strengthened and, following the plan of Ing. Beretta, provision was made to move the mule track that led to Palazzolo[12]. A few years later De Cupis made this suitable for vehicles as far as the little square in front of the Priory. This released his property from the right of way constituted by the seventeenth-century stairway that linked the Villa and the Priory[13].

Subsequent years also saw the obliteration of Navone's architectural layout of the church as part of the 1730 restoration, in particular the façade and the church bell-towers (figs. 121-123). Other small extensions, such as the construction of a chapel for use by the seminary students, are also attributable to this period.

---

[9] The historical notes treated here are merely functional to the themes of the planning choices made in the restoration of Palazzolo; the historical events which affected Palazzolo are amply covered in Chapter III.

[10] V.E.C. "Palazzola" File, Scr. 97. 1, 1. C, "*Misure di apprezzamento dei lavori da muratore eseguiti dal Signor Luigi Santangeli nella villa di Palazzola presso Rocca di Papa – a termini della lettera 12 febbraio 1916*".

[11] Ibid., "*IIo Misura ed apprezzamento dei lavori di muratura eseguiti da Luigi Santangeli presso Palazzola per le riprese del muraglione di sostegno a termini della lettera del 14 settembre 1916*".

[12] Cf. *Deliberazione del Consiglio Comunale di Rocca di Papa n. 49 del 17. 06. 1915*, V.E.C., "Palazzola" File, Scr. 97. 1, 1. A.

[13] Right from his first letters to the then Rector of the Venerable English College, Mgr. Hinsley, De Cupis, as prospective buyer, offered to build for Palazzolo, at his own expense, a new, convenient entrance suitable for vehicles, to restore the belevedere with cypresses and to build a new stairway for pedestrian access, which, obviously, came from the old and awkward stairway. V.E.C., *Palazzola*, 97. 4.

121. Plan of the present-day house: ground floor (V. E. C., Relief by M. Silvestri, 1998).

122. Plan of the present-day house: first floor (V. E. C., Relief by M. Silvestri, 1998).

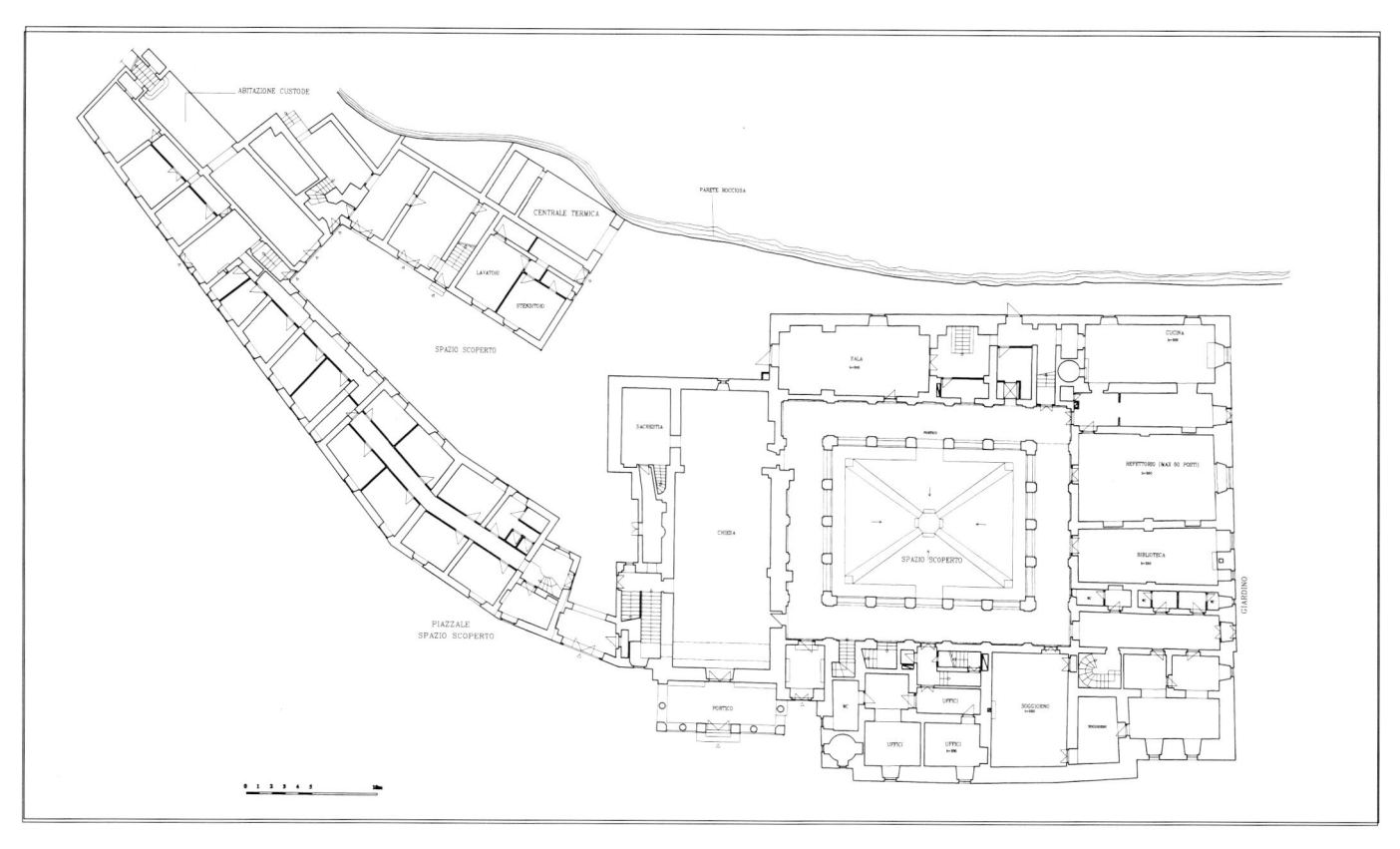

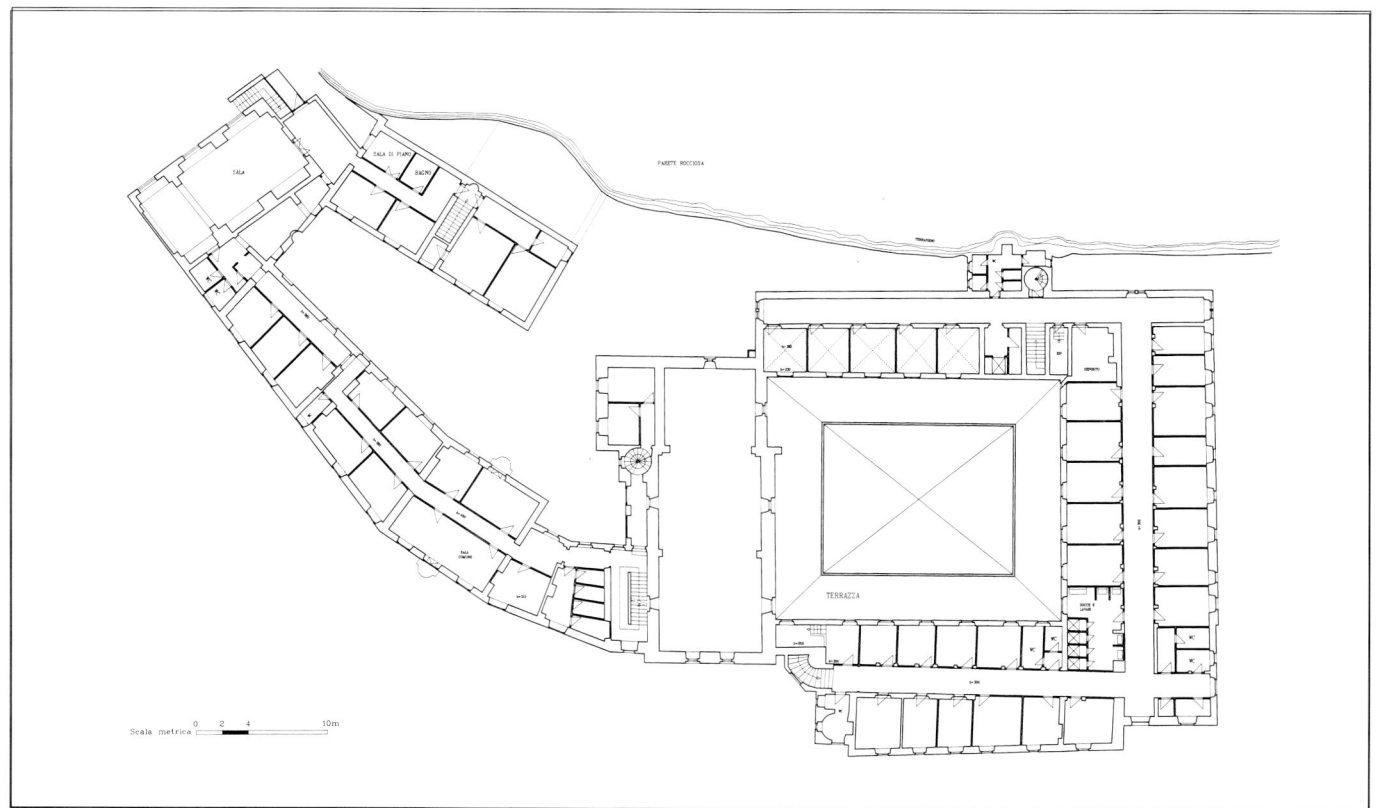

123. Plan of the present-day house: mezzanine (V. E. C., Relief by M. Silvestri, 1998).

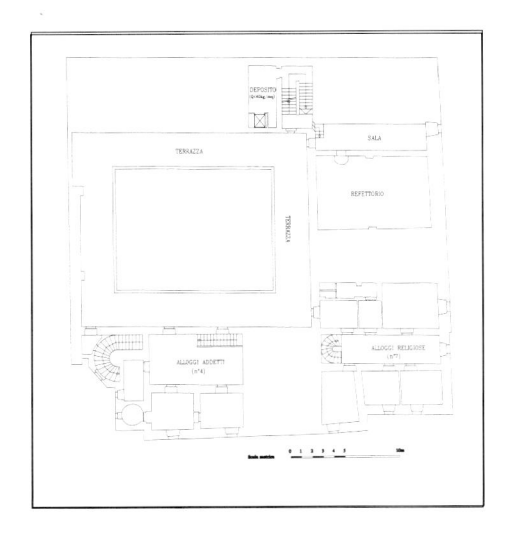

[14] The use of whitewash to imitate travertine on the peperino of the Alban Hills is a characteristic which is found again and again, above all in 17th and 18th century monuments. Such use begins to decline at the end of the 19th century, an era which also saw a re-evaluation of the natural appearance of the material and the realisation of works in *lapis veliternum* (the façade of the Crocefisso at Rocca di Papa, the façade of the small temple of Acqua Santa at Marino, etc.). With such a change in taste, in the 20th century thought was rarely given to restoring the whitewash on the stone, so that many stone monuments have come down to us deprived of colour imitating travertine. Their re-appearance, even in the presence of clear traces on the monument and incontrovertible historical documents, is not widely appreciated by the local populace, by now strangers to a practice which was effectively a reduction in the value of the local stone.

If the devastating twentieth-century restorations had not been carried out, it might have been reasonably possible, in the midst of the eighteenth-century order conferred on Palazzolo by Fonseca, to identify the focal constructive phase on which to base the Jubilee restoration. In fact, even though those restorations were largely a matter of restructuring what was there, this project represents the latest and most coherent attempt at a functional and formal ordering of Palazzolo. This is due to the homogeneous character and clear underlying intention aimed at giving the whole building a new shape and a typological and aesthetic interpretation. But the serious alterations carried out on the baroque restoration, particularly on the church, coupled with the losses suffered from the last years of the nineteenth century onwards, made every attempt to refer back to this phase misleading.

Carefully analysing the content of the eighteenth-century work, and excluding the new construction built especially for the use of guests, there is a sense of a superstructure, almost a type of *maquillage* planned to re-adorn the pre-existing structures; this is particularly clear in the arrangement of the great supporting wall of the terrace garden. In effect, it was a completion and revision of the preceding structure, an example where such a completion is really put into effect, seen in the system of slits for water drainage in the garden. In fact, inserted in quadruple rows in the retaining wall, they performed a purely visual role, for the great majority of them were 'blind', since the masonry buttonholes ended in an older wall lying behind.

Another *escamotage* of which there are faint traces is the general use of whitewash on local stone to imitate travertine. It was widely used in the course of the eighteenth-century work, and probably introduced in the seventeenth. The Cistercian complex on top of the pre-existing Roman remains could not be restored to a dignified baroque aspect without work on the peperino appearance abundant at Palazzolo; nor could one imagine any other system to bring about and unite the different decorative elements introduced in the eighteenth-century (coats of arms, cornices and facings) and the previous appearance of the building[14]. This light covering, to which much of the final result was due, must have been one of the first elements to deteriorate; from the documents that have come down to us, it is hypothetical that after just a few years the grey peperino was showing again; but times changed and no-one was concerned any longer about fighting the natural process of colours fading in order to protect an aesthetic requirement motivated by links to specific historical circumstances.

In this specific case I decided, as planner, to consider Palazzolo's appearance today as an indisputable fact, with all the losses, changes and alterations that have happened. Beyond considerations of whatever might be possible, or the right and proper chronological interpretations, I limited myself to recovering the elements believed to be essential and characteristic of the development of the work, both in as much as they kept to the logical planning that had produced them and that they had to do with the formal capacity with which they had been conceived and accomplished.

The parts which were most affected by the alterations due to the ancient nature of Palazzolo were obviously all those which constituted the interface with the outside: the façades, the roofing, the external layout; those very same structures where there was a lack of maintenance and which, considered in relation to the risk of loss and analysed in terms of cost-effectiveness, offered the best results in terms of resources and public interest. Furthermore, the positive and greater effect on the surrounding countryside of the restoration of the walls and façades, the terrace garden and, above all, its long retaining wall, seemed undeniable. It was a work extending into the surrounding natural and almost autonomous context of the Priory, in its merit as a wall of the ancient path that led to Albano; it was also necessary to salvage the significance and form of the garden, the old conventual garden ennobled by Fonseca's eighteenth-century restoration which had gradually degenerated into a multi-purpose area, where the most varied means of supporting the house, from the cultivation of vegetables to the deposit of various materials, lived happily side by side with the traces of the past.

The decision to work on external parts of the complex also allowed for an increase in the potential beneficiaries, from the restricted circle of frequent visitors to Palazzolo to a wider range of residents and tourists, whose presence in the area is a response to a wider sphere of interests, deriving both from the natural context, which has already been mentioned, and the proximity to the Papal residence.

The work

Within the general frame of reference four areas of work were identified[15]:

— the Priory façades;
— the roof of the church;
— the supporting wall;
— the terrace garden.

The work was preceded by historical research and a large survey of the estate. The research in particular, essentially of an archivistic nature, led to a deeper knowledge about Palazzolo, and also opened interesting insights into certain situations, personalities and monuments linked in some way to the place; the updating of available data, the unpublished documents that emerged, together with the rich pictorial evidence, form a truly independent result of the completed restoration. This book offers that research to experts to carry out further examinations and explore links[16].

The survey of the parts of the estate to be restored was integrated during the course of the work with the data from the site itself, as in the case of traces of ancient openings which emerged from under the plaster on the lake-side façade of the Priory. Surveys of a more specialist type were then carried out for specific areas such as the garden, where elements of vegetation were revealed, sampled and restored in a graphic representation[17].

[15] The work, directed by the author, with the collaboration of the surveyor Danilo Mattei and architect Marco Dolce, began in the summer of 1998, with the aim of finishing by November 1999. The firms responsible were: Archires S.r.l. (church roofs and restoration of the façades); Giuliano Roversi (restoration of the wall and terrace garden); Professional Green S.r.l. (restoration of the greenery); Security: architect Maria Luisa Del Giudice.

[16] The historical research was under the direction of Dott. Alberto Crielesi, author of various theses on the subject and who in this book publishes the results in Chapter III. Despite the scarce fame of Palazzolo today, perhaps also due to its secluded position, the archives of the religious Orders it belonged to contain numerous valuable documents despite being scattered over time. Analysis of the original sources, especially some manuscripts and various inventories which have come to light, some furnished with maps, allowed the reliable reconstruction of the historical and artistic history of Palazzolo; cf. *Archival and documentary sources* and *General Bibliography*.

[17] The survey of Palazzolo and the on-site graphic-documentary assistance were carried out by architect Marco Silvestri (ARCHIMIA Studio); all the documentation was rendered graphically with the information-technology support system AUTOCAD.

124. The roofs of the church and choir at the back affected by the restoration.

Besides the research stage outlined above, the usual series of checks and tests were carried out during the course of the work, with the aim of getting to know more about specific aspects: from stratigraphic tests of the plaster aimed at verifying the presence of old colours, to targeted borings to check the state of the masonry; from inspection of the spaces between the Roman supports on which the garden was built, to the final excavations looking for traces of the original water system in the garden.

More detailed studies were then carried out in relation to the individual areas that required specific specialisations, such as the botanic study with the appropriate plant health analysis of the substances in the garden[18] or the gnomic checks on the sundial on the south-east façade of the Priory, which was restored[19].

The roofing

This work concentrated on the church roof (figs. 124-125). The roof was directly placed on the pointed vault and the removal of the old roof made it possible to check the height to which the pointed vault was filled in. An interesting detail to emerge was a plugged opening in the tower next to the church itself, linked to the top of the roof by a flight of steps, perhaps intended for maintenance purposes (fig. 126); even if the overlapping of the side of the roof at the opening of the tower seems to suggest an addition to the church which partially obscured the lancet window, the correspondence between the height of the impost of this opening and that of the roof, the perfectly-centred staircase corresponding to the little door and the interruption of the marble dripstone which functioned as a gutter be-

[18] For the project on the flora component in the garden, assistance was provided by Dott. For. Giampietro Cantiani who, besides carrying out the sampling and the health analysis of the flora, also provided technical indications on the necessary future treatment.

[19] The tests were carried out by Ing. Lucio Baruffi who presents the results in Chapter V of this book.

125. Work on the roof of the church nearing completion.

126. Church roof: detail of the stairway discovered in the filling in of the vault.

127. Church roof: detail of the connection between the stairway and an ancient opening in the tower.

128. Back wall of the nave, with the restored marble cornice.

THE RESTORATION 143

129. The church with the adjacent guest quarters.

tween the slope of the roof and the wall of the tower, indicate that this passage had a valid functional purpose (fig. 127).

Of particular importance are the church's stone cornices, made of solid white marble, with smooth edges and bush-hammered caissons. On the rear façade of the nave a large part of this stone moulding was lost, and badly replaced with mortar wedges; with the remaining blocks strengthened, the missing part was restored using original materials and techniques. A block of marble compatible with the original was chosen, and twelve pieces were cut, worked, and put in place, thus restoring the missing piece of moulding (fig. 128).

Restoration of the façades

The restoration project looked at the façades in the oldest part of the Priory, those pre-dating the eighteenth-century additions; the façade of the guest-house had recently been painted by the owners (figs. 117-118).

The work consisted in a general overhaul of the plaster which had undergone much general reconstruction. Due to the state of decline of the materials and their extensive detachment from the supporting masonry, it was decided not to simply strengthen it. The mediocre quality masonry itself was at an advanced level of decay due, not only to the predictable impoverishment of the mortar, but also to the layers of the successive work done over time. Underneath the plaster, there was an overlapping system of openings with the consequent plugging of old windows which, at times, gave rise to breaks in the masonry itself[20].

Having considered the general construction of the masonry, reinforced strengthening was avoided because of the clear difference in flexibility between the metal and the actual materials there. Strengthening risked worsening the overall response of the structures because

[20] Important changes in the system of openings came to light above all in the southern façade of the Priory, which down the centuries had been subject to successive extensions; the stone moulding interrupted at the height of the second floor, corresponding to the windows, is visible evidence of this.

144 CHAPTER IV

130. West façade of the Priory: strengthening the wall by the 'pick-and-dip' method.

131. Preparing the mesh for the re-plastering.

132. Part of the documentary survey of the peperino architraves to be replaced.

of the differentiation in performance of the materials concerned. The result would be certain damage to the masonry of uncertain origin. Where prominent cracked caissons came to light, as, for example, in the corners of the building or in the upper floors, where there was serious decline combined with the considerable reduction of the supporting section, work focussed on restoring the wall and strengthening in specific areas. The aim was to restore some compactness and continuity to the masonry as a whole, using traditional materials and techniques or those at least compatible with the existing structures, proceeding with restoration and 'pick-and-dip' rebuilding, using whole bricks for the most serious cracks (figs. 130-131). Metal was used in the restoration only once: in the windows of the highest floors, where for the most part there were cracks in the architraves. It was not just

THE RESTORATION 145

133. Detail of the peperino ashlar which make up the oldest facings.

a matter of replacing the solid peperino blocks they were made of, as it was also necessary to reduce the weight of the overhanging wall, putting the supporting role onto metal joists inserted into the appropriately restored wall (figs. 132-134).

As regards the restoration of the architectural and decorative elements present, string courses, facings, mouldings and coats of arms, affected by micro-biological attacks and the general phenomenon of layers peeling away, progress was made using methods of stone restoration according to the cycle of biocidal treatment and preventive strengthening, cleaning by various methods depending on the nature and toughness of the deposits, plastering of the gaps and treatment of the plastering of the joints, and final protective application. Taking into account the physical and mechanical characteristics of the peperino (*lapis albanus*) and its state of preservation, the standard cycle of cleaning and strengthening, just like the level of restoration and the choice of materials for it, was calculated according to the various areas of work and the function of the object being restored. For example, in the case of the ashlars with a structural function, if their state of decline meant they could no longer guarantee maintaining such a function, it was decided, except in very limited cases, to go ahead with the replace-

134. Crack in the keystone of one of the stone arches on the second floor.

ment of the piece with similar material. In all other cases strengthening and micro-strengthening work was carried out using fibreglass pivots, micro-injections of microlite and applications of ethyl silicate via absoprtion (figs. 135-141).

However much the state of preservation and the advanced decline called for technical solutions gauged according to need, as often happens the problems on this project which needed unravelling did not stem from technical problems but ones of a more formal nature. As mentioned above, tests carried out on the stone showed the presence of whitewash imitating travertine on some window and door facings (fig. 142); this distempering must also have been carried out on the great peperino convex moulding which runs lengthways along the lakeside façade, since, under a layer of plaster relating to successive interventions, the same treatment came to light in a short section (fig. 143). The whitewash attributable to the eighteenth-century work was never restored and repeated, judging at least from the scarcity of the traces found, even if the microclimactic conditions present tended to accelerate the fading process of the paint. On the other hand, the same painting, almost completely disappeared, was perfectly visible in some work carried out in the second half of the nineteenth century, according

135. Marble moulding belonging to the cornice of the front façade of the church; the advanced state of decay is evident.

136. West façade of the Priory: micro-consolidation of the peperino corbels of the little balconies.

137. Marble cornice of the church: strengthening with fibreglass pivots.

138. Reconstruction of a stone cornice: framework for the mortar.

139. Reconstruction of a cornice in reinforced mortar nearing completion, before the layer of superficial finishing touches.

140. Peperino cornice in the choir: mortar reconstruction of some gaps.

141. The same cornice completed.

142. Traces of whitewash on a peperino facing on the south face.

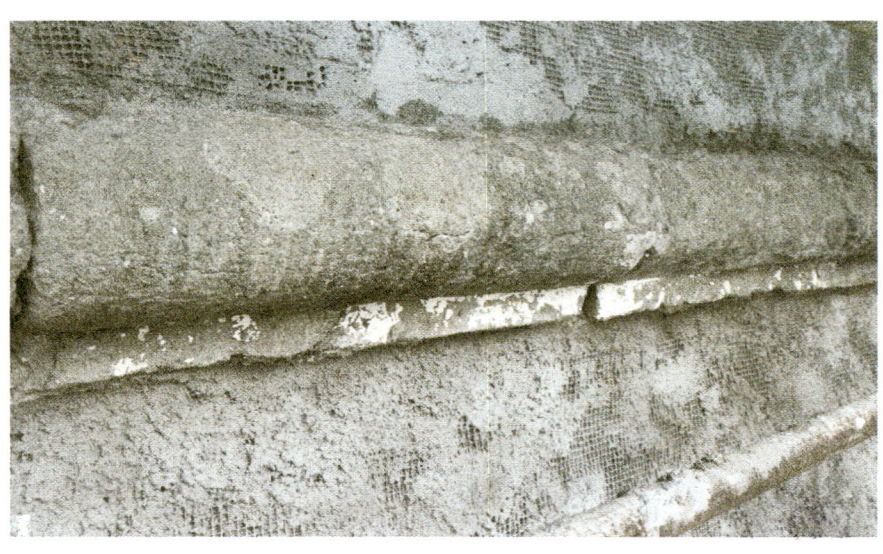

143. East face: traces of whitewash discovered beneath the plaster on the lower dentil peperino moulding.

146. Detail of the building adjacent to the church after restoration.

147. Façades after the completion of the restoration: the façade of the Priory looking towards the lake and overlooking the path.

144. The date '1863' carved on one of the arches on the second floor of the Priory.

145. Fragment of coloured plaster discovered in the back wall of the choir, in the highest part and largely protected by the cornice.

150 CHAPTER IV

to the date "1863" carved by unknown workers at the time (fig. 144); therefore, if desired it would have been easy at that time to take steps to re-paint the existing window facings, too. Instead, there is no trace of it at all.

The loss of the whitewash on the stone, just like on the plaster on the containing wall of the garden, gradually and progressively allowed the building material, the peperino, to regain its colour. From the point of view of colour, it again merged into the surrounding environment, the high cut of the rock and the caves, from which the stone was taken to build the Priory. This sort of "re-appropriation" by nature, when compared to the material and colours of the architecture, led me to evaluate very carefully the practicality of restoring the eighteenth-century aspect of the complex, to which were certainly attributable both the whitewash imitating travertine and the small traces of "sky-colouring" found in one place on the south façade of the building[21]. Furthermore, I had to consider whether the eighteenth-century order intended by Fonseca, with many of the baroque artefacts lost, could be revived with any certainty simply from the chromatic make-up of the finish on the façades; and further, whether the appearance acquired by the eighteenth-century work was meant to be preserved for no more than twenty or thirty years, in view of the difficult environmental conditions and the unexpected management problems that arose. These have always been present throughout Palazzolo's history, as the historic documents show in such an unmistakable manner.

Such considerations, together with an awareness of the short-lived nature of a whitewash produced using traditional methods in an environmental context such as that of Palazzolo, convinced me of the inappropriateness of restoring the eighteenth-century colours. By now they were no longer part of the original context, and, in any case, related to only one of the building phases at Palazzolo, which, for reasons outlined above, was not meant to be favoured at the expense of others.

Therefore, the stone was restored by ensuring it could be seen in the condition it was in at the start of the project. Provision was made simply for reconstructing its mechanical and design characteristics, following the working procedures already mentioned. With regard to colour, it was decided to use a colour-tone close to that present elsewhere at Palazzolo, further confirmed by traces of old painted plaster which came to light beneath the great moulding of the apsidal wall of the church (figs. 145-153).

Restoration of the garden wall

To a lesser extent, the same problems affected the containing wall of the terrace garden, the perfect offshoot of the south façade to which it was stylistically linked simply by a stone moulding, the only architectural element common to the façade of the Priory and this high wall.

Distinguished by a lakeside façade 108 metres long and of vary-

---

[21] A unique trace of just a few square centimetres of a colour came to light about a metre underneath the roof overhang of the façade facing the lake. Even though it had changed over time it could be explained as "sky-colouring". However, the heavy decline of the plaster on the two particularly exposed restored façades caused the almost total loss of the colours which, in other more sheltered areas of the complex, such as the cloister, showed a colour gradation of shades of ochre and yellow. Scarce traces of ancient plaster were also discovered on the apsidal wall of the church but there was no confirmation of the presence of "sky-colouring".

[22] "*Nel muraglione grande dell'Orto di 500 palmi di lunghezza, e 100 di altezza*", Cf. A.P.A., *Nota e Resumo delle spese e fabbriche insigni fatte e dirette dal R. mo P. Fr. Giuseppe Maria de Fonseca d'Evora*, ms., fasc. 1-35 n. 12. 1873.

148. The southern façade of the Priory, overlooking the garden, before restoration.

149. The garden façade after restoration.

150. Garden façade before restoration: detail of the right-hand door with inscriptions.

151. Detail of fig. 150 after restoration.

152. Garden façade after restoration: detail of the inscription concerning the 1730 restorations.

153. Garden façade after restoration: detail of one of the stone tablets on the façade.

ing height, depending on the course of the path - the old and important route to the Capuchin Priory at Albano - which skirts it[22], the wall was in a most advanced state of decline (figs. 154-156). Originally plastered, the ravages of time and the effects of the micro-climate had by now eaten into the supporting structure. The mortar was deeply eroded, leaving the ashlars themsleves with no support between them. Some jutted out in full-relief, partly already lost or in a state of collapse (figs. 157-158).

However, the restoration of the plaster, clearly necessary both from a technological-maintenance and philological point of view, posed an undeniable problem of abrupt change to the image that had been built up over decades, a period which, even if brief in the history of restoration, is appreciated with some sensitivity by the perception of at least two or three generations of visitors to Palazzolo. These visitors are used to the romantic and somewhat decadent im-

THE RESTORATION 153

154. The great, long supporting-wall of the terrace garden, as it looked before the start of work.

155. The rampart: detail showing the decay caused by the loss of the plaster.

156. South side of the wall: only the end stretch had preserved any plaster from a restoration.

157. West side of the rampart, marked by deep erosion of the mortar.

158. West side of the rampart: detail of the stone cornice.

154 CHAPTER IV

159. View of the final stretch of the containing wall, south face.

160. Re-plastering: trying out examples.

161. West side of the wall on completion of the work.

THE RESTORATION 155

162. The drafting of the plaster highlighted the slit pattern, arranged in four lines and alternating between them.

163. South side of the wall following restoration.

164. The restored wall as seen in a panoramic view from a distance.

156 CHAPTER IV

165. Corner monument on the wall before restoration.

166. The same after restoration.

167. Corner monument: detail of the coat of arms with tablet recalling the work of Fonseca, after restoration.

168. South side of the wall: detail of the garden boundary wall.

169. Coat of arms on the south side after restoration.

170. Coat of arms on the west side after restoration.

THE RESTORATION 157

171. Recovery work on the ancient slits.   *172. Restoration with bush-hammered peperino.*

173. Restoration of gaps in the peperino cornice.

age of the great stone garden wall, which penetrates deeply into the forest, decaying amongst the luxuriant vegetation which not only surrounds it but which has settled in and feeds on its very mortar[23] (fig. 159).

A type of plaster was therefore sought whose characteristics, from a material and chromatic point of view, were not too different from the stone, thus reducing the visual impact of the long wall plunging into the wood. Work proceeded on the plaster, composed of minute particles of inet material and appropriately sifted colouring (fig. 160), by applying a high transparency protective additive coat with soil, instead of proper painting. The aim was to tone the colour towards a chromatic effect in keeping with the surrounding environment, thus reducing the difference provoked by the sudden change of image as a result of the plastering of the vast surface, leaving an "unfinished" effect (figs. 161-164).

The drafting of the plaster brought to light the system of slits for water drainage from the terrace garden above, which has already been mentioned. The majority of these openings, as has already been said, have no practical function as they are linked only to the thickness of the eighteenth-century support and stop at the brickwork behind, part of the pre-existing wall, perhaps the work of Friar Marziale. However, in their four lines they run the length of the wall, creating a sort of weft which reduces the monotony of the wall. Together with the stone elements such as the long cornice, which has a clear role as a visual point of reference to the changes in height, they constituted the superstructure with which Fonseca wished to ennoble even this purely functional wall.

The constructor's mark was put on the most durable travertine, in the three coats of arms placed one on each side of the wall, and

---

[23] The state of preservation left no doubts about the lack of work done since the 18th century restoration, apart from some strengthening work done on a 17-metre long stretch at the start of the 20th century. This was also confirmed by the absence of any relevant documents about this. But there is no doubt that the retaining wall was plastered: a simple examination of the masonry technique and the traces of rendering present confirm this. They are incompatible with the supporting masonry, as is the insufficient thickness to complete the plan of a peperino convex moulding. Finally, in some 19th century depictions the plaster treatment on the retaining wall is still visible.

the third on a commemorative plaque in the corner looking towards the papal residence at Castel Gandolfo[24] (figs. 165-167).

Fonseca's attention to the "surroundings" calls for a little digression on the landscape merit of the work. This stems from an awareness of the intrinsic interpenetration between architecture and its context and from the habit of using a dimensional scale which passes over the specific object of the work in favour of the landscape. Following on from the work of Friar Marziale in the preceeding century, the restoration of the wall, when evaluated in conjunction with other work of which there are faint traces along the ancient Palazzolo path, seems in reality to be a work of urban re-appraisal, a fully equipped panoramic route, where the succession of architectural and natural elements - the rock tomb, the enclosure wall of the Priory, then the church and the garden wall, the caves and the wood[25] - acts as a border to the landscape element represented by the scene of the lake with the papal villa on the right. To make the walk easier, there was a system of fountains, often adorned with coats of arms recording the author of such generosity; where the dimensions conveyed a certain monotony, as on the garden wall, architectural devices were used to provide variation: the system of slits, the coats of arms on the corner, the sheer profile of the wall at the entrance to the Priory garden, clearly visible from the outside thanks to the triangle of masonry which, ending in spiral curves and lightened by two windows, still provides a frame for a coat of arms (fig. 168).

Almost submerged by the luxuriant vegetation, the three coats of arms on the garden wall were restored[26] (figs. 167-170). They were in varying states of preservation, or, as in the case of the coat of arms on the corner of the garden wall, of considerable decline. There were deep, small cavities and gaps inside which vegetation had taken root, with the result that over time some pieces of stone had fallen. The walls were particularly susceptible to microbiological attacks, especially in the upper parts. The restoration was done using biocidal compresses, the cleaning with amonium carbonate compresses, and the finish with micro-sandblasting and aluminium oxide at 120 Mesh. The widespread microcapillarity of the stone suggested that it would be advisable to strengthen it using ethyl silicate and, when the work was complete, with the drafting of a final protective coat[27].

As regards the drainage slits, steps were taken to recover all the original pieces and to restore those missing using similar material, treating the surface with granulation. For the long moulding it was a matter of restoring both with solid peperino and mortar, depending on the size of the gaps (figs. 171-173).

The garden

The garden, an eighteenth-century transformation of the pre-existing gardens, is part of a vast terrace with a supporting wall referred to in some detail above (figs. 174-175).

It is a simple rectangle, squeezed between the drop in height towards the lake and the cut in the rock out of which this space was

[24] Besides the three coats of arms on the wall and those placed in the Priory by Fonseca, there is a fourth which adorned a fountain located in the boundary wall leading to the Priory, on the path going down to the lake. Only the masonry framework of the fountain remains, situated in the lay-by level with the Roman tomb; even if it is in a very ruined state, the little coat of arms is preserved (fig. 111).

[25] Just as in the case of the Priory, it was a matter of re-appraisal and embellishment of existing work. The path, an ancient Roman route, was completely re-done in the course of the previous century, in connection with the exploitation of this area due to Urban VIII's accession to the papal throne. The tradition of a papal presence in Castel Gandolfo is due to him. In a letter dated 27 April 1662, Archbishop Egidio, writing to his brother the Cardinal on the occasion of a recent visit to the Villa by Alexander VII, stated: *"The Pope, the same day he came, after eating went out to see the new stairs built above the new road close to the church"*. A.C., II, A. 19, n. 4.

[26] The restoration of the coats of arms and the memorial tablets on the wall was carried out by Giovanna Mangia Bonella under the remit of the work entrusted to the Roveri Company. She was also responsible for the restoration of the stone of the garden fountain.

[27] The final protective coat used 290 Wacker in white spirit, in a proportion of 1 to 2; the biocide used was Preventol; the strengthening used a bi-component resin Epoj CTS filled with pozzolana, and then with superventilated pozzolana and hydraulic lime Lafarge and travertine dust.

174. The containing wall during the restoration work – view from above.

175. The same visual perspective following restoration.

hewn in ancient times. The garden measures 108 by 34 linear metres, an almost perfect ratio of 1:3 between the two sides. The design is characterised by two principle pathways running parallel to the longer side and intersected by perpendicular little avenues, sub-dividing the space into six grassy *parterres* surrounded by box-hedges (figs. 176-178); the end is laid out with a little formal garden made more attractive by a deep fountain with a mixed design of straight and curved lines at the centre, positioned in relation to the virtual pivotal point of the path. It is exactly in the sight-line of not just the meridian axis of the garden, but also with the entrance gate visually framing the large cave which is the real backdrop to the scene (fig. 179).

The charm arising from having attached such a suggestive natural element to the layout of optical cross-references which characterise all the views of the garden was lost not just with the sudden fall of a rock close to the mouth of the cave some decades ago, but above all by building the swimming-pool and changing rooms precisely on the "fountain-cave" axis (figs. 180-182). It is worth noting how the very design of the fountain, in particular the central element which arises out of the fish pond, simulating a rocky spur onto which vegetation has been grafted, maintains a strong link to the "natural" aspect.

Despite such a simple layout, the use of some of the large flower beds for cultivation, the lack of maintenance of the greenery, particularly the box-hedges, and the grafting of extraneous vegetation and improper use of the beds hindered immediate understanding of the constituent plan (figs. 183-184). Aside from recovering the form and safeguarding the physical integrity of the architectural material and flora present, the principal object of the restoration was really to restore and appreciate the formal origin underlying this garden.

The re-reading of the foundation plan was furthered by the adoption of planning devices such as the paving of the little avenues and the opening of service passages in the hedges which border the *parterres*, in precise relation to the visual axes (fig. 185). Effectively, this allowed a re-interpretation, in its widest possible sense, of the structural paths, highlighting their culmination in the doors which give access from the Priory to the garden at the north, and, at the other end, in stone seats inserted into the parapet (figs. 186-191). In relation to these latter, two visual elements were also introduced: two pairs of cypresses which, flanking the seats, enhance the visual boundary. In fact, one of the two seats consistent with the plan was still there. Once this master plan had been realised, it was inevitable that at the end of one of the two lengthways axes of the garden, the back of the second seat would be found beneath the plaster. Hence it was possible to restore its functional and formal role, replacing the lost parts by rebuilding the stone seat, following the example preserved there (fig. 192).

The "door-seat" design is also borne out by the principal horizontal axis to the two lengthways avenues, framed by a double line of *laurus nobilis*. The first of these little avenues, nearest the Priory, has part of the original paving and some ancient fragments walled in the containing parapets of the laurel flower beds (figs. 193-195).

Just as at the Villa Colonna above, it is probable that at least some of these fragments were re-used in the early part of the twentieth cen-

176. The garden before restoration.

177. The garden after the work.

THE RESTORATION 161

178. Marco Silvestri. The garden of Convento di Palazzolo, 1999; hand-painted watercolour plan (Soprintendenza Beni Ambientali e Architettonici del Lazio).

162 Chapter IV

179. The restored fountain in the garden.

180. Visual axis from the garden fountain looking towards the cave. Today, the view is hidden by the man-made changing-rooms for the swimming pool.

181. View from the swimming pool towards the garden; in the background, the high wall which fixes the entrance boundary.

THE RESTORATION 163

Agosto 1639

Indice della presente Pianta

A. Forma Antica de Romani, che porta li scoli della Montagna al Fontanile solo in quatro Mesi dell'Anno, quando più, quando meno

B. Altro Braccio di Forma, che non porta Acqua, e di doue i Padri sperano portar una porzione sperduta, non solo in d.º Fontanile, ma alla lor Peschiera

C. Fontanile nel terreno del Conuento, che riceue l'acqua della Forma A, e che riceuerà quella anche della forma B, quando sarà unita, e doue circa 30 anni fà à pena messa rispe. in un angolo è sopra lo scolo già leuata, e alle quanti restorono capaci i S.ri Barbarini

DD. Nouo Condotto di piombo p. portar l'acqua noua nella Peschiera della forma B

E. Peschiera fatta di nuouo nel terreno de PP.

F.F. Condotto, che dal Fontanile C porta l'acqua al Bottino Barbarini accomodato ora da PP.

G. Bottino Barbarini chiamato il Centauro doue Sono contornati l'Assi, come in tutti l'altri Bottini, e ciò de Consenso de PP.

H. Nuouo Fontanile che fanno i PP. fuori della Clausura p. Comodo di Passaggieri

I. Forma che porta l'acqua alla villa Colonna, e al Conuento di d.i PP.

L. Bottino della villa Sud.ª

M. Vascone dello scolo di d.º Bottino

N. Nuouo Condotto di questo Bottino alla Peschiera E

O. Orto del Conuento

P. Giardino d'Agrumi

Q. Grottoni del Conuento, che ora s'includono nella Clausura

R.R. Muro della Clausura, che Serra e gira l'Orto e Giardino

S. Nuouo Portone in f.ª la Strada d'Albano, e dirimpetto al Fontanile

T. Portone che diuide l'Orto dal Giardino

V.V. Muro della villa Colonna che la separa dal Conuento e suoi Orti

X. Segno fin doue è arriuato il Muro nouo che à da diuidere il Giardino e Fontanile

Y. Condotto che porta il ritorno della Peschiera al Fontanile H, e d. la al Bottino e Condotti Barbarini

Z. Dimostraz.ne del Fontanile con le due Bocche di ritorno, una delle quali sup.riori contrasegnata n.º 2 p. Seruigio del Conuento, e l'altra inferiore contradistinta col n.ª 1 che porta lo scolo al Condotto Barbarini, e sopra del quale appunto vi era anchinato un Asse

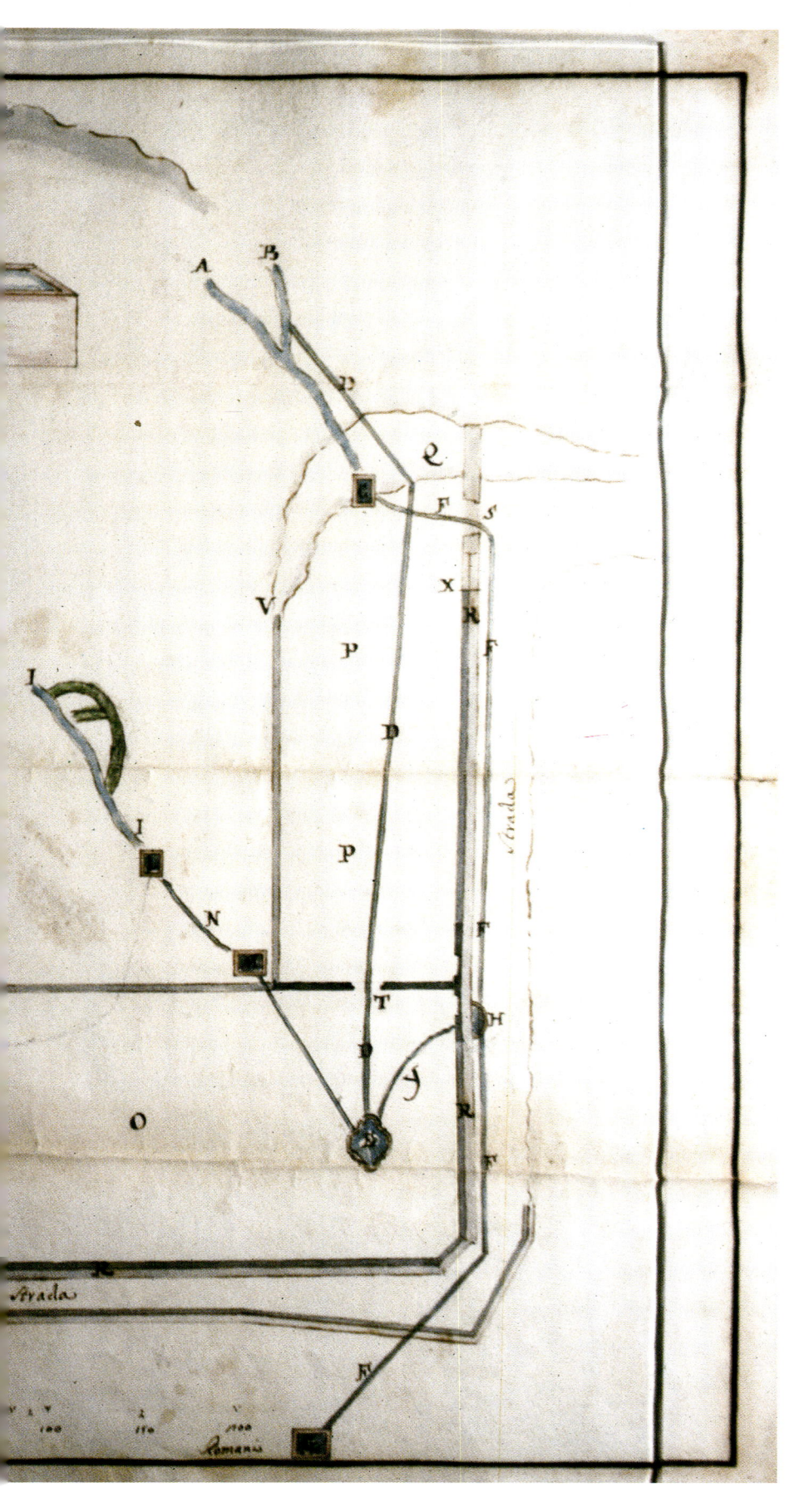

182. GIANDOMENICO NAVONE, 1739; the map shows the water system intercepting the springs which supplied, among other things, both the Navone fountain and a little fountain situated on the path, for use of passers-by (Rome, S. Francesco a Ripa Archives).

THE RESTORATION 165

183. General view of the garden before the work began.

184. The garden before the start of the work.

185. Plan for the work on the garden.

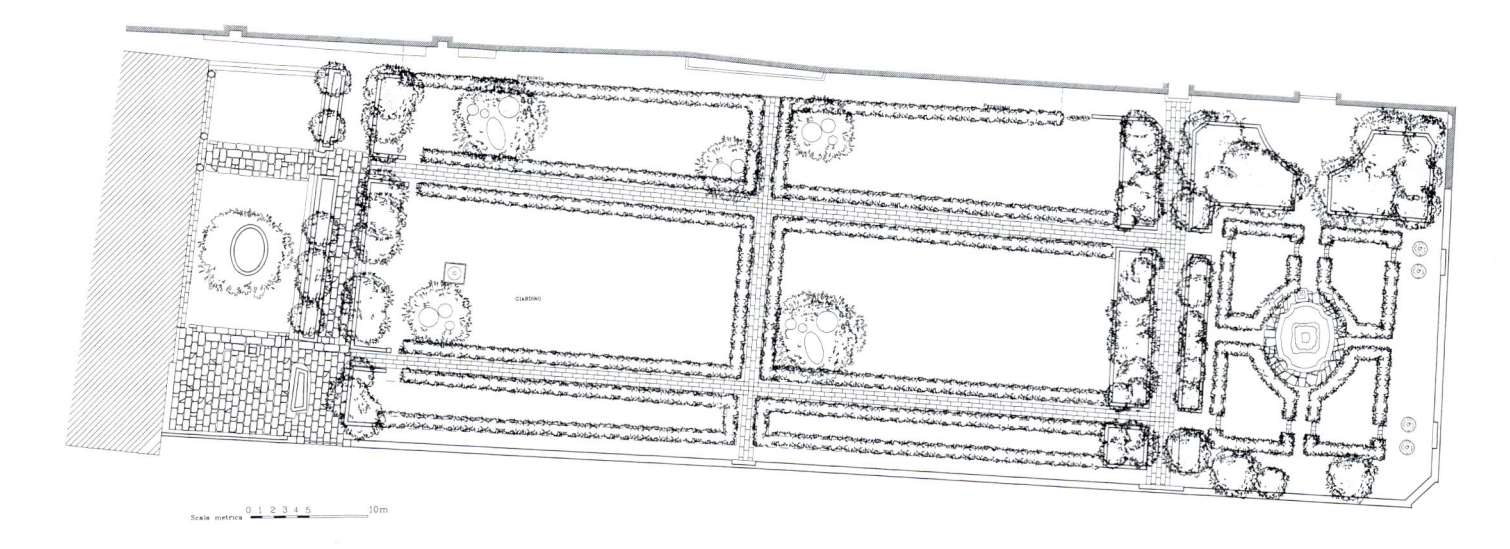

166 CHAPTER IV

186. View along one of the visual axes, ante operam.

187. Garden path after the work.

tury. A certain number of peperino pieces, dating largely from the late seventeenth-century, and some old marble fragments, are in fact still preserved both in what is today the Villa "del Cardinale"[28] and at Convento di Palazzolo. Over the course of time, they were re-used here to make garden seats and in other parts of the complex, or simply abandoned in the middle of the flower beds. At the start of the restoration work, concise cataloguing and a photographic record was made of all the pieces present before they were moved (figs. 196-199).

The great quantity of material, mostly architectural mouldings in full-relief, balustrade fragments, spheres, small columns, trophies and pedestals, must have corresponded to a re-ordering linked to the last decade of the 17th century, of which no documentary evidence remains. The definite attribution to this period of highly-refined stone artefacts such as the two washbasins in the sacristy and in the garden,

[28] Cf. In this publication Chapter II by G. Ghini, referring to the ancient settlement of Palazzolo.

188. External garden path before the work.

189. The same path afterwards.

[29] To the same gate could have belonged the coat of arms with the Colonna emblem preserved at the Villa del Cardinale, re-installed under the sundial on the side of the little tower facing the lake (fig. 220).

[30] A.V.T., D. ANTONIUM SEVEROLUM, *Acta Apostolice, ac Generalis Visitationis Tusculanem episcopatus ac Diocesis (...) anno Domini* 1660, ms. f. 118. The premature demolition of the small columns (1735) and the thickness of the marble justifies in part their almost total disappearance. In the course of time some of them were remounted in the well head in the cloister itself, some in the garden, and, later, some in the large arched windows illuminating the corridors.

dated 1693 (figs. 90-91), and the quantity of fragments that have come to light, one dated 1696, would suggest that important work was carried out in that period, at least from a decorative point of view. Some of these finds come from previous decades, such as the great main gate placed at the entrance to the garden, the work of Friar Marziale, to whom might be attributed the great ashlar making up one of the keystones preserved there[29]. Finally, according to what can be deduced from documentary sources[30], some of the material can be linked to the cloister, initially decorated with marble columns dismantled during work in the eighteenth-century

168 CHAPTER IV

190. Overall view of one of the visual axes; in the foreground are the trophies re-used in the passageways between the hedges.

THE RESTORATION 169

191. Final layout of the bottom of the garden.

192. Reconstruction of the seat nearing completion.

193. Transverse path near to the formal garden, shaded by an avenue of laurels; view looking towards the lake.

194. The same path looking in the opposite direction; just as with the garden's longitudinal axes, the end points are made up of a door and a seat.

195. Transverse path close to the house, with the remains of ancient paving.

THE RESTORATION 171

196. Work in progress in the garden; in the foreground, memorial fragments from various places.
197. Peperino memorial stone bearing an inscription and dated 1696.
198. A little fountain in the garden, re-using a salvaged piece of stone as a base.

[31] A.F.R., (Palazzola File I), "*Inventario del 22 guigno 1810...*": "*Tavolini quattro di peperino con sedili*".

[32] The remains of the table-top shown in the photograph published here can be found re-set in the pavement of the little pathway, not far from the original setting of the table itself.

[33] A.S.A.D.P., fasc. 110, fasc. 106-14, M. SALUSTRI, *Stima dei fondi rustici e fabbricati di proprieta del Governo di Portogallo, posti nel territorio del Comune di Rocca di Papa, Mandamento di Frascati, Provincia di Roma*, Albano Laziale, 29 October 1880: "*Above the pillars of the internal portico of the courtyard tower stand some peperino plinths on which rest spheres of the same stone or remains of the trophies and such like*".

The same fate befell some of Fonseca's work, leaving just some fragmented pieces and stone fragments. This is the case, for example, of the splendid peperino tables installed in the garden, described in the 1810 inventories[31], and of which there remains a precious photograph from the early years of the 20th century (figs. 200-201)[32]. Finally, again from the cloister, there are the remains of some trophies and peperino spheres of which some examples can still be seen. They were perhaps dismantled when the property changed hands in the early part of the 20th century and in the course of the consequent work already mentioned. They were still mentioned by Salustri in the careful assessment carried out for the Portuguese Government in 1880[33].

In the absence of precise dates which would allow hypothetical reconstructions by anastylosis of the stone material abandoned in the Priory garden, and given that the preservation of such material was a primary objective, particularly given that further knowledge may emerge, it was deemed necessary to sort a number of pieces, both for their formal characteristics and their uniqueness, and because of the presence of important elements, such as inscriptions. The pieces of greatest importance were housed inside the Convent.

The less valuable pieces, some of which were present in great numbers, such as, for example, the trophies made up of small parallel-piped mouldings, were inserted into the new layout of the garden, thus continuing the tradition, so often in evidence at Palazzolo, of reusing material. In particular, the cubic trophies were used in relation to the open passages in the hedges along the paths, filling in the cuts made (figs. 190-191). The other pieces were placed near the side service passages of the hedges, or in the transverse path close to the house, an area extensively used and already largely made up of materials from different places (fig. 202).

Having taken the basic decisions, the real work on both the architectural and the botanical aspects of the garden consisted first of all in the preliminary removal of inappropriate elements, such as additional flower beds or recent paving. Next came the restoration work itself on the main stone artefacts, such as the fountain, the coats of arms, the decorative elements, the stone benches and the stone cov-

199. Stone fragments dispersed throughout the garden.

erings on the parapets and the little containing walls of the flower beds (fig. 203).

The need for new paving on the pathways came from seeing the path in the context of the layout of the garden as a whole, reducing the width so as not to interfere with the health of the hedges which bordered them. All the other remnants of the ancient paving close to the Priory were left *in situ*, where they had been tightly arranged and brought together in the first half of the twentieth century (figs. 195, 204).

Special attention had to be paid to the fountain, a deep, buried tank bounded by an oval of straight and curved lines, the work of Giandomenico Navone. Out of the fish-tank emerges a kind of pinnacle on a base of four uneven peperino pillars. On these are great peperino ashlars shaped in such a way as to resemble the rock with some sculptured flowers and leaves; on the top there is a valuable white marble bowl with two fish wrapped around it. The break between the peperino rock and the marble bowl would seem to suggest

200. One of the four stone tables made during the eighteenth-century restoration, still in existence in the first years of the twentieth century; fragments of the top of the table can be traced in the paving of the path in the photograph (Foto Moscioni 1915-19, Photographic Archive of the Vatican Museums).

201. Fragment made up of an octagonal base, perhaps originally a base of one of the stone tables.

that it is once more a case of something being reused, but not properly completed, as if it was put there for the time being (figs. 205-207).

The state of deterioration varied depending on the materials and their position with respect to the water. The marble of the upper tank had a porous and incompact aspect, with widespread dense, grey microbiological growths. On the edge there were both grey roundish formations with whitish or yellow edges, and yellowish incrustations, which, when cleaned, were like calcium oxalites.

The part emerging from the water was completely affected by extensive carbonate deposits which were noticeably thick on the parts less affected by the flowing water. The state of the stone was worsened by black cement plaster and recent cracks in the peperino where roots had penetrated (figs. 208-210).

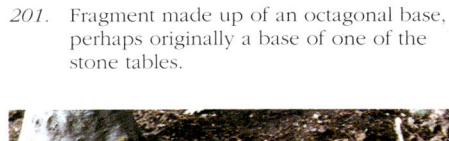

THE RESTORATION 173

202. One of the little walls in the garden after restoration.

203. Peperino covering before restoration.

204. New paving slab placed at the crossroads of the paved pathways.

Cleaning was done to levels that the materials could tolerate, even to the detriment of the final effect. The white marble was cleaned with compresses of cellulose pulp and ammonuim carbonate, finished with a microsandblaster with aluminium oxide at 180 Mesh, accompanied by biocidal treatment. It was decided not to focus on the calcium oxalite incrustations, so as not to spoil any of the stone material where there was no break. The peperino, which was only treated with a microdrill to reduce the layer of carbonate and then with a microsandblaster and aluminium oxide at 120 Mesh, had a whitish covering in some places due to salt infiltration. This could only be removed by working on a surface that would have to be lost, so this method was not adopted. The final result confirmed the appropriateness of such a decision, since the perfectly acceptable level of cleaning achieved meant that none of the stone surfaces were lost, as

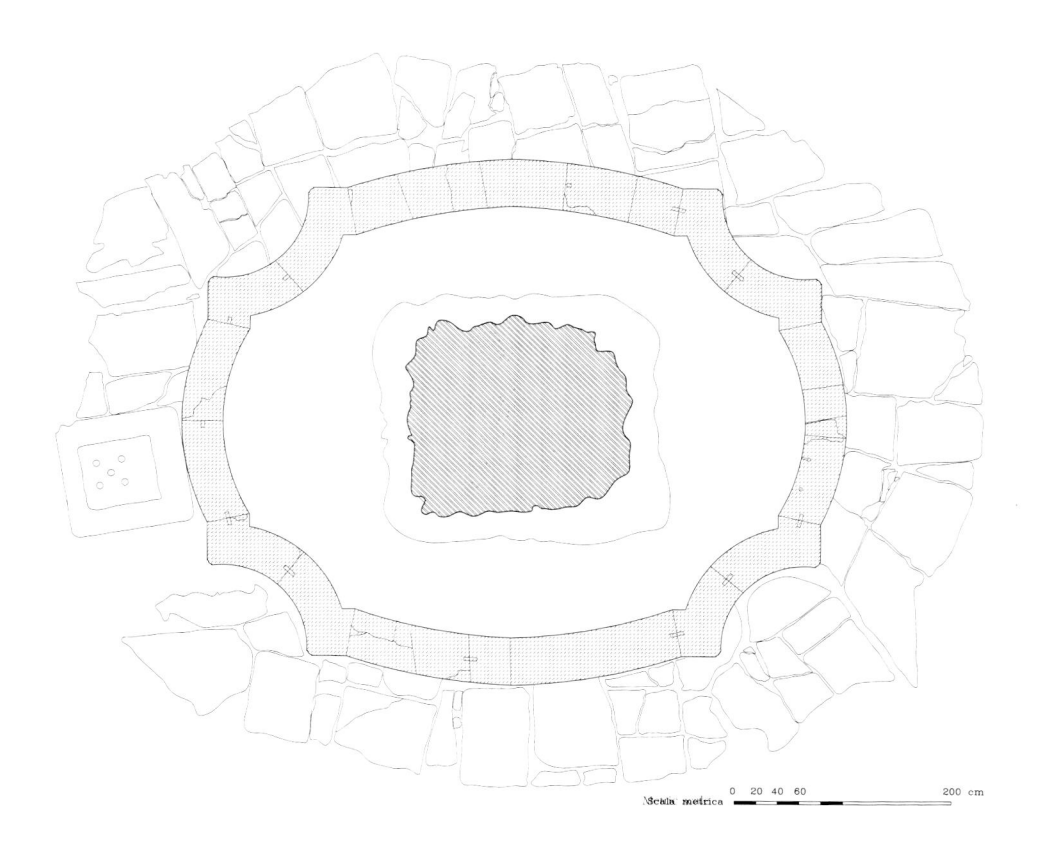

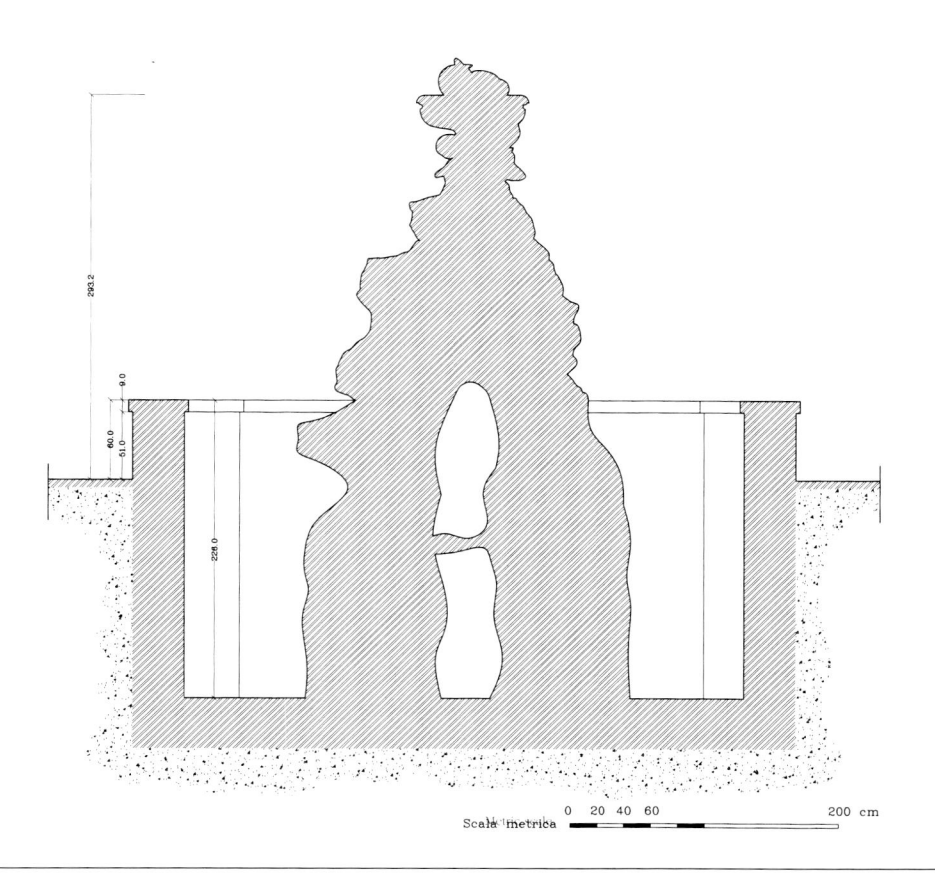

205. The fountain: plan and section
(Soprintendenza Beni Ambientali e Architettonici del Lazio: relief by M. Silvestri, 1999).

THE RESTORATION 175

206. The fountain: elevation (Soprintendenza Beni Ambientali e Architettonici del Lazio: relief by M. Silvestri, 1999).

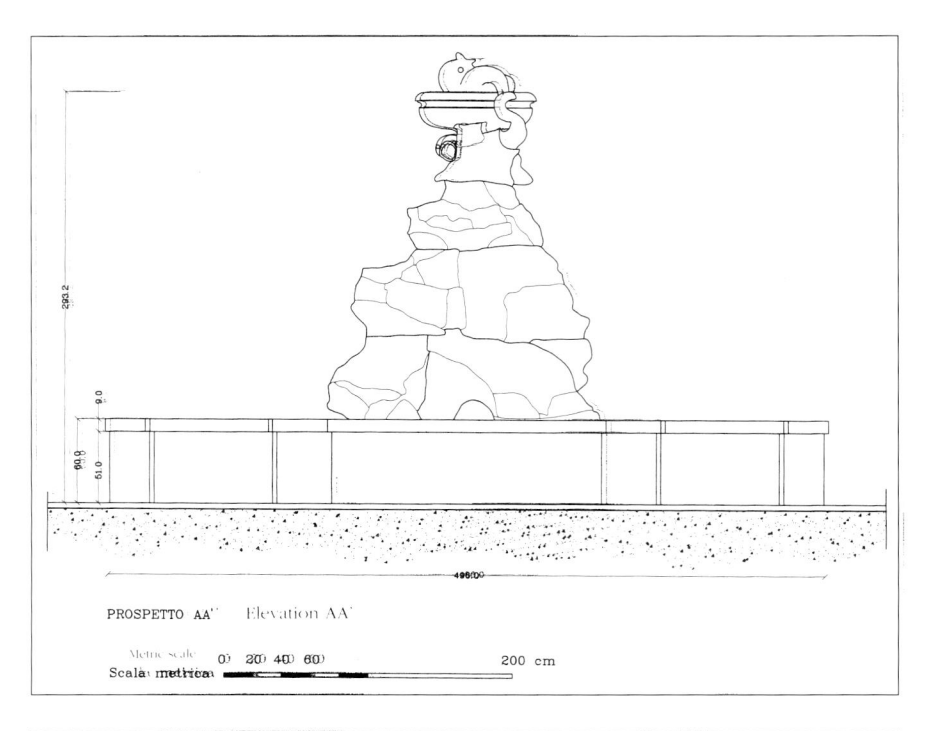

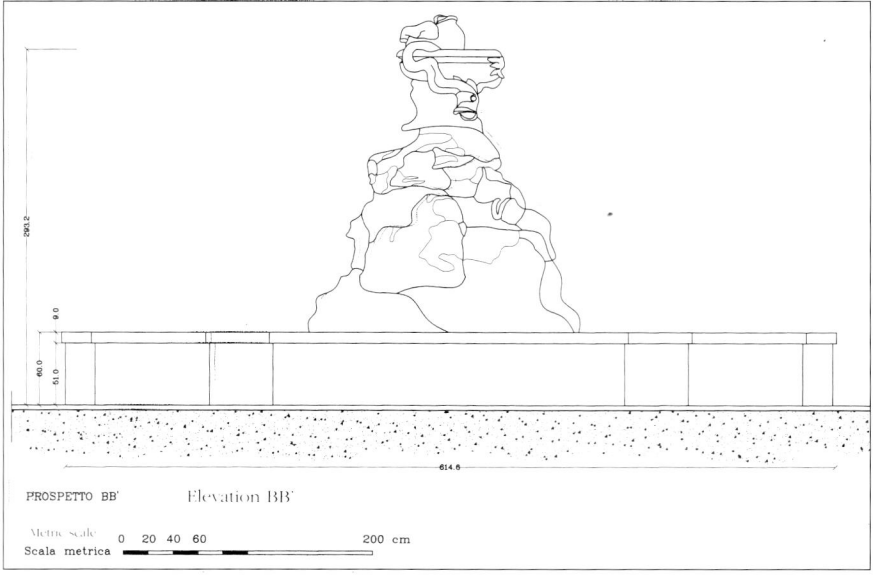

is obvious from the moulded carved flowers and the chisel carving still perfectly visible on the peperino.

Similar problems were encountered on the rim of the tank, made up of great pieces of moulded peperino marking the edge of straight and curved lines. The non-functioning of the drainage hole of the overfull fishtank, with the subsequent rise of the water level beyond the filled-in tank, caused seepage into the protective parapet. Furthermore, the disordered state of the ashlars and the decline of the external plaster allowed roots to get into the wall, resulting in the almost complete detachment of the plaster. Once the water

207. The fountain: central feature rising out of the tank.

208. The fountain: detail of the marble bowl on the top.

209. The fountain: detail of the peperino rocks, before restoration.

plant had been overhauled, the plaster, both outside and inside the tank, had to be completely re-done. The plaster inside was protected with waterproof products, subject to the dismantling of the stone edge of the fountain. The ashlars were numbered and laid out at the foot of the fountain, and then put back on the restored wall. They were cleaned and the missing parts restored and subsequently moulded (figs. 211-214).

Parallel with the architectural work, work was also carried out on the plants in the garden. Scarce maintenance, particularly with regard to the occasional shaping and pruning of the hedges, the health and nutritional care of the plants, along with the more or less wild grafting of extraneous vegetation, meant that the garden had a character of naturalness and abandonment. In particular, the laurels (*Laurus nobilis*), grouped in relation to the two cross-way paths, showed various signs of malformation, and some were dried or dead; even the box-tree (*Buxus sempervirens*), which had plants of a great age, had long stretches showing signs of wilting because of the strong competition from the numerous species of plants that had developed within the hedge itself.

As said before, at the start of the project the plants were catalogued and filed. The aim was to provide knowledge of the botanical composition of the garden and a complete and updated picture of the individual examples present. The inventory provided knowledge of the specific composition of the trees, the number of examples present, and individual analysis of their biological, structural and health characteristics with a view to planning the necessary care and maintenance.

In total, a census of 142 plants was taken, belonging to 18 different taxonomies. Their specific distribution is reported in the following table.

Common name	Scientific name	Number of examples
Laurel = L	*Laurus nobilis*	108
Cypress = Cu	*Cupressus sempervirens*	9
Common lime-tree = T	*Tilia x vulgaris*	3
Rose = R	*Rosa sp.*	3
Cherry tree = C	*Prunus avium*	2
Hibiscus = I	*Hibiscus syriacus*	2
Crape myrtle = Li	*Lagerstoemia indica*	2
Apple tree = Me	*Malus domestica*	2
Oleander = Ol	*Nerium oleander*	2
Apricot tree = A	*Prunus armeniaca*	1
Silk tree = Al	*Albizzia julibrissin*	1
Arizona Cypress = Ca	*Cupressus arizonica*	1
Persimmon = K	*Diospyros kaki*	1
Cherry Laurel = La	*Prunus laurocerasus*	1
Myrtle = M	*Myrtus communis*	1
Walnut = N	*Juglans regia*	1
Olive tree = O	*Olea europea*	1
Yucca = Y	*Yucca gloriosa*	1
		142

210. The fountain before the start of restoration work: detail of the outside of the tank.

211. The rim of the tank after the removal of the plaster, affected by seepage and by root systems.

212. Detail of the internal protective plaster of the tank, completely detached.

213. Dismantling and numbering of the covering slabs of the rim, laid out at the foot of the tank.

214. Re-assembling the peperino rim.

215. Detail of the end section of the visual axis with the passages in the hedges and the final arrangement of the seat and cypresses.

216. Removal of the old stumps of the laurel flower beds.

As the table shows, the most numerous group is that of the laurels, but there were also some examples of traditional fruit trees, such as cherry, apricot, persimmon, apple, olive, walnut and pear; there are then some notable examples worth preserving - common cypress (*Cupressus sempervirens*), hybrid lime-tree (*Tilia x vulgaris*) and walnut (*Juglans regia*).

The plants were allocated an identifying number in relation to their position in the garden, marked on a plan, and on the survey report, containing the necessary information and an indication of the work needing to be done. Things then progressed according to a seasonally structured work-plan: first of all the dead trees and shrubs were felled, and wilting or extraneous greenery was removed, along with the shrubs to be relocated; at the same time, the worn out tree stumps, which had encroached mostly on space intended for the rows of *Laurus nobilis* (fig. 216), were removed. Maintenance largely involved pruning, weeding - removing dry and malformed branches, and balancing by the shortening and proportioning of the foliage - and fertilising. At the appropriate time, replanting took place, mainly in the two rows of laurels, distinguished by two arboreal rows for which 19 trees were replanted. Four cypresses were then placed at the end of the little paths, thus making a sort of end portal (fig. 215).

The system of *Buxus sempervirens* hedges had been radically affected by the lack of pruning which should have preserved its alignment in a set shape. So it was necessary to replant a total of fifty metres of hedge. In the rest of the garden, there was internal and external reclamation of the hedges from competing plant species; the land was cultivated to improve conditions for air and water circulation, fer-

217. Overall view of the great central lawns following restoration.

218. Overall view of the central section of the garden following restoration.

tilisation was carried out and an irrigation system was prepared to guarantee a quick revival of both the existing and newly-planted plants.

The work was completed with the agronomic cultivation of the areas bordered by the hedges and the installation of a ready-made lawn (figs. 217-218).

With all the extraordinary work done in restoring shape to the garden, clearly the problems are now ones of ordinary maintenance, essential for the preservation of the plant heritage both from an aesthetic-ornamental point of view and a biological-cultivation angle. So once the project was finished, the owners were given a manual containing indications about the work to be done on the various elements of the garden: lawns, trees, shrubs; indications about the work done, such as fertilisation, irrigation, regeneration of the lawns, pruning and shaping, cultivation of the land, obviously including appropriate timescales.

Maintenance is particularly important in botanical restoration work, not only in order to preserve what has been achieved, but also to achieve the set objectives. In fact, work on the flora needs time consistent with the life-cycles of the material being worked on. In the case of Palazzolo, for example, the plan to restore the rows of *Laurus nobilis* to the original shape of a gallery could clearly not be completed within the timeframe of the restoration. Once the thinning out, pruning and replanting has been done, it is now a matter of waiting for the replanted specimens to grow and see how the guides put on the young branches can bring the foliage to the desired position.

In a few years time, we hope to be able to enjoy perfectly shaped galleries in a still well-kept garden, in the harmonious and relaxing layout of a prestigious terrace over the lake which has always distinguished it.

V. Restoration of the sundial at Palazzolo
Lucio Baruffi

A brief note about sundials

The first notions of time certainly led our ancestors to consider and count simply the alternation between day and night. Later, it would have been noticed that shadows get shorter until the sun reaches its greatest height and then lengthen until sunset. To better observe this phenomenon an upright pole would have been put up in a sunny open space, noting that on every clear day (from sunrise to sunset) the shadow of the end of the pole followed a curve. As the days passed, the curve went further away from or drew closer to the base of the pole itself, depending on the season, while maintaining the same course. Continuing the observation and marking on the curve the points closest to the base of the pole, it will have been noticed that the marks were all aligned on the segment of a straight line passing through the base itself: thus the sundial was born.

The straight line, which on the different days of the year indicates midday local time, was called the 'meridian', a term then extended also to sundials which show only midday and was sometimes used incorrectly to refer to sundials with more hours. The Greeks called these γνωμον, the Romans 'solarium', the English 'sundial', the Germans 'sonnenhur', the French 'cadran solair' and the Spanish 'reloj de sol'.

The other hours of the day are also represented by segments of lines, called 'hour lines', all passing through one point, the 'Meridian Centre'.

With regard to the trajectories traced on the various days by the shadow of the end of the pole, today we know that they are cone-shaped with different forms (hyperbola, ellipses and circles) depending on the position of the clock, and that they are repeated twice a year.

In this chapter the term 'table' is used to describe the surface occupied by the graphics (as in modern clocks) and 'sundial' for the whole, including any base, the quadrant, the pole and the decorations. The surface of the table can be flat or slanted (spherical, cylindrical, cone-shaped or even not easily assimilated on a plane).

The position of the table can be vertical, sloping (compared to the vertical), horizontal, as well as meridional (directed exactly towards the pole of the other hemisphere), oriental (directed towards the east), or occidental (directed towards the west). The first three arrangements define the inclination; the last three indicate the exposure, what in the gnomonic field is called the 'declination of the dial'; the positioning is defined by the association of one of the first three with one of the latter three.

The basic example described at the start is a flat, horizontal table; the declination is not specified since in this case it does not exist. A rod of definitely fixed shape, length and inclination has replaced the rudimentary pole, assuming the generic name of 'stile' or 'gnomon' from the Greek γνωμον. It is often subject to the decorative whims of the builders. Technical terminology refers to it as 'orthognomon' if it is perpendicular to the sundial table, or 'axognomon' or 'polar gnomon' if it is parallel to the earth's axis. The axognomon intersects the quadrant in the centre of the Meridian and its shadow is subsequently superimposed on the hour lines.

219. The cloister of Convento di Palazzolo; above, to the right, can be seen the little tower with traces of the sundial that has almost disappeared.

Besides the meridian, there is another distinctive line, the 'horizon line', which, depending on the exposure of the table, indicates the rising or the setting of the sun, or even both.

The earth's axis is tilted at 23° 27' on the ecliptic plane, a curve which the centre of the Earth covers in a year around the sun. There are two other important planes of reference for sundials: the horizontal, used right from the outset, and the vertical, also chosen for the Meridian. These two planes, according to preference, are assumed as points of reference for the quadrants with different inclinations.

As has been said, the hour lines indicate the hours, but they can also be marked corresponding to fractions of an hour, such as the quarter and half-hour. Until the appearance of mechanical clocks, sundials were the most trustworthy way of telling the time and until the 19th century were irreplaceable for setting clocks. This explains their presence in many old buildings.

Until the end of the 18th century in Italy people used *Italic Time*, which sub-divided the day into 24 equal hours starting from sunset; *Babylonian Time*, which sub-divided the day into 24 hours starting from sunrise; and *Transient Time*, which sub-divided the day into 12 night-time hours, from sunset to sunrise, and 12 day-time hours, from sunrise to sunset. As is well-known, the length of night and day are equal only at the equinoxes, while on the other days of the year they vary in opposite ways. Consequently, the length of the daytime hours of Transient Time differs from the nightime ones and varies during the year.

Modern Time sub-divides the day into 24 equal hours starting at midnight. Until the 18th century the hours used were those indicated by the hour lines corresponding to the position of the sun spaced out by multiples or sub-multiples of 15° azimuths (read at the Equator). Time thus marked is called *True Time* (TT); if the 12 hours correspond to the passage of the sun over the meridian of the place it is called *Local Apparent Time* (LAT).

Due to the obliqueness of the earth's axis and the peculiarity of the earth's orbit, the length of these hours varies during the year. At the end of the 19th century, with the adoption of *time zones*, *Median Time* (MT) was introduced, obtained by replacing the true sun with an imaginary one which travels over the equator in a uniform motion. In this case, the hours on the quadrant are indicated by an *analemma* (a curve in the form of an 8), rather than by line segments.

Furthermore, in every time zone the first hour begins from solar midnight at the centre of the zone: thus we have *Median Time in the Time Zone* (MTTZ), adopted in modern clocks; for Italy the MTTZ is that of Central Europe (CET).

The sundial at Palazzolo

At Palazzolo, there are two sundials. The one in the Villa Colonna (del Cardinale), restored in 1924 and now more or less illegible, is orientated towards the south-east and should mark Modern Time (fig. 220); the other, object of the present restoration, is situated on the south-east facing side of the former Priory (fig. 221); since this is

220. Villa Colonna (del Cardinale), sundial on the south wall of the tower.

221. Convento di Palazzolo, garden façade; the sundial after restoration.

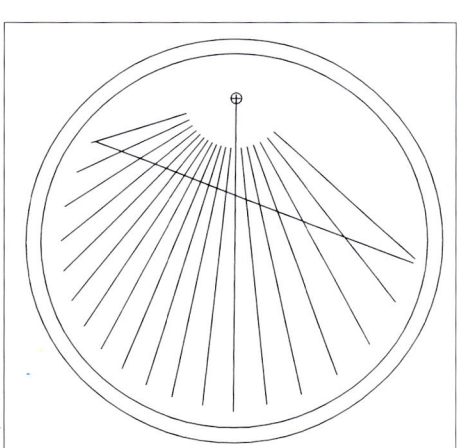

222. Drawing of the actual sundial.

223. Chart showing the bearing.

Charts for sundial calculations

Bearings taken on 6/10/99

tab. 1			
	degrees	radians	minutes
Latitude N 41° 44'.468 =	41.74113	0.72852	
Longitude E 12° 41'.448 =	12.6908		50.7632

Linear measurements (see fig. 226)

tab. 2	
	cm
C - 1 =	72.1
C - 2 =	61.3
C - 3 =	55
C - 9 =	44,6
C - 19 =	118
C - 13 =	47,9

tab. 3	
	cm
C - 1' =	25.10
C - 2' =	25.00
C - 3' =	24.10
C - V =	29
C - 1" =	86.00
C - 2" =	97.00

tab. 4			
	cm		cm
1 - 2 =	14.3	6 - 11 =	14.3
1 - 3 =	24.3	6 - 12 =	24.3
1 - 4 =	32.1	6 - 13 =	32.1
1 - 5 =	38	6 - 14 =	38
1 - 6 =	43.2	13 - 15 =	43.2
6 - 7 =	4.5	13 - 16 =	4.5
6 - 8 =	8.8	13 - 17 =	8.8
6 - 9 =	13	17 - 18 =	13
6 - 10 =	17.2	17 - 19 =	17.2

CHAPTER V

the wall slightly sloping to the buttress, the surface of the wall with the face of the sundial has been corrected so as to seem vertical.

There also used to be a mechanical clock with counterweights in the little tower containing the seventeenth-century staircase linking the Priory to the Villa Colonna (fig. 129). The clock, which has now disappeared, could be read easily from the Priory cloister itself, especially convenient when the weather was bad. It is interesting to note that, from the outset, mechanical clocks were associated with meridians which, given the times, also had a role as sample clocks.

The face as reproduced in fig. 222 had no gnomon and was partially erased. Once the restorers had cleaned the plaster and filled in the gaps, the sundial appeared as a disc of about 2 metres in diameter bordered by an ochre circular strip of about 7 metres. The equinox line and 19 line segments, for the hours and the half-hours, could be just made out. These latter extended and did not intersect at one point (The Meridian Centre) as they should have done, but rather converged on a hollowed out, uneven area a few centimetres in diameter, the result of removing the base of the gnomon. Besides the loss of the original gnomon, all the hour markings, which should have been present, had disappeared. There was also no trace of the horizon line.

The only trace of the diurnal curves (in this case hyperbola) was the equinox line, as noted, and the absence of any other trace shows that this was due to a specific choice made by the designer.

No documentation about the sundial was found, so therefore nothing is known about its construction. However, the fact that the hour lines do not meet at one point, and the absence of the diurnal curves, lead to the interesting conclusion that the maker did not use precise methods such as those geometric, already in use from ancient times, or analytical, still little known even today. Instead, he had traced the design from points marked directly on the face. In fact, if one is happy with whatever the outcome might be, tracing the lines only needs bearings to be taken four days a year (two for the hour lines and two for the equinox line), while every diurnal curve needs at least as many bearings taken as the number of hour lines marked in a specific day. The absence of the sun in one of the chosen days means the postponement of the exercise until the sun returns with the same declination, in the hope that the sky will not be covered. Using this method to trace the curves can take more than a year. We imagine that this is what the unknown constructor did.

The course of the equinox line, which rises from right to left, is marked by a meridian directed between the East and the South, that is *oriental*, as confirmed by the tests carried out. In conclusion, the sundial restored at Palazzolo has a flat, vertical and oriental table.

Surveys on the sundial

In order to recover the original missing data, the measurements shown in fig. 223 were taken; the reference numbers in the tables are those indicated in fig.226 starting from hour VI in relation to the intersections of the hour lines with the equinox line:

224. Charts for sundial calculation.

Chart for sundial calculations

Chart for sundial calculations. Bearings taken on 6/10/99

Tab. 5			
Bearings	CET	xp	yp
6/10/99		cm	cm
1	10h 55' 55"	-0.05	-9
2	11h 34' 00"	-2.34	-9.67

Tab. 6		
Insert in calculating l		
from Δ1	from Δ2	from Δ3
1.43046	1.43639	1.42617
0.71505	0.71786	0.71395

Calculated parameters

Tab. 7			
	degrees	radians		l = cm
Δ1 =	20.4628	0.357	10h 55' 50"	22.42
Δ2 =	21.0876	0.368	11h 34"	22.41
Δ3 =	20.2150	0.353		22.42
x^s =	20.77	0.363		
				22.33

l = cf. connection and d = 44.85 (tab. 8)
Δ = from the projected face
Δ = from the projected face
(Δ from Acad and equation of the equinox line)
(from Acad where s = equinox line)
(used in the tests and carried out)

Tab. 8	
d = cm	44.87
d = cm	44.85

actual Acad, distance of s from C, Meridian Centre
calculated Acad, distance of s from C, the Meridian Centre

Tab. 9			
Xc = cm	Yc = cm	D = cm	dial-plate
8.366	21.351	32.070	22.9314
8.643	21.435	32.196	23.11201
8.256	21.316	32.021	22.86101
		31.94	22.64

(D = axognomon)
(from Δ1 where l = 22.42)
(from Δ2 where l = 22.41)
(from Δ3 where l = 21.41)
(where l was used in tests and carried out)

– fig. 223 table 3 – distance of C from the beginning and end of some hour lines;
– fig. 223 table 2 – distances between C and some points on the equinox line;
– fig. 223 table 4 – distance between some points on the equinox line;
– fig. 224 table 8 – distance **d** of C from the equinox line;
– fig. 223 table 3 – distance of C from point **V** of the circular strip (fig. 225).

Examination of the existing graph leads to the following conclusions:
– the hour line closest to the vertical is not inclined by the angle corresponding to the hour distance of the place from the centre of the time zone, but is itself almost vertical, and so is therefore marked to indicate Local Apparent Time.
– the hour line XII, the meridian, which must be vertical, has turned out to be rotated by half a degree towards the antimeridian hours; this has not compromised the calculations, but leads to a 3-minute error in reading them, which has been taken into account in the correction tables.

With the relevant measurements it was possible to draw up a preliminary formulation (fig. 226).

225. Original and theoretical graphs.

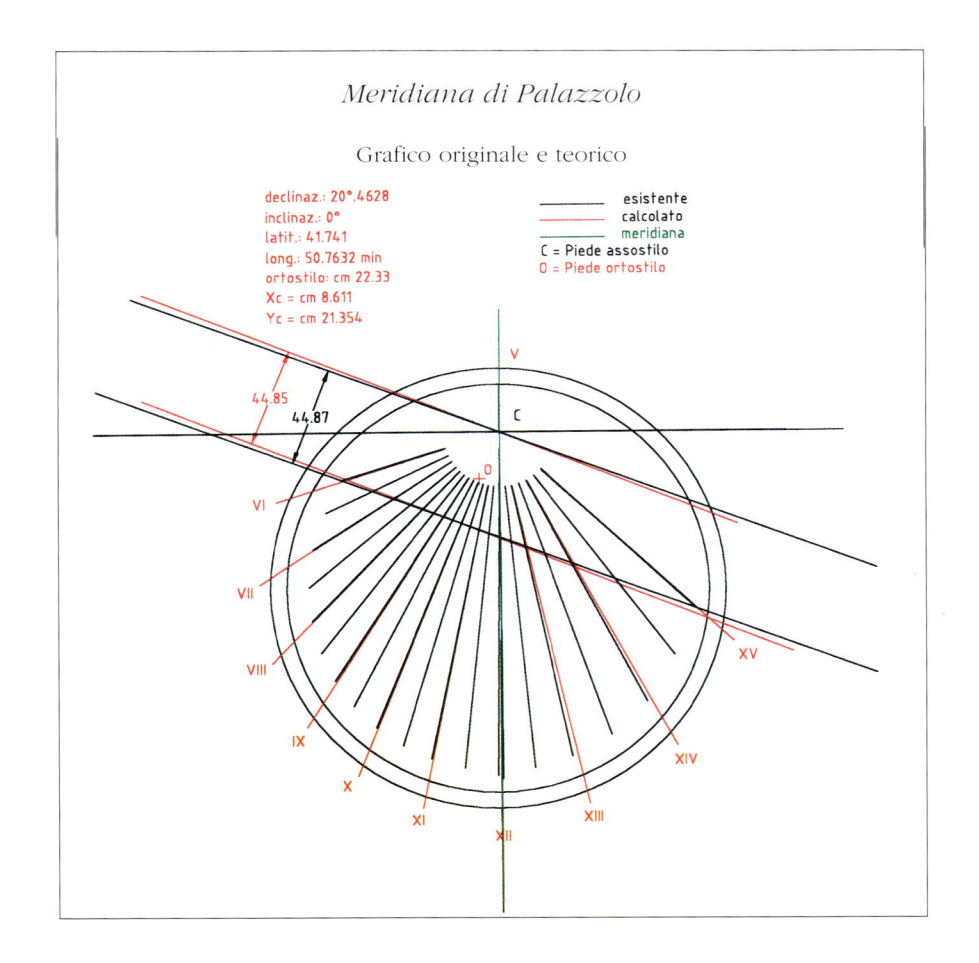

Surveys to define the geographical co-ordinates of the site and the orientation of the meridian

From the map of the Italian Geographical Institution and the confirmation of the G.P.S. (Global Positioning System) the geographic coordinates of the site are as follows:

Longitude East: 12° 41'. 448 – Latitude North: 41° 44.468

Tests showed that the evenness and verticality of the surface were satisfactory. As shown in table 5 of fig. 224, two hourly bearings were taken on the same day to determine the surface declination. The time was read on a radio-controlled clock and a bearing taken with a 10 centimetre sample gnomon on a suitable vertical slab (fig. 227).

In the calculations, the use of distance **d** for the reconstruction of the gnomon demands that the positions of the Meridian Centre and the equinox line be precise. But here it was not the case. In order to define the Meridian Centre with sufficient approximation the hour lines were provisionally extended as far as the junction with the others and the point at which these mainly concentrated was chosen as the centre. The position of the equinox line was assumed to be right, it not yet being possible to compare it with mathematical results.

226. *Preliminary formulation*

Palazzolo sundial

Preliminary formulation

Scala 1/20

227. Survey work in progress.

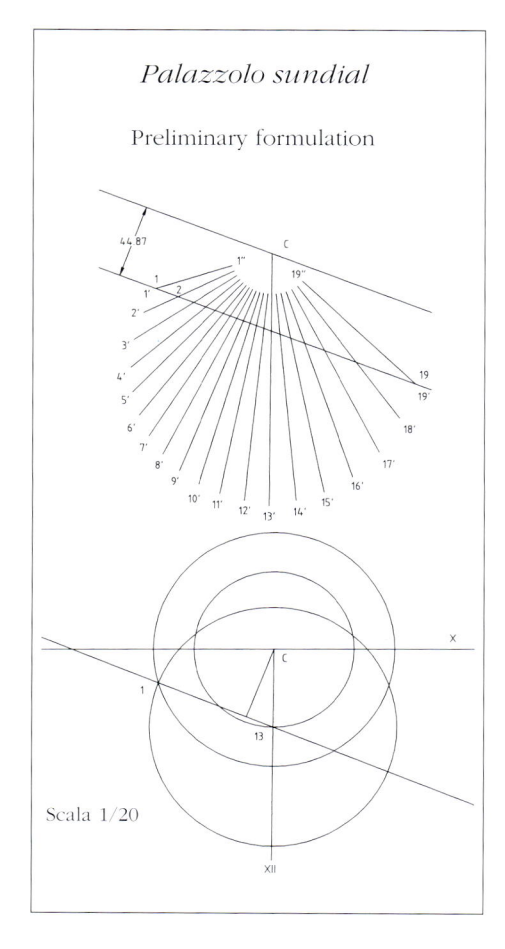

Calculating the orientation of the surface and the orthognomon

Translating the data gathered into calculation language[1], the values Δ_1 and Δ_2 are arrived at, shown in table 7 of fig. 224; these two values are compared with the value Δ_3, analytically arrived at via the original graph; from these three Δ_1 was chosen, $= 20°.4628$, which is closer to Δ_3. With the gnomon missing and the exact position of the base of the orthognomon (gnomon perpendicular to the vertical) or the axognomon not being marked it was necessary to work out from the mutual position of the hour lines and equinox line both the length **l** of the orthognomon and the co-ordinates of the Meridian Centre

$$Xc = -l\, tg\, \Delta \quad Yc = l\, tg\, \varphi\, /\, cos\, \Delta$$

In table 9 of fig. 224 it has been worked out: $Xc = 8.256$ and $Yc = 21.318$

So, the gradient st^Y of the projection of the stile on the table (dial-plate) with respect to the vertical (*meridian line*) is:

$$st\wedge Y = arctg\, X_c\, /\, Y_c = 21°\, 10'$$

With the notation φ = latitude of the site, starting from the equation of the equinox line

$$x\, cos\, \varphi\, sen\, \Delta - y\, sen\, \varphi - l\, cos\, \varphi\, cos\, \Delta = 0$$

one gets the following equation, from which **l** can be taken, since the distance **d** has already been measured:

$$l = -d\, /\, (tg\, \Delta\, cos\, \varphi\, sen\, \Delta + tg\, \varphi\, sen\, \varphi\, /\, cos\, \Delta + cos\, \varphi\, cos\, \Delta)\, /\, (cos^2\, \varphi\, sen^2\, \Delta + sen^2\, \varphi)^{0.5}$$

In table 7 it can be seen that **l** = 22.42 cm is obtained from $\Delta 1 = 20°,4628$; in the tests with an adjustable orthognomon it was found that the measurement most adapted to the existing graphic was **l** = 22.33 cm; this measurement, differing less than a millimetre from the one calculated, was used in the construction of the new axognomon in the constructive design shown in fig. 228.

The length of the polar axognomon **S** is therefore

$$S = = 31.94\, cm$$

The slope **i** of the axognomon with regard to the face comes out at:

$$\mathbf{i} = arcsen\, l\, /\, S = 44°\, 20'$$

Calculation of the theoretical meridian

At this stage, with all the necessary parameters noted, the theoretical meridian and its graph can be calculated through the general equations of the sundial[1].

The hour and equinox lines, the only lines provided for in this sundial, can be traced through points according to the angles they make with the cartesian axes.

With the second method, through an hour line **t** the angle x^t with the axis X the following equation can be obtained:

The equinox line can be traced with at least two points obtained from one of the two equinoxes.

$$x\wedge t = arctg\, \frac{cos\Delta cos\eta - sen\Delta\, cos\xi\, sen\varphi}{cos\xi\, sen\varphi}$$

228. Executive design for the gnomon.

Examination of the graphs

For an immediate comparison fig. 225 shows both the graphic designed on the wall and the theoretical one. Note that the meridian line (hour XII), corresponding to that traced on the face, is not vertical as it should be but is rotated towards the antimeridian hours by about half a degree.

It is also possible to compare the declination Δ_1, adopted by the existing meridian, and Δ obtained instrumentally from the solar shadow; in fact, stating **s** to be the equinox line and measured on the face the angle x^s, one arrives at

$$\Delta_1 = \arcsen (tg\ \varphi * tg\ x\wedge s)$$

The resulting difference, $\Delta < \Delta 1,$ is about half a degree.

Fig. 225 also shows appreciable angular differences between some hour lines on the face and those that were calculated. In the table in fig. 229 the hourly differences due to the angular inaccuracies for all the hours and half-hours marked on the face were calculated; the same hourly differences were also noted in the histogram in fig. 230 (the values indicated cannot be interpolated).

[1] Lucio Baruffi, "*Orologi Solari – Trattato Pratico Teorico*" Roma 2001, unpublished – § 3.8a

229. Correction chart.

Palazzolo sundial
Correction chart

The hours are those on the sundial
The (original) angles x^t are formed by the X axis of the hour lines on the sundial
The (calculated) angles x^t are formed by the X axis of the hour lines calculated and drawn up on the computer
The fault is the difference between the correct CET at the time shown and the actual time

ora indicata	effettivo x^t°	effettivo γ (rad)	corretto x^t°	corretto γ (rad)	differenza gradi	differenza min	min	sec
VI	17,18	0,299848	17,798	0,310634	0,61800	2,47200	2	28,32
VI 1/2	25,36	0,442615	25,904	0,452110	0,54400	2,17600	2	10,56
VII	32,78	0,572119	33,268	0,580636	0,48800	1,95200	1	57,12
VII 1/2	39,74	0,693594	39,996	0,698062	0,25600	1,02400	1	1,44
VIII	45,79	0,799186	46,205	0,806429	0,41500	1,66000	1	39,6
VIII 1/2	51,66	0,901637	52,013	0,907798	0,35300	1,41200	1	24,72
IX	57,01	0,995012	57,530	1,004088	0,52000	2,08000	2	4,8
IX 1/2	62,36	1,088387	62,858	1,097079	0,49800	1,99200	1	59,52
X	67,78	1,182984	68,094	1,188465	0,31400	1,25600	1	15,36
X 1/2	73,04	1,274788	73,332	1,279885	0,29200	1,16800	1	10,08
XI	78,20	1,364847	78,663	1,372928	0,46300	1,85200	1	51,12
XI 1/2	83,95	1,465204	84,185	1,469305	0,23500	0,94000	0	56,4
XII	89,40	1,560324	90,000	1,570796	0,60000	2,40000	2	24
XII 1/2	95,44	1,665742	96,209	1,679164	0,76900	3,07600	3	4,56
XIII	101,91	1,778665	102,959	1,796974	1,04900	4,19600	4	11,76
XIII 1/2	109,35	1,908518	110,338	1,925761	0,98800	3,95200	3	57,12
XIV	117,65	2,053380	118,461	2,067534	0,81100	3,24400	3	14,64
XIV 1/2	126,94	2,215521	127,387	2,223323	0,44700	1,78800	1	47,28
XV	136,89	2,389181	137,095	2,392759	0,20500	0,82000	0	49,2

230. Correcting the readings.

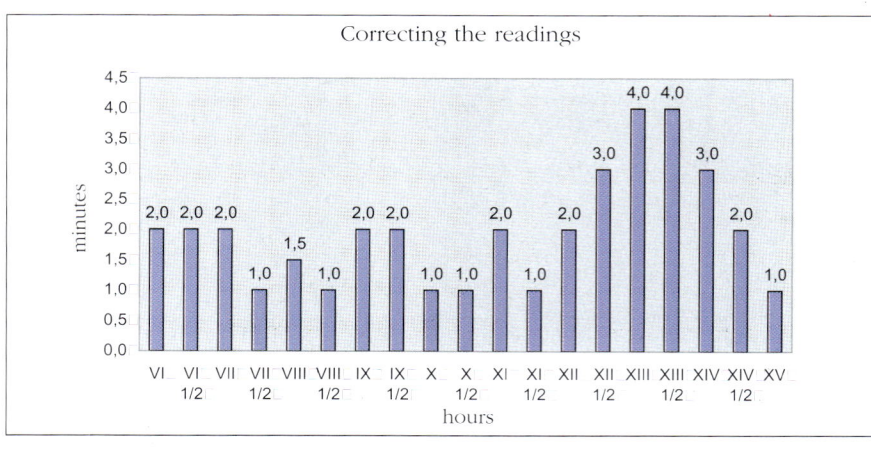

231. Conversion graph from Local Apparent Time to Central European Time.

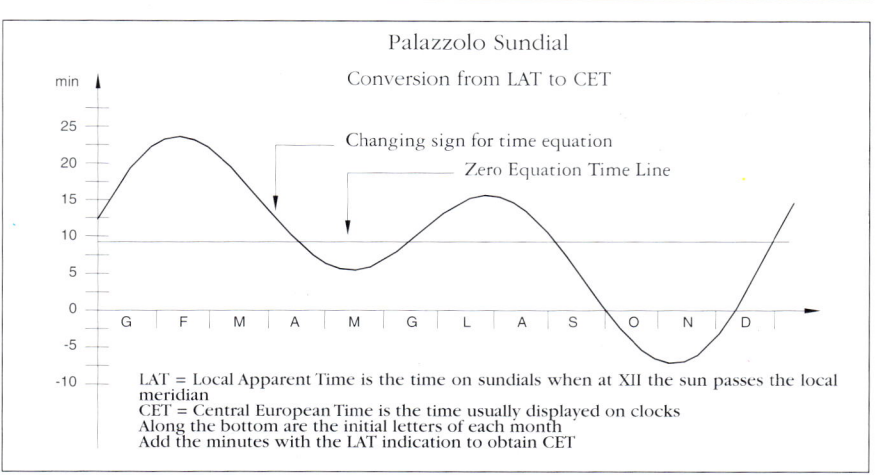

Palazzolo Sundial
Conversion from LAT to CET

LAT = Local Apparent Time is the time on sundials when at XII the sun passes the local meridian
CET = Central European Time is the time usually displayed on clocks
Along the bottom are the initial letters of each month
Add the minutes with the LAT indication to obtain CET

232. Conversion chart from Local Apparent Time to Central European Time.

Palazzolo sundial
Conversion LAT - CET

long. fuso			long. sito		fuso - sito	scala
min. sec.	°	'	min. sec.	min	min	
60	12	41,448	50 45,792	50,7632	9,2368	1,00

giorno	equaz. tempo min	correzione min	giorno	equaz. tempo min	correzione min
0	-3,184	12,4208	190	-5,107	14,3438
5	-5,461	14,6978	195	-5,776	15,0128
10	-7,564	16,8008	200	-6,235	15,4718
15	-9,445	18,6818	205	-6,452	15,6888
20	-11,058	20,2948	210	-6,415	15,6518
25	-12,372	21,6088	215	-6,115	15,3518
30	-13,367	22,6038	220	-5,553	14,7898
35	-14,030	23,2668	225	-4,740	13,9768
40	-14,363	23,5998	230	-3,693	12,9298
45	-14,374	23,6108	235	-2,436	11,6728
50	-14,079	23,3158	240	-1,000	10,2368
55	-13,505	22,7418	245	0,582	8,6548
60	-12,682	21,9188	250	2,276	6,9608
65	-11,642	20,8788	255	4,038	5,1988
70	-10,423	19,6598	260	5,828	3,4088
75	-9,068	18,3048	265	7,609	1,6278
80	-7,614	16,8508	270	9,335	-0,0982
85	-6,103	15,3398	275	10,960	-1,7232
90	-4,576	13,8128	280	12,448	-3,2112
95	-3,077	12,3138	285	13,757	-4,5202
100	-1,641	10,8778	290	14,845	-5,6082
105	-0,309	9,5458	295	15,676	-6,4392
110	0,885	8,3518	300	16,222	-6,9852
115	1,907	7,3298	305	16,452	-7,2152
120	2,731	6,5058	310	16,348	-7,1112
125	3,333	5,9038	315	15,898	-6,6612
130	3,698	5,5388	320	15,099	-5,8622
135	3,817	5,4198	325	13,961	-4,7242
140	3,690	5,5468	330	12,503	-3,2662
145	3,328	5,9088	335	10,751	-1,5142
150	2,747	6,4898	340	8,750	0,4868
155	1,978	7,2588	345	6,549	2,6878
160	1,052	8,1848	350	4,202	5,0348
165	0,015	9,2218	355	1,772	7,4648
170	-1,086	10,3228	360	-0,672	9,9088
175	-2,198	11,4348	365	-3,069	12,3058
180	-3,275	12,5118	370	-5,353	14,5898
185	-4,259	13,4958			

Correction = - time equation - (zone – site)

Converting True Local Time to Central European Time

The time shown by normal clocks in Italy is CET (mean time in Central Europe), that is a mean time in relation to the meridian of the time zone and an imaginary sun which appears to rotate around the Earth at a constant angular speed. On Palazzolo's sundial the hour lines indicate the LAT (Local Apparent Time), that is time in relation to the local meridian and to the true sun, whose apparent speed of rotation around the Earth is not uniform; this leads to different time readings between a meridian at Local Apparent Time and a normal clock (see fig. 231 referring to the zero line of the Equation of Time).

For a specific longitude, the difference between the Local Apparent Time and the Median Time of the time zone at the same moment is called the *Equation of Time*, wich subtracted algebraically from TT gives MT.

The table in fig. 232 shows the conversion values calculated for a year with a cadence of one day every five; fig. 231 shows the graph for a quick conversion from Local Apparent Time to Central European Time.

233. The gnomon installed.

Restoration work on the sundial

As already noted, the sundial's quadrant, which was simply painted plaster, was strengthened and restored, the grooves of the lines were picked out again and the colours restored; on the circular strip around the edge of the face the hours were re-written in Roman numerals corresponding to the hour lines (fig. 221).

In remaking the lost gnomon, account was taken of the fact that it had to be of the axognomon type, parallel to the earth's axis, since it had originally been fixed in the Centre of the meridian. The aim was to produce a simple gnomon, like the quadrant itself.

Fig. 228 shows the design for the gnomon, done with precision instruments. The proposal was to use brass, which in time darkens but does not stain. The base has a hole allowing for accurate assembly and the pole of the gnomon can be taken down easily. It was all set up from the base on exact lines checked with the calculated position and fixed to the face with removable wall-plugs. The 31.94 cm pole is perfectly straight, has a diameter of 8 mm and is partially tapered towards the end in order to allow a more precise indication of the hour. In its position, the axis of the pole coincides with that of the theoretical polar stile (fig. 233).

Specifications of the sundial

To sum up, the distinctive data of the sundial after restoration are as follows:
– Longitude 12° 41'.448 East
– Latitude 41° 44'.468 North
– Vertical, flat face
– Declination of the face 20° 27'.768 East
– Diameter of the face 20 cm
– Brass axognomon type gnomon, can be dismantled
– Length of the stile 31.94 cm
– Inclination of the stile from the flat surface 44° 20'
– Inclination of the dial-plate compared to the vertical 21° 10'
– Graphic elements: equinox line and 20 hour lines
– Time system: Modern Time in Local Apparent Time
– Indication of hours and half-hours between 0600 and 1530

Reading the time

The sundial is arranged to show Local Apparent Time. The moment at which the reading of the time shown is exact is when the centre-line of the stile's shadow coincides with the hour line. Since it was decided to leave the original hour lines with their inaccuracies, Local Apparent Time is slightly distorted. To know the precise time it is necessary to add the differences shown on the y-axis of the histogram in fig. 230 or in the table in fig. 229. From the international adoption of time zones and mean time, Local Apparent Time is no longer commonly used, but can be converted to Central European Time by adding algebraically the differences shown in the table in fig. 232 or the minutes on the conversion chart in fig. 231.

APPENDICES

Archival and documentary sources

Archives

ROME

Central State Archives
F. CARTA, "Relazione intorno ai lavori di intervento e consegna della Biblioteca", ms., Fondo Biblioteche Governative e non Governative, envelope 160, 1, 1880.
Rocca di Papa, Palazzola, mss., Fondo Antichità e Belle Arti, Beni Corporazioni Religiose soppresse, B 24, n. 64, SF 32.
Camerale, Diverse II, Fondo Antichità e Belle Arti, B 9, n. 226, 1807.
Lettera Dir. Gen. Fondo Culto, ms., Fondo Antichità e Belle Arti, II Versamento, envelope 255, n. 4437.
Giustificazioni di Tesoreria e dai Mandati Camerali, (16 May 1661).
Not. Ac. Tommaso Paluzzi, 1661, vol. 4982, ff. 237.

Vatican Secret Archives
Jura diversa, ms., Holy Roman Rota, 493, 1796.
Sacr. Cong. Stat. Regul., Relationes 39, Osservanti, F4, 1650.
Archive of the Portuguese Legation to the Holy See, ms. n.1, box 9, pack 2.
Secretary of State, Portuguese Nunciature, Segnatura: 57 (1700), 59 (1702), 60 (1716), 63 (1705), 64 (1706), 65 (1707), 67 (1709), 68 (1710), 69 (1711), 70 (1712), 71 (1713), 72 (1715), 73 (1716), 74 (1717), 75 (1719/20), 76 (1721), 85 (1728), 96 (1741), 97 (1742), 100 (1745), 101 (1746), 102 (1747), 104A (1744f.).

Archive of the Reverenda Fabbrica of St Peter's
Liste mestrue e gustificazioni, vol. 86, II piano, serie IV.

Capitoline Archives
Notai, ms., C.C., Section 8, vol. 70.

Historic Archives of the National Academy of S. Luca
Vols. 46, 47, 166.

Archives of the Roman Province of the Friars Minor
Relations with Portuguese Administration, ms., Palazzola Estate.

Aracoeli Provincial Archives
Brief (of the nomination of Evora by Benedict XIII, Proc. Gen. Dell'Ordine), ms., vol 83, n. 14, 1727.
"Contro le pretenzioni del Palmini Falegname", ms. vol. 83, n. 13 (18th century)
Ms., (description of the visit by Ebora), vol 83, n.12, 1735.
Palazzola File, "Memorie e fatti storico-cronologici del Monastero e della Badia Nullius di S. Maria di Palazzola nel Territorio Albanense", ms., 1737.
Palazzola File, "Nota e resumo delle spese, e fabriche insigni fatte, e dirette dal R.mo P. Fr. Giuseppe Maria De Fonseca D'Evora incominciando dall'anno 1715…", ms., fasc. 1-35, 1738.
"Necrologium sive Mortilogium Almae Observantis Provinciae Romanae…", ms., n. 30 (1894).
Palazzola File, "Carte Varie".
O. A. CASABASCIANA, "Memorie di avvenimenti appartenenti alla Provincia Romana dei frati minori osservanti incominciando dall'anno 1612…", ms. 8, f. 87f.

S. Antonio dei Portoghesi Archives
Contas 1736-1788, n. 3.
Copiados, ms., 1748-1801.
A. DE COUTO OLIVEIRA, "Situacao Juridica des Portugueses em Roma e sua Igrazia", undated.
"Inventario de tudo que seacha neste Archivio", ms. A.A. 20, 157, letter A, nn. 6-7.
Livro dos Instumentos…, ms., 1682-1756.
Livro dos testamentos, ms., E.E. 1.
"Memoire, couvent et Eglise de ste Marie des Neiges a' Palazzola", ms., n. 36, 1, 1873.
P. MIGUELE DE CHUNA (copy of), "Memoire sovre os conventos de Sancta Maria de Palazzola e Sancta Liberata e Biblioteca de Aracoeli", ms., n. 1-35, n. 14, (19th century).
L. WADDING, undated manuscript, n. 1-35.
M. SALUSTRI, "Stima dei fondi rustici e fabbricati di proprietà del Governo del Portogallo…", Mandamento di Frascati, Provincia di Roma, n. 110, n. 106-14, 1880.
"Palazzola ristrutturata ovvero descrizione dell'origine della chiesa e convento di S. Maria di Palazzola percorso di sette secoli", undated manuscript.
Palazzola Estate, Various Papers.

S. Francesco a Ripa Archives
"Depositiones… esaminator in causa vertente PP. Min. Conv. Palatiola Barberinos", ms., Palazzola Estate, file 1, issue 1, n. 10.
F. GIORGIO MARZIALE, "Descrittione del Convento di Palazzola fatta dal P.re Frà Giorgio Martiale Deffinitore Perpetuo della Provincia inore Osservante", Anno 1670, ms., Palazzola Estate, issue n. 12.
Relazione del guardiano (19th century), ms., Palazzola Estate, file 2.
"Spese della Fabrica del Vnble Convento di Palazzola fatte dal R.mo Evora l'anno 1738", ms., AFR 124, 1738.
Palazzola File I, "Inventario del 22 giugno 1810".

Palazzola File II, various letters.
Venerable English College Archives
Palazzola Archive, 3, 23-24; 2C9; 6A.
Palazzola File, Scr. 97, 1ff.

FRASCATI

Tuscolano Episcopal Archives
JOANNEM BAPTISTAM DE' ALTERIS, Acta Apostolicae ac Generalis Visitationis Tusculanem episcopatus ac. Diocesis…, ms., 1636.
D. ANTONIUM SEVEROLUM, Acta Apostolicae ac Generalis Visitationis Tusculanem episcopatus ac. Diocesis, ms. f. 118. 1660.
F.M. DE ASTE, Visitationes Civitatis et Diocesis Tusculanae…, ms., 1703.

Aldobrandini Archives
"Planta, et descriptio Status, ac Territorii Prioratus Albani", in "Carte relative al Priorato…", Doc. Stor., 35/147/2.

MARINO

Archives of the Basilica of S. Barnaba
G. TORQUATI, Studi Storico Archeologici sulla città e sul territorio di Marino…, ms., 3 vols., undated.

SUBIACO

Colonna Archives
Letters of Egidio Colonna, ms., Misc. II A 19, 24; II A 71, 26; II A 24, 62; 24, 56; 19, 4;
III AA 193, 34; 73, 343; 73, 265r-270v;
KB 6, 24;
III B, 19, 4; 15, 37; 29, 19; 4, 42;
III BB 773, 15, 32; 15, 106; 20, 100; 54, 87 Parchment Archive.
III BB Paper Archive, file 55, n. 20.
Misc. Stor. II A 4, 74 cc. 509-513, 19, 23; 19, 26, 71, 20;
II C A 27.17
III KB 6, 24;

PORTUGAL, LISBON

National Archives of Torre do Tombo
Santo Antonio Alvarà de Lecenca para fundacao de hum convento dedicado ao dito Santo na Villa de Mafra, ms. 1, 35, Chancelaria de D. Joào V, 1711.
Antonio Soares de Faria…, ms. 1, 42, Chancelaria de D. Joào V, 1714.

Libraries

ROME

Vatican Apostolic Library
Disegni e Piante diverse, Chigiani Manuscript, P.VII, 12 and 13.
Cod. Ottoboniano 2116
E. STEVENSON (Junior), ms., Cod. Lat. 19559, ff.114ff.
"Castello Gandolfo e Ariccia – Per Fabriche – 1659 al 1666", Arch. Chigi n. 3652.
CASSIANO DAL POZZO, Barb. Lat., 1871, f. 39.
"Memorie di Mons. G. Speroni", Vat. Lat., n. 9896, f.115.

Angelica Library
Atti Arcadici, ms., Archives of the Arcadia National Academy
Fatti degli Arcadi, ms., III, IV, Archives of the Arcadia National Academy.

Casanatense Library
Memorial to Pope Clement XI…, ms., vol. Misc. 221, 2, (c. 1716)

PORTUGAL, LISBON

National Library
Ms. 157, Col. Pombalina.
Ms., Cod. 418, Col. Pombalina.
Folheto de Lisboa, ms., B.N.L., Res. Cod. 554, 1742-45.
L. MONTEZ MATTOSO, Anno Noticioso e Historico, ms., vols. 2,4, B.N.L., Res. Cod. D. 8065/6, 1740-42.
Mss., Reservados, Caixa 41, n. 7, doc. nn. 16.72, 78, 82.

Palazzo d'Ajuda National Library
Ms. 49 (18th century)
Ms. 54.
Fondi Redondo.

PORTUGAL, EVORA

Public Library
Mercurio Historico de Lisboa, niss. Cod. CIV 1-11 to CIV 1-20, 1743-50.

Unpublished works

L. BARUFFI, *Orologi solari Trattato – Manuale*, unpublished, Rome 2001.
C. DE CUPIS, *La villa e l'eremo del Cardinal Girolamo Colonna (senior) sul lago d'Albano*, undated, (copy with A Crielesi).

Bibliography

AA.VV., *Geomorphological features of Latian Volcano* (Alban Hills, Italy), in "Geologica romana", Vol. XIII, Roma 1974.

AA.VV., *Un Parco naturale regionale nei Castelli Romani*, Velletri 1980.

AA.VV., *L'Ariccia del Bernini*, Ariccia 1998, cat. della mostra omonima, Ariccia 10 ottobre-31 dicembre 1998.

B. AMENDOLEA, *I due ninfei del Lago Albano in alcuni disegni ed incisioni del XVII, XVIII e XIX secolo*, in "Documenta Albana", II s., 9, 1987, pp.29-49.

H.C. ANDERSEN, *Dagbøger*, 1825-1875 (a cura di R. Olsen e H. Topsoe-Jensen), København 1971-1976, Vol.I, pp.220-224.

ANDREA DA ROCCA DI PAPA, *Sunto storico dei Conventi Case e Monasteri appartenenti all'antica Provincia Romana dell'Ordine dei Minori*, Roma 1898.

ANONIMO, *Regola del Nostro Santo Padre S. Francesco con le Costituzioni Generali per le Province Riformate Cismontane de' Minori Osservanti*, Napoli 1643.

ANONIMO, *Tributo d'ossequio al Reverendissimo Padre Giuseppe Maria d'Evora dell'Ordine de' Minori Osservanti...*, Arezzo 1736.

S. ANSALDI, *"Una pala di Antoniazzo Romano"*, in L'Arte, XL, 8, 1937, pp.192-196.

A.P. ANZIDEI, A.M. DE SANTIS, A.M. BIETTI SESTRIERI, *Roma e il Lazio dall'età della pietra alla formazione della città*, Roma 1985, pp. 156-157.

Archeologia a Roma nelle fotografie di Thomas Ashby 1891-1930, cat. Della Mostra (Roma, 1989), Napoli 1989.

A. ARNOLDUS-HUYZENDVELD, *Nota preliminare sull'interpretazione di Alba Longa come "dorsale illuminata dal sole"*, in "Documenta Albana", II s., 21, 1999, pp.25-42.

P. ARRIGONI – A. BERTARELLI, *Piante e vedute di Roma e del Lazio conservate nella raccolta delle stampe e dei disegni. Castello Sforzesco*, Roma 1939.

T. ASHBY, *Dessins inédits de Carlo Labruzzi*, in "Melange d'Archeologie et d'Histoire", XXIII, 1903, p.398.

ID., *Classical Topography of the Roman Campagna*, in "Papers of the British School at Rome", 1910, V, p.27.

T. ASHBY – J. GARVIN, *"The history of Palazzola"*, "The Venerabile", I, 4, 1924, pp.289-297; II, 1, 1924, pp. 3-13; II, 2, 1925, pp.132-146; II, 3, 1925, pp.222-230.

A. AYRES DE CARVALHO, *A escultura em Mafra*, Mafra 1956.

L. AUVRAY, *Les registres de Grégoire IX*, Parigi, 1896-1955, vol II.

A. BALLAND, *Une transposition de la grotte de Tibère à Sperlonga: le ninfeo Bergantino de Castegandolfo*, in "Mélanges de l'Ecole Française de Rome, Antiquité", LXXIX, 1967, pp.421-502.

J.J. BARTHELEMY, *Mémoires sur les anciens monuments de Rome*, in Mémoires de Littérature... de l'Académie Royale des Inscriptions et Belles Lettres, Paris 1761, p. 588.

R. BATTAGLIA, *Due architetti borrominiani in S. Lorenzo in Piscibus di Roma*, in Bollettino d'Arte, XXXI, ifi, 1938, pp.370-375.

G. BATTELLI, *Ratones decimarum nei secoli XIII e XIV, Latium*, Città del Vaticano 1946, p.15 n. 3

B.G. BEDINI, *Breve prospetto delle abbazie Cistercensi d'Italia*, Roma, 1944, p.143.

ID., *Le abbazie Cistercensi d'Italia – S. Maria di Palazzola*, Casamari 1966.

I. BELLI BARSALI – M.G. BRANCHETTI, *Ville della Campagna Romana*, Lazio 2, Milano 1975, pp.309-310.

A. BERTOLOTTI, *Esportazioni di oggetti di Belle Arti da Roma in Spagna e nel Portogallo nei secoli XVI, XVII, XVIII*, Archivio Storico, Artistico, Archeologico e Letterario della città e provincia di Roma,III,1878-79, 99. 281-285.

G. BIZZARRI, *La Città di Paliano. Il castello di Zancati*, Roma 1915, pp. 34-35.

E. BOAGA, *La Soppressione Innocenziana dei piccoli conventi in Italia*, Roma 1971.

E. BONOMELLI, *I papi in campagna*, Roma 1953.

G. BORGHINI – S. VASCO ROCCA (a cura di), *S. Antonio dei Portoghesi*, Roma 1992.

G. BOTTAI, *Diario 1935-1944* (a cura di B. Guerri), Milano 2000, p. 488.

M. BRANCIA DI APRICENA, *Le committenze di padre Josè Maria de Fonseca ed Evora a Roma e nel territorio*, in "Giovanni V e la cultura romana del suo tempo", Roma 1995, pp.153-184.

ID., *Il Complesso dell'Aracoeli sul Colle Capitolino*, Roma 2000, p.228.

F. CALABRESE, *Il recupero delle ville colonnesi a Marino*, in "Ville e Parchi nel Lazio", Lunario Romano, Roma 1984.

L. CANINA, *Esposizione storica della Campagna Romana*, Roma 1839.

ID., *Gli edifizj antichi dei contorni di Roma*, Roma 1856.

I.M. CANIVEZ, *Statuta Capitolorum Generalium Ordinis Cistercensium*, Lovanio 1933-1941, vol.II, p.171.

B. CAPMARTIN DE CHAUPY, *Découvert de la Maison de Campagne d'Horace*, Roma 1767, vol. II, pp. 109-113.

F. CARAFFA, *Il Monachesimo a Roma (e nel Lazio) dalle origini al secolo XX*, in "Monasticon Italiae", Cesena 1881, vol.I, p. 148 n. 128.

F. CARUSO, *Cartario di S.Maria in Campo Marzio (986-1199)*, Roma 1948, p.55.

CASIMIRO DA ROMA *Memorie istoriche delle Chiese e dei Conventi dei Frati Minori della Provincia Romana*, Roma 1744 (1845), pp.321-346.

V. CASTELLANI – W. DRAGONI, *Opere arcaiche per il controllo del territorio: gli emissari sotterranei artificiali dei laghi albani*, in "Gli Etruschi maestri di idraulica", Perugia 1991 (a cura di M. Bergamini), pp.43-65.

F. Castelo Branco, *Lisboa Seicentista*, Lisboa 1956.

A. Cavallaro, *Antoniazzo Romano e gli Antoniazzeschi. Una generazione di pittori nella Roma del Quattrocento*, Udine 1992.

C. Cecamore, *Il santuario di Iuppiter Latiaris sul Monte Cavo: spunti e materiali dai vecchi scavi*, in "Bullettino della Commissione archeologica comunale di Roma", XCV, 1993, pp.19-44.

C. Ceschi, *Teoria e storia del restauro*, Roma 1970.

F. Chiarelli – G. Morelli, *Palazzola*, tesi di Restauro II, Facoltà di Architettura, Università di Roma "La Sapienza", Prof. G. Miarelli Mariani, Roma 1988-89.

P. Chiarucci, *Colli Albani, Preistoria e protostoria*, in "Documenta Albana", I s., 5, 1978, pp.167-168.

Id., *Rinvenimenti presso il lago di Albano*, in "Quaderni del Centro di studio per l'archeologia etrusco-italica", 1981, 5, pp.191-197.

Id., *Materiali dell'età del bronzo nelle Acque del Lago di Albano*, in "Quaderni del centro di studio per l'archeologia etrusco-italica", VII, 1985, pp.36-39.

Id., *Nuovi materiali e recenti scoperte della civiltà laziale nell'area albana*, in "Quaderni del Centro di studio per l'archeologia etrusco-italica", VIII, 1987, pp. 205 ss.

Id., *Indagini sul lago Albano*, in "Documenta Albana", II s., 9, 1987, pp. 19-28.

Id., *Nuove considerazioni su alcune sostruzioni in opera poliginale sui Colli Albani*, in "1° Seminario nazionale di studi sulle mura poligonali", Alatri 1988, pp. 65-69.

Id., in A. Pasqualini (a cura di), *Alba Longa Mito Storia Archeologia*, Atti dell'Incontro di Studio Roma- Albano 27-29 gennaio 1994, Roma 1996, pp. 326-329.

Id., *Il villaggio delle macine sommerso nelle acque del Lago Albano*, in "Bullettino di Archeologia Subacquea.", n.1-2, Anno II-III, Roma 1995-96, pp.175-183.

Id., *La documentazione archeologica pre-protostorica nell'area albana e le più recenti scoperte*, in "Alba Longa" 1996, pp.1-27.

Id., *Viabilità arcaica e luoghi di culto nell'area albana*, in "Alba Longa" 1996, pp. 317-333.

P. Chiarucci, T. Gizzi, O. Melasecchi, *Albano città del Grand Tour*, "Documenta Albana" n. 20, Albano 1998.

L.A. Chracas, *Diario Ordinario*, Roma (sec. XVIII).

C. Civitelli, R. Funiciello, M. Parotto, *Caratteri deposizionali dei prodotti del vulcanismo freatico nei Colli Albani*, in "Geologica romana", Vol. XIV, Roma 1975.

F. Coarelli, *Dintorni di Roma*, Bari 1981.

Id., *Gli emissari dei laghi laziali*, in "Gli Etruschi maestri di idraulica", Perugia 1991 (a cura di M. Bergamini), pp.35-41.

M. Cogotti, *Il Convento di Palazzola*, in R. Cipollone-S. Cancellieri (a cura di), *Il Giubileo 2000 alle porte di Roma-Monumenti ritrovati nel Lazio*, Roma, 1999, pp.62-64.

A. Coppi, *Memorie Colonnesi compilate*, Roma 1855, pp.269-271.

L. Crescenzi, *La Villa di Domiziano a Castel Gandolfo: nuove prospettive*, in "Quaderni del Centro di studio per l'archeologia etrusco-italica", IV, 1981, pp.181 ss.

L. Crescenzi – E. Tortorici, *"Alba Longa"*, in *Enea nel Lazio, Archeologia e Mito. Bimillenario virgiliano*, cat. della Mostra, Roma 1981, pp18-19.

G.M. Crescimbeni, *Catalogo de' Pastori Arcadi per Ordine di Annoverazione*, Roma 1690-1728.

Id., *Ristretto de/la istoria della celebre Adunanza degli Arcadi*, (1719),London 1804.

Id., *Storia dell'Accademia degli Arcadi...*, (1712), London 1804.

A. Crielesi, *Santa Maria "ad Nives" di Palazzolo*, Velletri 1997.

Id., *L'eredità del Fonseca a S. Maria ad Nives di Palazzolo*, in "Castelli Romani", a.XXXV, Num. Monogr. 1995.

Id., *Santa Maria ad Nives di Palazzolo*, in "Analecta Tor", vol.160, 1997, pp.233-264.

Id,. *Palazzolo, Splendori e miserie dell'antica abbazia nullius di S.Maria della Neve*, in Lazio ieri e oggi, A. XXXIII, nn.11-12, 1997, pp.338-370.

Id., *Palazzolo sul Lago di Albano, Splendori e miserie dell'ex abbazia nullius di S.Maria della Neve durante i secoli*, in Lazio Insolito, Montecompatri 1998, pp.22-30.

Id., *Fra Giorgio Marziale di Ponzano*, in "Atti del Convegno: Ponzano di Fermo tra Medioevo e Rinascimento", Ponzano 19 luglio 1998, pp.20-33.

Id., *Il pittore Fra Pietro da Copenaghen al secolo Albert Kuchler*, Roma 1999, p. 28.

G.C. Crocchiante, *L'Istoria delle chiese della città di Tivoli*, Roma 1726, p.213.

S.J. De Pasqueira, *Palazzola (Um convento portguez na Italia)*, Porto 1904.

G.M. De Rossi, *Bovillae*, in "Forma Italiae", R.I. vol.XV, 1979, p.290.

D. De Sanctis, *Columnensium procerum imagines et memorias nonullas...*, Romae 1675.

G. Digard e altri, *Le registres de Boniface VIII*, Parigi 1884-1935, III, p.100 n. 4096.

F. Dionisi, *L'artistico sepolcro rupestre non è del console Cornelio Scipione Ispalo*, in "Studi Romani", XVII, 1969, pp.405-424.

C. Enggass – R. Enggass (a cura di), N.Pio, *Vite dè Pittori, Scultori ed Architetti moderni*, (1724), Città del Vaticano 1977.

D. Esposito, *Tecniche costruttive murarie medievali*, Roma 1997, p. 79.

F. Federico – I. Fontana, *L'organizzazione dei Cistercensi nell'epoca feudale*, Casamari 1988, pp.257-265.

J.A. Ferreira, *Memorias archeologica historicas de Cidade do Porto*, voll. 2, Braga 1923.24.

J.M. P.Fonseca Ab Ebora, *Romana Reductionis in pristinum pro Ven. Conventu...*, Roma 1707-1722.

A. Forbiger, *Handbuch der Alten Geographie*, Leipzig 1822-1848, II, pp. 322-456.

M. Fornaseri, A. Scherillo, U. Ventriglia, *La regione vulcanica dei Colli Albani*, Roma 1963.

G. Frascarelli, *Iscrizioni portoghesi che esistono in diversi luoghi di Roma*, Roma 1868.

A. Galieti, *Contributi alla storia della diocesi suburbicaria di Albano Laziale*, Città del Vaticano 1999.

G. Ghini, *Prospezioni subacquee nei laghi albano e nemorense*, in Bullettino di Archeologia Subacquea", n. 1-2, Anno II-III, Roma, 1995-96, pp. 185-191.

P.G. Gierow, *The Iron Age Culture of Latium: Excavation and Finds; 1, The Alban Hills*, Lund 1964.

O. Gigli, *I beni ecclesiastici negli Stati Romani*, Firenze 1862.

A.M. Giorgetti Vichi (a cura di), *Gli Arcadi dal 1690 al 1800. Onomasticon*, Roma 1977.

M.O.R. Giovan Battista Da Monza, *Regola del serafico Padre S. Francesco fondatore dell'Ordine dei Minori spiegata in forma di dialogo*, Napoli 1647. 1963.

P. Francesco Gonzaga, *De origine Seraphicae Religionis Franciscanae*, Roma 1587, p.183.

C. Gualdi, *I Monti Albani*, Roma 1962.

C.M. Guarinoni, *Le chiese Parrocchiali di Rocca di Papa*, Rocca di Papa 1998, pp. 31-38.

L. Guerrini, *Il monumento rupestre di Palazzola*, in "Archeologia Classica", XXI, 1969, pp. 227-245.

A. Guidi, F. Di Gennaro, M. Pacciarelli, *Rinvenimenti di età pre e protostorica a Grottaferrata e a Monte Cavo*, in "Quaderni del Centro di studio per l'archeologia etrusco-italica", 1, 1978, pp.84-86.

A. Guidi, in *Enea nel Lazio, Archeologia e mito*, cat. della Mostra, Roma 1981, pp.88-94.

Id., *Alcune osservazioni sul popolamento dei Colli Albani in età protostorica*, in "Dialoghi di Archeologia", IV, 1982, pp.31-34.

G.S. Hedberg, *Antoniazzo Romano and his School*, I, New York University, 1980.

L. Holstenii, *In Italiam Antiuam Philippi Cluverii Annotationes*, Roma 1666, p. 180.

C. Huelsen, *Le chiese di Roma nel Medio Evo. Cataloghi e appunti*, Firenze 1927.

G. Incisa Della Rocchetta, *Notizie sulla fabbrica della chiesa collegiata di Ariccia (1662-1664)*, in "Rivista del R. Istituto d'Archeologia e Storia dell'Arte", I, Roma 1929-1930, pp. 349-392.

L. Janauschek, *Originum Cistercensium*, Vindobonae, 1977, p.244.

F. Joannis A Capistrano, *Novissima pro Cismontana Minorum Familia Generalium Costitutionum*, Roma 1827.

A. Kirker, *Athanasii Kircheri Latium id est. Nova & parallela Latii tum veteris tum novi descriptio*, Anistelodami 1671.

C. Labruzzi, *Le Antichità di Albano delineate da suoi avanzi*, 1854.

E. Langlois, *Le registres de Nicolas IV*, Parigi 1886, p. 10.

R. Lefevre, *L'Abbazia medievale di Palazzolo sul lago Albano*, in "Lunario Romano", Roma 1987, XVII, pp.173-191.

Id., *Storia e storie dell'antichissima Ariccia*, Ariccia 1996, pp.154-161.

P. Litta, *Famiglie celebri d'Italia*, 2, IX, Milano 1837.

A. Lo Bianco (a cura di), *Pietro da Cortona 1597-1669*, Catalogo della mostra omonima, Roma 1997.

T. Lombardi, *Storia del francescanesimo*, Padova 1980.

G. Lugli, *Le antiche ville dei Colli Albani prima dell'occupazione domizianea*, in "Bullettino della Commissione archeologica comunale di Roma", 42, 1915, pp. 251-316.

Id., *La Villa di Domiziano sui Colli Albani. Topografia generale*, in "Bullettino della Commissione archeologica comunale di Roma", 1917, pp. 29 ss.

Id., *La Villa di Domiziano sui Colli Albani: Le costruzioni centrali*, in "Bullettino della Commissione archeologica comunale di Roma", 46, 1918, pp.3-68.

Id., *La Villa di Domiziano sui Colli Albani. Le costuzioni sparse*, in "Bullettino della Commissione archeologica comunale di Roma", 47, 1919.

Id., *La Via Trionfale a Monte Cave e il gruppo stradale dei Colli Albani*, in "Memorie della Pontificia Accademia romana di archeologia", I, 1923, p. 258.

Id., *Dove sorgeva Alba Longa?*, in *Studi Minori di Topografia Antica*, Roma 1965, pp. 353-358.

G. Mollat, *Jean XXII (1316-1334). Lettres communes*, Parigi 1921-1947, III, p.13 n. 10417.

J. Mabillon, Annales O.S.B., vol.6, Lutetiae Parisorum 1739-1745.

F. Manoel Da Esperanca – F. Fernando Da Doleda De, *Historia serafica da Ordem dos frades menores de S. Francisco na Provincia de Portugal*, Lisboa 1656-1729.

R.F.P. Marchant, *Fundamento duodecim Ordinis Minorum S. Francisci*, s.l.e., 1657.

G. Marocco, *Monumenti dello Stato Pontificio e relazione topografica di ogni paese, Lazio e le sue memorie*, Roma 1853, vol.VIII, pp. 164-165.

A. Mastrigli – G. Pelami, *La scoperta archeologica di Albalonga*, Marino 1968.

F. Milizia, *Memorie degli architetti antichi e moderni*, II, Bassano 1785.

M. Missirini, *Memorie per servire alla storia della Romana Accademia di San Luca fino alla morte di Antonio Canova*, Roma 1823.

V. Misserville, Il dott. Arnaldi a Palazzolo, in "Castelli Romani", a.VII, n.9, settembre 1962.

G.B. Mittarelli – A. Costadoni, *Annales Camaldulenses*, Venezia 1755, I, P.119.

M.G. Moeri, *Vite degli Arcadi illustri*, Roma 1751.

Id., *Adunanza tenuta dagli Arcadi per la morte del Fedelissimo Re di Portogallo Giovanni V*, Roma 1751.

Id., *Memorie Istoriche dell'Adunanza degli Arcadi*, Roma 1761.

O. Montenotesi, *La biblioteca del convento Aracoeli e le sue vicende. Ricordi storici*, La Madonna d'Aracoeli, Roma 1949.

G. Moroni, *Dizionario di erudizione storica-ecclesiastica*, Venezia 1840-1861.

F. Negri Arnoldi, *Maturità di Antoniazzo*, Commentari, 16, 1965, pp.225-244.

A. Negro, in *L'Arte per i Papi e per i Principi nella campagna romana: grande pittura del '600 e del '700*, I, cat. della Mostra, Roma 1990.

F. Nerini, *De tempio ed coenobio SS. Bonifacii et Alexii*, Roma 1752, pp. 484-486.

N. Neuerburg, *L'architettura delle fontane e dei ninfei nell'Italia antica*, Napoli 1965, pp. 158-159.

A. Nibby, *Analisi storico-topografico-antiquaria della carta dei dintorni di Roma*, voll.3, 2° ed., Roma 1848-1849.

G. Noehles, *Antoniazzo Romano, Studien zur Quattrocento malerei in Rom*, Phil. Diss., Mùnster 1973.

A. Paravicini Bagliani, *I testamenti dei cardinali del Duecento*, Roma, 1980, p.115.

T. Paris (a cura di), *L'Area dei Castelli Romani*, Roma 1981.

A. Pasqualini, *I miti albani e l'origine delle Feriae Latinae*, in Alba Longa 1996, pp.217-253.

E.S. Piccolomini, *Commentaria rerum memorabilium*, Milano, 1984.

G.B. Piranesi, *Le Antichità Romane*, Roma 1756.

Id., Le *Antichità d'Albano e di Castel Gandolfo*, Roma 1762-1764.

E. Portal, *L'Arcadia*, Palermo 1922.

P. Pressutti, *Regesta Honorii papae III*, Roma 1886, I, pp.CX-CXI.

M. Prou, *Le registres d'Onorius IV*, Parifi 1888, n. 49.

P. Quieto, *Giovanni V di Portogallo e le sue committenze nella Roma del XVIII secolo*, (La pittura a Mafra, Evora, Lisbona, Bentivoglio) 1988.

S. Quilici Gigli, *A proposito delle ricerche nella ubicazione di Alba Longa*, in "La Parola del Passato", 38, 1983, pp.140 ss.

N. Ratti, *Storia di Genzano*, Roma 1797.

A. Remiddi, *Velletri. Memorie storiche*, voll.2, Velletri 1982.

A. Ricci, *Rocca di Papa, appunti d'Arte e Storia*, Roma 1927.

G.A. Riccy, *Osservazioni archeologiche sopra un antico mausoleo consolare incavato nel Monte Albano presso il convento di Palazzolo*, Roma 1828.

A. Rocchi, *De coenobio Criptoferratenai eiusque biblioteca et codicibus praesertim Graecis commentarii*, Tusculi 1893.

E.A. Safarif, (a cura di), *Galleria Colonna in Roma*, 1998.

L. Samoglia, *Benedetto XIV e il Portogallo*, Giornale di Studi Padovani, dicembre 1977.

P. Scatizzi, *I Colonna signori di Genazzano*, in A. Bureca (a cura di), *Il Castello Colonna di Genazzano*, Roma 2000.

F. Scoccia, *Ponzano nel Cinquecento*, Monte Ottone 1995, pp. 94-99.

A. Scotti, *L'Accademia degli Arcadi in Roma ei suoi rapporti con la cultura portoghese nel primo decennio del 1700*, Bracara Augusta XXVII, 63, 1, 1973, pp.115-130.

G. Tomassetti, *La Campagna Romana Antica Medioevale e Moderna*, vol.II, Roma 1910, pp. 159-178.

G. Tomassetti, *"La Campagna Romana Antica Medioevale e Moderna"*, (1910-1926), nuova ed. a cura di L. Chiumenti – F. Bilancia, Firenze 1979-80.

L. Totaro (a cura di), E.S. Piccolomini, *I Commentarii (1584)*, voll. 2, Milano 1984.

G. Tucci, Savo, A. Giovannoni, *Paliano. Monografia storica*, Tivoli 1933.

G. Ucelli, *Le navi di Nemi*, Roma 1950, pp.39-56.

F. Ughelli, *Italia Sacra sive di Episcopis Italiae*, Venezia, 1717-1722, 1, col. 259 ss.

S. Vasco Rocca – G. Borghini – P. Ferraris, *Roma lusitana – Lisbona romana, guida alla Mostra*, Roma 1990.

V. Vecchj, *Collezione di 24 vedute quasi tutte inedite rappresentanti monumenti e luoghi celebri esistenti nelle vicinanze di Roma disegnate dal vero dal Dott. Vincenzo Vecchj...*, Roma 1866.

U. Vichi, *La chiesa di S. Antonio dei Portoghesi in Roma*, Il Santo, N.S. 7, 1967, pp.339-354.

G.B. Vignato, *Storia di Benedetto XIII dei Frati Predicatori*, vol.2, Milano 1952-53.

R. Voss, *Du mein Italien*, 1910, trad. di V. D'Onofrio, *Visioni D'Italia*, Lanciano 1912, p.41.

L. Wadding, Annales *Minorum seu Trium Ordium a S. Francisco Institutorum*, ed. Roma 1731,1794.

R. Wagner-Rieger, *Die italienische Baukunst zu Beginn der Gotik*, vol.2, Graz 1956.

P. Zani, *Enciclopedia metodica critica-ragionata delle Belle Arti*, Parma 1822.

G. OFM Zucconi, *La Minoritica Provincia Romana dei SS Apostoli Pietro e Paolo*, Roma 1969.

Id., *La Provincia Romana dei Frati Minori dei SS.Apostoli Pietro e Paolo*, Roma 1972.

Index of names

Adriano VI 85
Agliardi Antonio cardinale 126
Agnese (o Agnesina) di Montefeltro 82, 84, 85, 86
Agnifili Amico 85
Agostino Chigi 96, 100, 101
Aldobrandini famiglia 109
Alessandro VII 34, 92, 94, 96, 98, 100, 105, 107, 109, 114
Alessio da Roma 105
Algardi Alessandro 82
Amico, cfr. Agnifili Amico
Andrea Basili da Rocca di Papa 126
Angeletti Raimondo 138
Annibaldi famiglia 25, 26
Antoniazzo Romano (o Antoniazzo) 77, 80, 129
Antonio del Grande 94
Arnaldi Carlo 128, 138
Arrigucci Luigi 29, 30, 32, 87, 88, 110
Ashby Thomas 63
Augusto 49, 55
Aurelio da Roma 85
Barberini famiglia 120
Barberini Maffeo card., cfr. Urbano VIII
Barberini Taddeo 88, 96
Barthèlemy Jean-Jacques 55
Benedetto (abate) 72
Benedetto XIV 123
Bernini Gian Lorenzo 96, 100, 102, 103
Bernini Luigi 102
Betti Jacobo 98
Blunck Ditlev 125
Bødtcher Ludwig 125
Boguet-Didier Nicolas 28
Bolini Giovanni Maria 102
Boni Giacomo 50
Bonifacio VIII 71, 72
Bonifacio IX 73, 75
Bonomelli commendatore 129
Borromeo Anna 85
Bottai Giuseppe 129, 131
Breccioli Bartolomeo 87
Bufalini Giulio 90, 91
Caetani Gaspare 90, 91
Calcini Antonio 61
Canali cardinale 129
Capizucchi Francesco 90
Capizzucchi Papirio 90
Capmartin de Chaupy Bertrand 55
Caporilli 127
Capranica cardinale 76
Carlo Duca dei Marsi, cfr. Colonna Carlo
Carlo VII 118
Casimiro (Frà) da Roma 54, 55, 61, 77, 83

Cassiano dal Pozzo, cfr. Dal Pozzo Cassiano
Castelli Domenico 87
Castiglia Nicolò 85
Cellini Pico 129
Cesare Massimiliano 84
Chigi Agostino, 96
Chigi Fabio cardinale, cfr. Alessandro VII
Chigi Flavio cardinale 100
Cibo famiglia 123
Clemente XI 116
Clemente XII 118, 123
Clodio 48
Colonna famiglia 33, 75, 77, 80, 83, 90, 91, 131
Colonna Anna 88, 89
Colonna Antonio 25
Colonna Ascanio cardinale 33, 75, 76, 83, 84, 85, 86
Colonna Beatrice 83
Colonna Camillo 83
Colonna Carlo 34, 89, 90, 92, 94, 98, 107
Colonna Costanza 86
Colonna Egidio, cfr. Colonna Carlo
Colonna Fabrizio 75, 82, 83, 84, 85, 123
Colonna Federico 82, 84, 85, 86
Colonna Ferdinando 83
Colonna Filippo 33, 85, 86, 90
Colonna Gerolamo (o Girolamo) cardinale 29, 34, 86, 87, 88, 92, 110
Colonna Giovan Battista 92
Colonna Giovanni 75
Colonna Giulia 82
Colonna Lorenzo Onofrio 93
Colonna Marcantonio (II) 33, 86, 93
Colonna Marcantonio (IV) 86
Colonna Odoardo 75, 76
Colonna Prospero 75
Colonna Sciarra 83
Colonna Vittoria 83
Colonna-Gonzaga Flaminia 115
Conti di Tuscolo famiglia 26
Contini Giovan Battista 102
Cornelio Scipione Hispallo 56
Corsini Papa, cfr. Clemente XII
Cortese Guglielmo 100
Cortona da Pietro 86, 100
Dal Pozzo Cassiano 55, 74, 110
De Cupis Cesare 61, 93
De Cupis Guido 34, 95, 137
De Fonseca Pietro cardinale, cfr. Fonseca Pietro
De' Rossi Mattia 102
Dione Cassio 55
Domiziano 49
Egidio monsignore, cfr. Colonna Carlo

Enea 43
Esopo Apsyrtiano 55
Eugenio III 67
Faria Gentil Bernardino Antonio 126
Fearnley Thomas 125
Federico Duca di Urbino, cfr. Colonna Federico
Felice della Greca 102
Feltria Agnese, cfr. Agnese di Montefeltro
Ferrini monsignore 99, 104
Filippo I (Colonna), cfr. Colonna Filippo
Filodoro Domenico 128
Fiori Francesco 120
Fonseca da Evora, Josè (o Giuseppe) Maria de 41, 108, 110, 116, 117, 118, 123, 130, 131
Fonseca Pietro cardinale 120, 128, 129
Fontana Carlo 102
Fontes de marchese 117
Frà Marziale, cfr. Marziale Frà Giorgio
Francesco da Capua 77
Francesco da Viterbo 75
Frangipane Graziano 65
Garaste 118
Gaspare da Trevigliano 85
Gattoni Emilio 94
Gentilini 124
Gesualdo cardinale 79
Giarletti Francesco 124
Gimignani Giacinto 100
Giordano 75
Giorgio di Cesare di Giorgio 96
Giovanna d'Aragona 85
Giovanni V del Portogallo (o di Braganza) 117, 121
Giovanni XXII 72
Girolamo cardinale, cfr. Colonna Gerolamo
Giuseppe da Cavrago 124
Giuseppe de Fonseca da Evora, cfr. Fonseca da Evora, Josè Maria de
Gonzaga Francesco 55, 61, 79
Gozzadini cardinale 116
Gozzoli Benozzo 77
Gregorio IX 65, 67
Gregorio XVI 126
Grimaldi Vittorio 126
Guala Bicchieri cardinale 65
Innocenzo III 65
Innocenzo IV 24, 65, 67
Innocenzo X 89, 96, 99
Isidoro cardinale, cfr. Ruteno cardinale
Jacopa de' Settesoli 65
Jacovacci Domenico 35, 36, 38, 89
Küchler Albert 125
Labruzzi Carlo, 23

Lambertini Pinto Josè 127
Leoncello Cesare di Cave 85
Leone X 85
Luca Francia Giovanni di 75
Ludovico da Ferrara Frà 75
Maderno Carlo 87
Magnifico il, cfr. Chigi Agostino
Marchesano Giuseppe 128
Mario 100
Martiale Giorgio, cfr. Marziale Frà Giorgio
Martino V 75
Marzer Antonio 85
Marziale Frà Giorgio 35, 94, 96, 98, 100, 102, 103, 106, 109, 114
Marziali Giorgio, cfr. Marziale Frà Giorgio
Massimiliano I d'Austria 83
Masucci Agostino 121, 129
Mazzoleni Lorenzo 124
Mcmillan 129
Michele da Bergamo Frà 103
Monteverde 131
Montini 129
Mussolini Benito 129
Mutini Lorenzo 90
Navone Giandomenico 110, 120, 123
Nepalini mons. 105
Nicolò IV 70
Nicolò V 76
Onorio III 65
Onorio IV 70
Orsini Felice 86
Orsini Nicola 75
Padre Casimiro, cfr. Casimiro da Roma
Paganelli (abate), cfr. Eugenio III
Palloni Nilo 72
Paris Nazareno 126
Pasquale II 26
Paulucci cardinale 116
Pellegrino 85
Peruzzi Baldassarre 96
Piccolomini Enea Silvio, cfr. Pio II
Pierleoni Tommaso 73, 75, 86, 87, 110
Pietro da Cortona, cfr. Cortona da Pietro
Pietro di Collemezzo cardinale 67
Pinto Luiz 124
Pio II 55, 76
Pio V 79
Pio IX 126
Pio XII 129
Pira Lucilia 55
Piranesi Giovanni Battista 56, 122
Pizzardo cardinale 129

Pompeo Magno 48
Raffaello 96
Raggi Antonio 100
Rainaldi Girolamo 33
Ricciarelli famiglia 130
Riccy Giovanni Antonio 56
Romano Giulio 96
Ruteno cardinale 59, 76
S. Bernardo da Chiaravalle 67
S. Brunone 75
S. Carlo 85
S. Giacomo della Marca 107
Salustri Mariano 80, 126, 138
Salviati Caterina Maria Zeffirina 123
Santangeli Luigi 138
Santinovi Lorenzo 120
Savelli famiglia 25, 26
Savelli Giulio 100
Savelli Nicolò 25
Sconzani Ippolito 120, 132

Serafini Egidio 126
Silla 47
Sisto IV 77
Sisto V 79
Stefano da Roma Frà 75
Stefano de' Normanni (cardinale) 65, 67, 70
Tardini monsignore 129
Teodoro da Roma 85
Thomar, Antonio Conte di 126
Tintisona Biagio 99
Tomacelli Lucrezia 33, 85, 86, 90
Tomassetti Giuseppe 83, 93, 128
Tullo Ostilio 43, 45, 55
Urbano V 73
Urbano VIII 13, 26, 29, 34, 86, 87, 89, 99, 100
Van Wittel Gaspar 33, 115
Vecchi Vincenzo 63
Volpi Antonio 124
Waddingo 116
Zaccaria Papa 24

FINITO DI STAMPARE NEL MESE DI FEBBRAIO 2004
CHICCA DA IMPIANTI TIPOLITOGRAFICI
GANGEMI EDITORE SPA – Roma